Investing for Prosperity

Investing for Prosperity

A MANIFESTO FOR GROWTH

Edited by
Tim Besley and John Van Reenen

THE LONDON SCHOOL OF ECONOMICS AND POLITICAL SCIENCE

Published by LSE Academic Publishing

Published in association with London Publishing Partnership
www.londonpublishingpartnership.co.uk

ISBN 978-1-909890-02-2 (pbk.)

A catalogue record for this book is available from the British Library

This book has been composed in Lucida using T_EX
Copyedited and typeset by T&T Productions Ltd, London

Cover image: Dreamstime
Cover design: LSE Design Unit (lse.ac.uk/designunit)

Printed in the United Kingdom by Hobbs the Printers Ltd

Contents

Preface

What institutions and policies are needed to sustain UK economic growth in the dynamic world economy of the twenty-first century? After years of inadequate investment in skills, infrastructure and innovation, there are long-standing structural weaknesses in the economy, all rooted in a failure to achieve stable planning, strategic vision and a political consensus on the right policy framework to support growth. This must change if we are to meet our current challenges and the many more that will arise in the future.

The nation is scarred by the worst economic crisis in many generations and we are left wondering what the next half-century will bring and how to prepare for it. The pace of change is sometimes bewildering. The world's centre of economic gravity has been shifting eastwards, bringing a new global division of labour; innovation has created rapid change, with new online giants emerging from almost nowhere; the global crisis led to the demise of several financial behemoths overnight; and climate change may fundamentally alter the physical environment in which we live.

Despite the current gloom, the UK has many assets that can be mobilized to its advantage, including strong rule of law, generally competitive product markets, flexible labour markets, a world-class university system and strengths in many key sectors, with cutting-edge firms in both manufacturing and services. These and other assets helped to reverse the UK's relative economic decline over the century leading up to 1980. Over the course of the following three decades, they supported faster growth per capita than in the UK's main comparator countries: France, Germany and the US. These assets must be fostered and enhanced, as ill-conceived policies can cause collateral damage (by putting our universities at risk, for example).

This book argues that the UK should build on these strengths and, at the same time, address the inadequate institutional structures that have deterred long-term investment in order to support our future prosperity. This requires stable, well-informed policy frameworks anchored in a broad political consensus around a strategic vision for growth.

The LSE Growth Commission was born from despair and hope. In 2011 we were frustrated by the way in which public discourse was dominated by discussions about the pace of deficit reduction and whether 'austerity' is good or bad for the economy. Despite the fact that we had both participated in this debate (often with opposing views), we were determined to show that this was not the only game in town. Vital questions about the policies needed to foster long-term growth were being drowned out by increasingly acrimonious short-term arguments over fairly modest changes to monetary or fiscal policy.

To counter despair, we hoped to forge a stronger consensus over what was needed to bolster the supply side of the economy in the long term.

We approached a number of colleagues and friends with the idea of a Commission to 'boil the ocean' for growth ideas. The research director at the Institute for Government, Julian McCrae, was instrumental in focusing our attention on thinking through the practical politics: 'If your ideas are so good, why haven't they already been done?' And the huge enthusiasm for the idea of creating a Commission that we encountered helped us to attract outstanding commissioners from academia, at home and overseas, and from the public and private sectors.

We imposed on ourselves a strict time constraint of twelve months to produce a report in order to keep the analysis fresh and the proposals timely. Another important decision was to have open hearings in 'Select Committee' style, where we took evidence from a wide range of experts. This helped foster a sense of engagement and complemented the desk research by the excellent secretariat, headed by Miguel Coelho, and the closed-door sessions with a vast number of people from politics, academia, the business community and beyond.

The discussions at these public hearings and in private sessions were vital in producing sharp insights into the fundamental issues and into how we could navigate a path back to sustainable growth in the UK. They also shaped our appreciation of the core issues that needed to be addressed; we were increasingly struck by how a picture emerged of the UK's failure to focus on important aspects of investment in skills, infrastructure and innovation. And this appreciation shaped the emerging narrative of the report: a narrative that all of the commissioners signed up to.

The reforms we propose are crucial to respond to a rapidly changing world in which skills, flexibility, openness and receptiveness to technological change are becoming ever more important for long-term prosperity. Together, they constitute a 'manifesto for growth', which we urge people across the whole political spectrum to support.

Acknowledgements

We are grateful to the Economic and Social Research Council and the LSE's Higher Education Innovation Fund for generous funding. Our partnership with the Institute for Government, especially Julian McCrae, has been invaluable. The LSE Growth Secretariat, led by Miguel Coelho and consisting of Nitika Bagaria, Novella Bottini, Jennifer Kao, Isabelle Roland, João Pessoa and Anna Valero, has provided exceptional support for the Growth Commission. We are grateful to Romesh Vaitilingam for his help in drafting the report on which this book is based. Much useful input was also provided by Nigel Rogers. An enormous number of people have kindly submitted written and oral evidence for our research. We are particularly grateful to the expert witnesses who appeared at our five public evidence sessions and for the written formal submissions. All supporting documentation for this book can be found at www.lse.ac.uk/ growthcommission.

Tim Besley and John Van Reenen

Contributors

THE LSE GROWTH COMMISSION COMMISSIONERS

Tim Besley (co-chair of the commission) is School Professor of Economics and Political Science at the London School of Economics. He is also a visiting professor at the Institute for International Economic Studies at Stockholm University, a Research Fellow at the Institute for Fiscal Studies and a Program Member of the Institutions, Organizations and Growth Program of the Canadian Institute for Advanced Research. He has also served as an external member of the Bank of England Monetary Policy Committee.

John Van Reenen (co-chair of the commission) has been a full professor of economics at the London School of Economics and director of the Centre for Economic Performance since 2003. He has served as a senior advisor to the UK Prime Minister, to the Secretary of State for Health and to the European Commission.

Philippe Aghion is Robert C. Waggoner Professor of Economics at Harvard University, having previously been a professor at University College London, an Official Fellow at Oxford's Nuffield College, and an assistant professor at Massachusetts Institute of Technology.

Lord John Browne is a partner and the managing director of Riverstone and co-head of Riverstone's Renewable Energy Funds. Prior to joining Riverstone, he spent forty-one years at BP serving in turn as group treasurer, managing director and group chief executive of BP and Amoco.

Francesco Caselli is professor of economics at the London School of Economics and the director of the Macro Programme at the Centre for Economic Performance.

Sir Richard Lambert is chancellor of the University of Warwick. From 2006 to 2011 he served as director-general of the Confederation of British Industry. From 2003 to 2006 he was a member of the Bank of England's Monetary Policy Committee, and from 1991 to 2001 he was the editor of the *Financial Times*.

Rachel Lomax is a British economist who served as deputy governor of the Bank of England from 2003 until 2008 and was a high-ranking civil servant before that. She was permanent secretary of three government departments between 1996 and 2002: the Department of Work and Pensions, the Welsh Office and the Department for Transport. She was a vice president and chief of staff to the president of the World Bank in 1995–96 and she was the head of the Economic and Domestic Secretariat at the Cabinet Office in 1994.

Sir Christopher Pissarides is School Professor of Economic and Political Science at the London School of Economics. In 2010 he was awarded the Nobel Memorial Prize in Economic Sciences, jointly with Peter A. Diamond and Dale Mortensen, for his contributions to the theory of search frictions and macroeconomics.

Lord Nicholas Stern is the IG Patel Chair of Economics and Government at the London School of Economics, as well as being the director of the LSE's Asia Research Centre and the chair of the Grantham Research Institute. He has also served as the head of the Government Economic Service, as Second Permanent Secretary to Her Majesty's Treasury, as chief economist and senior vice president at the World Bank and as chief economist at the European Bank for Reconstruction and Development.

CHAPTER AUTHORS

Nitika Bagaria is a PhD student and research assistant at the Centre for Economic Performance.

Novella Bottini is an econometrician at the Legatum Institute, and was formerly a research consultant ('Productivity and Innovation') at the Centre for Economic Performance.

Miguel Coelho is Senior Economist at the Institute for Government and is head of the London School of Economics Growth Commission Secretariat.

Jennifer Kao is an Occasional Research Assistant ('Productivity and Innovation') at the Centre for Economic Performance.

João Paulo Pessoa is a PhD student and an Occasional Research Assistant ('Productivity and Innovation') at the Centre for Economic Performance.

Isabelle Roland is a PhD student at the Centre for Economic Performance in the Financial Markets Group.

Investing for Prosperity: Skills, Infrastructure and Innovation

By the LSE Growth Commission

In this chapter we summarize the core policy recommendations of the LSE Growth Commission. In the subsequent chapters we go into greater depth on each policy area, providing reviews of the literature and more detailed explanations of our recommendations. Chapter 2 details the economic story of the UK since the late nineteenth century, focusing on the relative revival after 1980, but also on continuing challenges in the present day. Chapter 3 details the analysis underlying primary and secondary schooling. Chapter 4 focuses on the relationship between infrastructure and growth, while chapter 5 dives into the details of how our proposed Infrastructure Bank would operate. Chapter 6 analyses the third major long-run issue: private investment, particularly in innovation. Finally, chapter 7 looks at how to move beyond GDP per capita and consider a key element of the distribution of income: median household income.

1.1 INTRODUCTION

At the beginning of 2013 the outlook for the UK economy remains highly uncertain. Output has been depressed for a longer period than it was even in the Great Depression, with GDP still below the peak level of early 2008.

Institutions once thought of as emblematic of the UK economy are under stress. The City of London has been tarnished by being at the centre of the global financial crisis that began in 2007 and worsened dramatically in late 2008. There are serious concerns about the ability of the institutions of UK economic policymaking to steer the economy out of nearly five years of stagnation and into a sustainable recovery.

Changes outside our national borders are also having a profound effect. The continuing crisis in the eurozone is weighing down on our major export market. Over the longer term, the emergence of China, India and

The views expressed here are those of the commissioners and do not necessarily reflect the views of the individuals or institutions mentioned above.

other countries as major economic powers is shifting the global division of labour and will challenge us in areas where the UK has historically enjoyed a comparative advantage.

Over a twelve-month period, the Commission has looked at the institutions and policies that should underpin growth for the next fifty years. We believe that it is vital to look beyond the next budget cycle, the next spending review and the next parliament. Although austerity is one of the current headline debates to which several of the commissioners have contributed, we are not focusing on the appropriate fiscal and monetary policy stance in the near term. Indeed, we fear that impassioned debates about the short term are clouding even more important debates over the longer-term direction of the UK economy.

We take an optimistic view, believing the UK economic framework to have many underrated strengths. Competitive product markets, flexible labour markets, openness to foreign investors and migrants, independent regulators and good levels of higher education have helped to reverse a century of relative UK decline prior to the three decades leading up to the crisis. They should continue to play important roles in the future.

But significant reforms are needed to address the major challenges that we face, including productivity levels that still lag behind those of other major countries. Effective reform requires learning from both our failures and our successes. Our primary failures are a lack of investment in the long term and a failure to tackle the rising inequality that accompanied the improvements in our growth performance before the financial crisis.

Policies for prosperity require providing the right conditions for investment in skills, infrastructure and innovation. This will not happen without creating institutions that are built to last and that diminish rather than exacerbate policy uncertainty. These institutions must support an economy that is both resilient to adversity and capable of seizing new opportunities.

This book discusses what should be done to build for the future by *investing for prosperity*.

A Caveat

The area we are tackling is huge, well trodden and daunting. Our value added is to bring together a range of perspectives from academia, policymaking and business. We draw on the best available research, but a recurring theme is the paucity of high-quality policy evaluation. Unfortunately, even when such evidence is available, it is too often ignored by policymakers.

Our Approach

We focus on our three long-term investments—skills, infrastructure and innovation—because

- there is a strong analytical basis for the claim that they are important for growth;
- there are some long-standing problems with UK performance in these areas;
- these problems are not being adequately addressed by the current trajectory of policy; and
- we have some concrete proposals for what needs to be done.

The book begins with an overall analysis of the UK's economic story to date. Then, in each of the main chapters, we describe why each investment matters for growth and offer a diagnosis of the UK's failure to invest sufficiently. This analysis underpins our policy proposals. We ask why adequate policy solutions have not already been implemented: political bottlenecks and institutional rigidities loom large in understanding this problem. Finally, we make the case for a new measure of economic progress. We also discuss the structures that are needed at the heart of government to drive the growth agenda forward.

1.2 THE ECONOMIC STORY OF THE UK[1]

The Growth Process

Economic growth is the increase in a country's capacity to produce goods and services. We care about such gains because they lead to improvements in citizens' material wellbeing through higher consumption, increased leisure time and/or improved public services. We prefer these fruits of growth to be as *inclusive* as possible rather than for them to be appropriated by a small, fortunate slice of society. Thus, all advanced economies have mechanisms for distributing the fruits of growth more widely through taxes, benefits and the provision of public goods such as education. Equipping citizens with skills gives them the best chance of participating in the process of growth.

Policies that have a small positive effect on the annual rate of economic growth can have a huge effect on long-term human wellbeing as these increases become compounded over time. An economy that grows at 2% per annum in real terms (which was the UK's average growth rate between 1830 and 2008) doubles its material living standards every thirty-five years.

---

[1] For a more detailed discussion see chapter 2.

3

The modern theory of economic growth argues that the world's potential to grow is determined in the long run by the accumulation of ideas—scientific, technological and managerial—that make it possible to do more with the raw materials that we have. Sustainable growth is not about increasing the basic labour input of the population but rather about finding ways to do new things as well as doing the same things more efficiently.

Creating a dynamic economy requires investment of three basic kinds: in people (human capital), in equipment and physical structures (infrastructure), and in new ideas and technologies (innovation). This book focuses on all three. Investment in education and research and development (R&D) helps to create new ideas and extend the technological frontier. But it may also help a country to catch up with leading-edge economies, making it possible for firms to learn about and absorb innovations from elsewhere.

The modern era of economic growth began around 1800 when a collection of economies, initially led by the UK, pulled away from the rest. The growth sparked by the industrial revolution was impressive, but what remains remarkable is how few countries emulated the success of the UK and, not long after, France, Germany, the Scandinavian countries and the US. This is because investment requires a supportive climate in which to flourish.

History shows that markets need government support, with predictable rules and regulations. Government also plays a key role in supporting a productive economy through encouraging investment in skills, infrastructure and new technologies. But whether a government is successful in this role depends on whether its intervention is geared towards the country's long-term economic needs. Without a focus on the long term, the powerful forces unleashed by market incentives cannot be harnessed for the common good.

There is no reliable evidence that the growth potential of an economy is limited by the size of government over the wide range we see in OECD countries. Indeed, the twentieth century witnessed a significant increase in the size and responsibilities of governments throughout the developed world alongside large and sustained increases in living standards. Different market economies can be economically successful with high or low levels of state spending: compare the Scandinavian countries with the US, for example.

Thus, demands for ever greater deregulation and reductions in government spending as a panacea for the UK's growth problems are misguided. Growth is less about the precise size of the state than whether the state is smart in the way that it regulates and spends. Having a government that plays a major role in the economy—as ours does in the UK—places a premium on well-designed policies that support growth. Achieving this is heavily dependent on having an institutional framework that supports good policy.

Growth is also shaped by global developments. In recent years, the international division of labour has expanded as countries such as China catch up with advanced economies, and in some areas take a lead. The UK faces pressure in a range of industries, particularly in the manufacturing sector, although over the medium term we should expect this to apply to parts of the service sector too. Such changes also create opportunities to move up the value chain and export to China and other emerging economies in areas where we can retain or gain a comparative advantage. Understanding where and how to collaborate and where to compete will be a crucial part of reinvigorating growth.

The challenge of restoring growth must also address a problem that faces all countries: managing climate change. An industrial revolution driven by the search for low-carbon technologies is likely to emerge as one of the most important areas for innovation in the coming years.

UK Decline and Rebound

It is sometimes remarked that the British are the only people who indulge in *Schadenfreude* about themselves, revelling in stories of national decline. This is perhaps the inevitable legacy of being the first industrial nation and the global superpower of the nineteenth century. Although the UK has enjoyed significant improvements in material wellbeing over the last 200 years, UK per capita GDP was in *relative* decline compared with other leading countries, such as France, Germany and the US, from around 1870.

At first, the UK's relative decline reflected an almost inevitable catch-up of other countries whose institutions created the right kind of investment climate. But by the late 1970s, as figure 1.1 shows, the UK had been comprehensively overtaken: US per capita GDP was 40% higher than that of the UK, and the major continental European countries were 10–15% ahead. The subsequent three decades, in contrast, saw the UK's relative performance improve substantially, so that by the eve of the crisis in 2007 UK per capita GDP had overtaken both France's and Germany's and the gap with that of the US had narrowed significantly.

Figure 1.2 shows trends in UK per capita GDP since 1950. After falling behind for most of the postwar period, the UK's performance improved

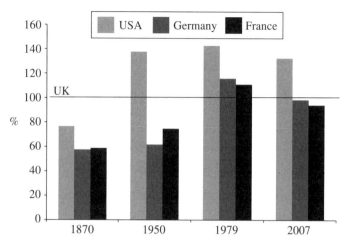

Figure 1.1. GDP per capita 1870–2007 (UK = 100).

Source: Crafts (2012). *Notes.* In each year the base is UK = 100 and each country's GDP per capita is relative to this. So a value of US = 120, for example, implies the US has a 20% higher GDP per capita than the UK. GDP per capita is expressed in 1990 International Geary-Khamis dollars.

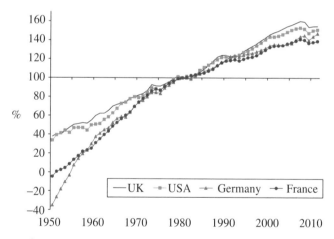

Figure 1.2. GDP per capita 1950–2011 (1980 = 100).

Source: Conference Board data, extracted on 8 June 2012. GDP is measured in US dollars, at constant prices and constant purchasing power parity, with a base year of 2011. For each country the logged series is set to 100 in 1980, so the level of the line in any year indicates the cumulative growth rate (for example, a value of 110 in 2001 indicates that the series has grown by $\exp(10/100) - 1 = 11\%$ between 1980 and 2001). The steeper the slope of the line, the faster that growth has been over that period.

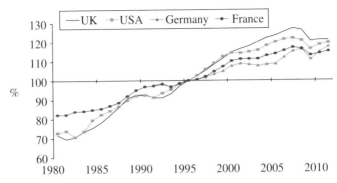

Figure 1.3. Trends in real GDP per working age adult 1980–2011 (1995 = 100).
Source: Conference Board data, extracted on 8 June 2012. GDP is measured in US dollars, at constant prices and constant purchasing power parity, with a base year of 2011. The number of working-age adults, which is obtained from the US Bureau of Labor Force Statistics, includes the civilian population aged over 16. The data for unified Germany is from 1991. For each country the logged series is set to 100 in 1995, so the level of the line in any year indicates the cumulative growth rate (for example, a value of 110 in 2001 indicates that the series has grown by exp(10/100) − 1 = 11% between 1995 and 2001). The steeper the slope of the line, the faster that growth has been over that period.

compared with other leading countries after the 1970s. Figure 1.3 focuses on the later years (partially correcting for demographics by looking at GDP per adult rather than GDP per capita) and shows a similar story: a strong relative performance, especially before 2008.

The improvement in GDP per capita can be broken down into increases in the employment rate (the proportion of the adult population that is working) and increases in labour productivity (GDP per worker or GDP per hour worked). Jobs growth in the UK was facilitated by an improvement in the functioning of the labour market through more activist employment policies and greater wage and job flexibility. But productivity growth was also impressive: among the G6 countries, the growth of UK per hour GDP was second only to that of the US in the decade to 2007, and the growth of the employment rate was better in the UK than it was in the US.

Some commentators have suggested that these productivity improvements were all based on one narrow sector: finance. But this claim is wrong. As figure 1.4 shows, productivity growth between 1980 and 2007 was *not* mainly due to the financial services sector. If we focus on the 'market sector' (by removing health, education, public administration and property—all sectors in which output is very hard to measure), productivity (real output per hour) grew at around 2.8% per annum between 1980 and 2007. Finance only accounted for 0.4% of the 2.8% annual productivity growth in the market economy between 1997 and 2007. Distribution

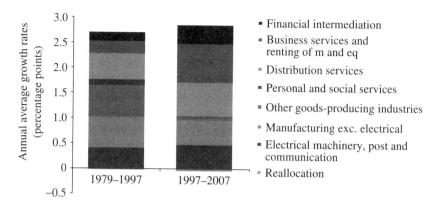

Figure 1.4. Finance directly contributed only a small part of market sector productivity growth.

Source: Corry *et al.* (2011), using EU KLEMS data. These numbers are for the 'market economy'. This excludes the sectors where value added is hard to measure: education, health, public administration and property.

and business services were much more important contributors to productivity growth.

Another way to see that the UK's positive pre-crisis performance was not driven mainly by finance is by looking at the two versions of GDP growth published by the Office for National Statistics (ONS). One uses an output measure based on summing value-added growth across industries, which could in principle be subject to a bias from overestimating output in financial services (although figure 1.4 shows that this is not a major issue). The second measure, based on the 'expenditure' side, adds up the growth of real consumption, investment, government spending and net exports. The output of financial services would only affect these calculations through an overstatement of net exports (at most 0.1% of GDP growth). If there is a discrepancy between these two measures of GDP, the ONS uses the expenditure-based measure. Since this is not biased by mismeasurement of financial services output, finance cannot have caused direct overstatement of GDP in the years before the crisis.

So if it was not all a finance-driven statistical mirage, what caused the improvements in UK performance? The answer is that policies mattered.[2] It is worth focusing on important policy *changes* to understand where the economic gains in figures 1.1–1.3 came from.

---

[2]There is good evidence that policy reforms helped to foster UK growth. Card *et al.* (2004) summarize the evidence from the Thatcher–Major era and Corry *et al.* (2011) summarize the evidence from the Brown–Blair era. OECD (2012a) shows the international evidence of how such reforms foster growth.

- Increases in product market competition through the withdrawal of industrial subsidies; movement to effective competition in many privatized sectors with independent regulators; a strengthening of competition policy (for example, through the 1998 Competition Act); and our membership of the European Union's (EU's) common market.
- Increases in labour market flexibility through reform of the public employment service, improving job search for those on benefits, reducing replacement rates, increasing in-work benefits and restricting union power.
- Openness to foreign business and global talent: restrictions on foreign direct investment were eased in the 1980s and restrictions on immigration relaxed in the late 1990s.
- Sustained expansion of the higher education system: the share of working-age adults with a university degree rose from 5% in 1980 to 14% in 1996 and 31% in 2011, a faster increase than in France, Germany or the US.

In spite of these policy successes, a number of long-term investment failures have not been tackled. The most important of these are a failure to invest in mid-level skills, a failure to build adequate infrastructure—particularly in transport and energy—and a failure to provide a supportive environment for private investment and innovation. There has also been a failure to distribute the fruits of growth more widely: alongside the improvements in the UK's growth performance in the three decades before the crisis, the country has experienced substantial increases in inequality.

Levels of inequality are much higher in the UK than in continental Europe and Japan. As it did in the US, UK inequality rose dramatically from the late 1970s onwards. Figure 1.5 gives one illustration of this phenomenon, showing (separately for men and women) the gap between the richest 10% of workers and the poorest 10% between 1979 and 2010. There was a large increase in wage inequality, especially in the 1980s. Although some of this was related to worldwide pressures from technological change and international trade, which have increased the demand for skilled workers, policies such as the weakening of unions and the lowering of welfare benefits also played a role. The distribution of income has widened and the median household's income (that is, those in the exact middle of the distribution) has risen more slowly than that of the average household. Hence, focusing on the median paints a less rosy picture of economic progress over the last three decades than looking at the average.

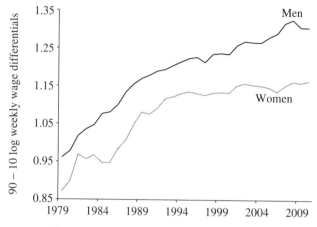

Figure 1.5. Wage inequality 1979–2010.

Source: Lindley and Machin (2013), using data from the New Earnings Survey (NES) and the Annual Survey of Hours and Earnings (ASHE) (a 1% sample of all UK workers). Difference in the natural logarithm of weekly wages of full-time (FT) workers at the 90th percentile (the richest tenth) and the 10th percentile (the poorest tenth).

Increasing inequality is not an inevitable by-product of growth, especially if policies are pursued that make growth more inclusive. A strong education system and an efficient labour market help people to participate in productive processes. Redistribution helps society to deal with the dislocation caused by innovation and globalization. Although the UK's tax and benefit system is progressive and softens earnings differences, lower marginal rates on the better off and reductions in real benefit levels during the 1980s exacerbated the degree of post-tax income inequality. This trend was reversed in the mid 1990s as in-work benefits became much more generous (for example, working family tax credits). In addition, the national minimum wage, introduced in 1999, helped to narrow inequality at the lower end of the wage distribution. But less has been accomplished in addressing other sources of wage inequality (e.g. skill-biased technological change), by improving mid-level skills, for example.

Decline Again After the Crisis?

In the wake of the crisis, the public mood has shifted from euphoria to depression with the general belief that the UK's previous economic success was illusory. We do not think that this is the case, but GDP is still around 3–4% below its early 2008 peak and the pace of recovery is slower than in every previous UK recession. The crisis has taken a severe toll on

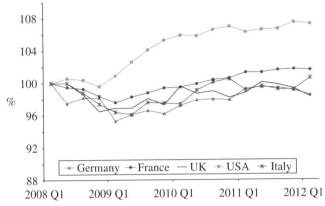

Figure 1.6. Output per hour (2008 Q1 = 100), seasonally adjusted.
Source: ONS (2012). US output per hour covers only the business sector.

all OECD countries, with the UK faring somewhat worse than average in terms of GDP but better than average in terms of jobs.

UK labour productivity has fallen since the crisis began and is about 10% below where it would have been had the pre-2008 trends continued. But as figure 1.6 shows, the UK is hardly unique in this: just about every OECD country has seen such a decline in productivity, with the only exception being the US, which had a much larger shakeout of jobs. This suggests that the causes of depressed productivity are common across the advanced economies rather than due to a UK-specific issue. Furthermore, as discussed above, the evidence in figure 1.4 shows that the pre-2007 productivity gains in the UK were not primarily due to the financial services bubble.

Many possible explanations have been put forward for the low output and productivity of the UK and other advanced economies since the onset of the crisis.

Demand-side explanations of the continued slow recovery emphasize that fiscal austerity has been a drag on growth, especially when it is pursued simultaneously by most advanced economies with interest rates stuck at close to zero. The UK government has so far kept to a tough austerity programme and that seems destined to last for a number of years. Low domestic demand has been exacerbated by a recession in the euro-zone, the UK's main export market, which is also struggling with fiscal retrenchment, banking crises and sovereign debt problems. This uncertainty has been compounded by the unresolved fiscal issues in the US.

The principal supply-side explanation of the slow recovery stresses the damage done by the shock to the financial sector.

- The first problem is that banks are repairing their balance sheets, which is making them reluctant to lend.
- The second problem is that small and medium-sized enterprises (SMEs) are finding it hard to access finance and this is inhibiting growth and new entry.
- The third problem is one of exit: while low interest rates and some forbearance by banks have led to fewer defaults by households and businesses, this has slowed the adjustment process. Many businesses and households would go bankrupt under normal market conditions.

Together, these three factors have created a problem of capital misallocation and debt overhang that may take many years to unwind. This weighs down on incentives to invest in housing and private capital.

These demand- and supply-side factors are interrelated. There is a risk that if high levels of unemployment persist for many years, the long-term unemployed will lose their skills, motivation and networks, thus reducing potential supply. If there are fewer innovative new entrants, this will drag down potential growth for many years.

Even though these factors create serious headwinds, standard growth theory and economic history suggest that permanent falls in the rate of growth are unlikely. For example, growth rates did not fall permanently after the Great Depression. Although there may be some permanent loss in the level of output, this loss has tended to be modest in most past recessions. Hence, although policy remains important in determining the speed of the recovery from recession, we do not believe that the crisis has revealed that the pre-2008 improvements in the UK's economic position relative to the EU and the US are likely to unravel.

Investment Failure: The UK's Fundamental Problem

The UK was once a paragon of investment. Around the time of the industrial revolution, major investments in roads, canals and railways supported growth and industrial transformation. For example, the turnpike trusts, which were created to extend the road network as well as canal-building programmes, harnessed private initiative to alleviate transport bottlenecks at a time when the absence of infrastructure would have been very damaging. In the late nineteenth and early twentieth century, the UK was also at the forefront of investment in electrification and sanitation, enabling dramatic gains in living standards. The UK had the structures needed to be adaptable to the economic challenges of the time.

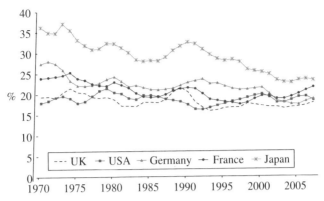

Figure 1.7. Investment as a percentage of GDP, 1970–2007.

Source: OECD (2012c). This indicator is calculated as the ratio of gross fixed capital formation to GDP. Data refer to the fiscal year.

The dynamism that saw the provision of infrastructure that enabled the growth of the UK as an industrial power has all but evaporated. Successive policy initiatives have failed to put in place adequate structures to support the identification, planning, implementation and financing of infrastructure projects, particularly in transport and energy. Thus, the inadequate provision of infrastructure now constitutes a persistent and major policy failure, one that generations of governments from all parties have failed to address.

The failure to provide infrastructure is matched by the failure of policy since the 1970s to address long-standing problems of low investment. In some cases, policy reforms may actually have made the problems worse. While it is well known that public and private investment rates have been slashed in the wake of the crisis (with public investment falling from £51.1 billion in 2009/10 to £26.7 billion in 2011/12), investment levels have in fact been low in the UK for many decades (see figure 1.7).

These problems of underinvestment are not confined to capital in the classic sense: indeed, they cut across aspects of skills, infrastructure and innovation. Despite a great deal of evidence about these problems and their impacts on growth (which we document in more detail below), successive governments have failed to address them effectively. Three problems loom large.

First, relatively large numbers of children are still exposed to poor-quality teaching and leave school inadequately prepared for the rest of their lives. In 2011, 58% of pupils in England got five good GCSEs (A*–C), including English and mathematics. But only a third (34%) of pupils from disadvantaged backgrounds (classed as those on free school meals or in

13

local authority care) achieved this benchmark. Improvements in human capital are arguably the best way to achieve more inclusive growth and to reverse increases in inequality without putting further pressures on the benefit system.

Second, infrastructure has been neglected, particularly in the areas of transport and energy. For example, more than a fifth of the UK's electricity-generating capacity will go out of commission over the next decade and Ofgem, the energy sector regulator, has warned of power shortages by 2015.

Third, the UK is home to one of the most dynamic world centres for financial services, yet the country seems unable to deliver adequate long-term finance for innovation and private investment. UK investment levels are significantly below those of other EU countries (see figure 1.7). In 2008 the UK's share of total GDP devoted to R&D stood at 1.8%, a lower proportion than in the US (2.8%), Germany (2.7%) and France (2.1%).

In spite of the evidence that low investment in skills, infrastructure and innovation imposes major constraints on growth, poor policies persist, as do institutions that fail to provide long-term frameworks for investment and action. The result is that although there were improvements before the crisis, UK productivity levels still lag behind those of other major countries. In 2011 UK per hour GDP was 27% below the level in the US, 25% behind France and 22% behind Germany.

Why does the UK fail to invest for prosperity? To understand this, we need to understand the nature of policy successes and failures and the institutions that support them.

Policymaking Success

Long-term investments require a stable policy environment within which investors can manage risk, since returns often accrue over decades, well beyond the typical parliamentary cycle. Stability is fostered by having a predictable policy framework, backed where possible by a cross-party consensus. Failure to create such conditions undermines investment, posing a serious impediment to growth. The evidence suggests that the UK has failed to create an enabling environment in a number of important areas for growth.

The problem of policy instability is compounded by a number of features of the political process.

- First, the time horizons of politicians are typically truncated as they are moved swiftly between ministerial posts and face the electorate every four or five years.

- Second, the adversarial nature of UK politics creates a tendency for policy switches (and subsequent reinvention) as governments change. Sometimes this means rebranding and reorganization. In some cases, there is genuine uncertainty about whether the policy framework that is in place will last. The pressure of bad publicity weighs heavily on political decisions and makes it harder for politicians to take unpopular decisions.
- Third, political debates often lack guidance from independent, evidence-based advice. For example, the civil service must maintain the confidence of ministers and is constitutionally barred from advising anyone but the government of the day. Civil servants' incentives appear to be more focused on helping to deliver policies than on helping governments (or others) structure their thinking in the longer-term interests of society as a whole.

Too often, the result is a costly cocktail of political procrastination, institutional churn and poor decision making. 'Celebrity reviews' are often set up to come to the rescue, sometimes as a genuine attempt to fill an institutional gap but more often to serve an instrumental purpose, leaving many of the key problems unaddressed.

In some policy areas, the UK has led the way in seeking innovative institutional solutions for designing and implementing policy more effectively. In many cases this has been achieved by creating a better balance between political discretion, technocratic input and predictable rules. Perhaps the longest standing is our system of common law, which has allowed independent courts to oversee the evolution of the law while operating at a distance from political interference. More recent examples include the following.

- The conduct of competition policy under the 1998 Competition Act and the 2002 Enterprise Act, which strengthened the Competition Commission and the Office of Fair Trading (OFT): these two institutions were made more independent and political lobbying was removed from decisions over large-scale mergers.
- The decision to give the Bank of England independence to set interest rates after 1997: a series of structures was put in place to allow for the idiosyncrasies of monetary policy, particularly the need for credible, long-term policy commitments based on sound and transparent expert advice. The UK went from having one of the most unstable macroeconomic environments in the 1970s and 1980s to having one of the most stable. While lessons are now being learned from the crisis, this approach is also being followed in 'macroprudential regulation' of financial markets.

15

- The regulators of privatized services, such as telecoms (Ofcom), energy (Ofgem) and water (Ofwat): these agencies aim to provide a framework of rules that safeguard the public interest along with a stable investment climate. They draw heavily on independent expert advice overseen by judicial process.
- The National Institute for Clinical Excellence, which has helped to create a better informed and less polarized debate around the choices of health treatments available within the NHS: the government rightly remains in charge of overall spending rules but no longer directly manages difficult detailed decisions where clinical expertise is of primary importance.
- The Migration Advisory Committee, which set up the points-based system for immigration; the Low Pay Commission, which advises on the minimum wage; the national Pay Review Bodies for public sector workers; and the Climate Change Committee. In all of these cases, expert opinion is used within a clearly defined framework.
- The Office for Budget Responsibility, which has taken over the UK's fiscal forecasting functions from HM Treasury: this new institution monitors the degree to which the government is on track to meet its own fiscal goals; it produces long-term assessments of fiscal sustainability; and it scrutinizes the Treasury's costing of budget measures. In these various roles, the Office for Budget Responsibility helps to strengthen the external credibility of fiscal policy and raises the quality of the political debate.

Two main lessons follow from these experiences.

- First, they have put politics in the right place. The strategic choices, rules and high-level objectives are set by government. Independent bodies make decisions based on the technical criteria laid down by politicians and are held to account by parliament. In so doing, these bodies have mitigated the problems of indecision and unpredictability that are important impediments to investment and growth. By focusing the politics where it should be, they improve accountability, transparency and democracy.
- Second, in these successful cases the political debate is supported by a framework for independent and transparent expert advice, with clear lines of accountability.

Throughout this book we discuss how these principles of policymaking success can be extended further to foster a better climate for encouraging investment in human capital, infrastructure and innovation.

In thinking about institutional ways to reduce policy instability, we also need to consider our relationship with Europe. We cannot predict what will happen with any degree of accuracy, but we will surely still have Europe as our main trading partner for the foreseeable future—and, as discussed above, the common market has been an important driver of productivity-enhancing competition. Hence, calls for Britain to leave the EU following a referendum are not only misguided, they create the very uncertainty that will damage investment and productivity right now. It is analogous to the needless self-inflicted wounds that the US is causing in its debates over the debt ceiling and the fiscal cliff.

The Structure of This Chapter

This chapter is about how the UK can create better conditions for investment. First, we show how the causes of lower UK productivity levels are linked to investment failures—in human capital (section 1.3), in infrastructure (section 1.4) and in private investment and innovation (section 1.5).

In each section we ask why the type of investment particularly matters for growth, and we document the UK's specific problems in these areas. We then give our recommendations, dividing these into the most important core policies first followed by some additional auxiliary measures. We also take up the challenge of answering the political economy question: why have these problems not been dealt with adequately before?

The last sections of the chapter suggest a better way of accounting for our progress in promoting inclusive growth (section 1.6) and include a call to all sides of the UK political spectrum to sign up to a 'Manifesto for Growth' (section 1.7).

1.3   HUMAN CAPITAL[3]

Why Human Capital Matters

Both economic theory and empirical evidence show that, in the long run, human capital is a critical input for growth. The growth dividend from upgrading human capital is potentially enormous and improving the quality of compulsory education is the key to achieving these gains. Evidence suggests that increasing UK school standards moderately (say, to the level of Australia or Germany) could put us on a growth path that would more than double long-term average incomes compared with current trends. An even more ambitious target—to raise our educational standards to

---

[3]For a more detailed discussion see chapter 3.

those found in world-leading countries, such as Finland—would generate even more spectacular gains. It is important, therefore, to frame debates about improving school quality as a growth issue.

There is a double dividend from improving human capital since many of the gains from growth would accrue to the less well off, thereby reducing inequality. Increasing the quality and quantity of the skills of disadvantaged children will make growth more inclusive through reducing the high levels of wage inequality in the UK (see figure 1.5 above). In addition to the benefits from lower inequality, reducing the fraction of poorly educated people will reduce the welfare rolls and the numbers caught up in the criminal justice system.

Although our principal focus is on education between the ages of five and eighteen, it is important to promote excellence in higher education and lifelong learning as well as dealing with other long-standing problems in vocational training, pre-school education and adult skills. We also suggest reforms in these areas.

A large number of international studies show that high-quality teaching is the key to improving schools. There are well-established positive effects from extra resources, improved buildings, higher pay (especially when linked to performance), extended provision of information technology and smaller class sizes, but these effects appear to be very modest in comparison with the large benefits that could be realized by increasing the quality of teachers.

Unfortunately, predicting who will be an effective teacher before they start working is very hard and is not well captured by the formal teaching qualifications held nor by the number of years in the profession. But once teachers have been in front of a class, parents, pupils and especially head teachers have a good idea of who the really excellent teachers are. In addition, there is now much more data on pupil progression. Thus, a system for improving the quality of teachers has to use information acquired from observing teachers at work and being responsive to their performance.

Diagnosis: The Problems of Education in the UK

The UK is mid-table overall in most international rankings of schools: it is mediocre in the internationally comparable tests in the OECD's PISA (Programme for International Student Assessment) scores (taken at age 15), although it does somewhat better in the more curriculum-based TIMSS (Trends in International Mathematics and Science Study) assessments (taken at ages 10 and 15). Indicators of the UK's average educational outcomes have shown significant improvements, some of which is down to grade inflation but some of which is real. Most impressive is the increase in the proportion of the workforce with a university degree, which increased from 5% in 1980 to 31% in 2011.

One major systemic failing in the UK education system is the 'long tail' of poorly performing schools and pupils compared with other countries, particularly at the secondary level. A significant part of the explanation for this is the stubborn link between pupils' socioeconomic backgrounds and their educational attainment. For example, a fifth of children in England on free school meals (a common measure of disadvantage) do not reach the expected level in mathematics at age 7 (Key Stage 1), and this proportion rises to a third by age 11 (Key Stage 2). The correlation between disadvantage and poor academic attainment is particularly strong in the UK. Our failure to provide adequate education to children from disadvantaged backgrounds constitutes a waste of human resources on a grand scale. It holds back economic opportunities and is detrimental to growth.

Disadvantaged children are found in many schools and generally perform poorly compared with their better-off peers even when located in better schools. Disadvantaged children lose out in schools for a number of reasons.

- Most schools face weak incentives to focus on their performance. Parental choice is seriously constrained by place of residence and, in particular, distance from home to school. Despite numerous initiatives to facilitate greater parental choice, including several changes to the schools admissions code, the ability to choose schools is still mainly a prerogative of better-off families who can buy houses near good schools.

- The framework for school inspections by the regulator, Ofsted, places insufficient emphasis on pupil performance across the range of achievement levels.

- Government 'floor targets' are themselves flawed.[4] They do not focus on the 'lower tail' within schools and so schools can meet them largely by ignoring the bottom third of pupils.

---

[4]According to the Department for Education, primary schools are underperforming unless one of the following criteria is met in English and mathematics: (i) at least 60% of pupils achieve the expected level (level 4) or higher; or (ii) pupils make the expected degree of progress between the end of infants (Key Stage 1) and the end of juniors (Key Stage 2). Secondary schools are underperforming if less than 40% of pupils achieve five good GCSEs—or equivalent qualifications—graded A*-C, including English and mathematics (this threshold will rise to 50% by 2015); or if fewer pupils make good progress in English and mathematics between Key Stage 2 and Key Stage 4 than the national average.

Current funding arrangements give more resources to local authorities in areas with more disadvantaged children. But the evidence suggests that these resources fail to reach those children effectively. One of the reasons for this is, for example, because much of this money is not ring fenced for individual schools or for disadvantaged pupils within those schools. In response to this, the Pupil Premium was introduced as a funding stream attached directly to disadvantaged children. As with an educational voucher, this should increase the incentives for schools to admit disadvantaged pupils and increase their financial resources. But although such payments are better targeted than standard local authority funding, survey evidence suggests that schools do not generally use these funds specifically to help disadvantaged pupils.

Another problem in schools is deficiencies in teacher recruitment and training. Selection into teacher training is tight at the beginning of the course but negligible thereafter. Tightening academic entry requirements still further is not the answer: such policies restrict the number of recruits without having a significant impact on teaching effectiveness.

Although, when it comes to school autonomy, the UK scores reasonably by international standards, autonomy remains limited because a large number of schools still operate under heavy constraints due to the power of local authorities. Local authorities are generally reluctant to allow popular schools to expand and underperforming schools to contract. Thus, in practice, most schools have a guaranteed intake, regardless of how they perform. This is changing under the expansion of the academies programme started by the last government and extended in the 2010 Academies Act by the coalition government. Academies have significantly greater freedoms in management (although, quite rightly, not the freedom to select their pupil intake on ability) and they are directly funded by the Department for Education.

School autonomy *combined with* a strong accountability framework centred on quality provides the best hope for improving school performance. There is evidence that more autonomous schools respond better to local parental choice, so increasing parental choice will not lead to higher standards unless there is also greater decentralization to empower head teachers. Accountability is also fostered through better governance and leadership through sponsorship from successful external organizations, such as universities or school networks.

Core Recommendations on Education

Our proposals go with the grain of the academies movement. But the system needs to deal more squarely with the UK's failure to develop the talents of disadvantaged pupils. We therefore propose some direct steps, particularly financial and non-financial incentives, to address this fundamental problem.

The 'academization' of the school system should deepen into a *flexible ecology*, building on aspects of the higher education system (see below). There are four integral parts: greater school autonomy, strengthened central accountability (transparent information and inspection), wider parental choice and more flexibility for successful schools and their sponsors to expand.

To improve school governance, leadership and management, it must become easier for outstanding sponsored academies to grow. Ideally, this operates at the school level by making physical expansion easier. But there may be spatial limitations, which is why expansion through the growth of networks of sponsored academies is also an important way to spread better practices. By the same token, it should be made easier for underperforming schools to shrink and, if they do not improve, to be taken over or, in extreme cases, closed down.

Changes that could be made to help to develop the talent of *disadvantaged pupils* include the following.

- Information on school performance needs to be changed to also reflect the performance of disadvantaged children within the school. Such changes should apply to league tables and targets and they should be more closely reflected in Ofsted's inspection regime. Improving the performance of disadvantaged children should be given a central role when Ofsted awards an 'outstanding' grade to a school.
- 'Floor targets' must be redesigned to become effective in addressing poor school performance and should be aligned with the guidelines defined in the framework for schools inspection. This should involve moving away from undifferentiated average performance targets (such as the current target, which requires 40% of pupils to achieve five A*–C passes at GCSE level). These are 'blind' targets that distort schools' incentives to target resources and support at those children who can more readily be expected to reach the predefined threshold.
- Contextual value added (school exam results adjusted for intake quality) should be published for each school for Pupil Premium children and for the medium-performing Key Stage 2 group.

The expansion of new sponsored academies should be focused on underperforming schools serving disadvantaged children. The original programme was shown to be very successful in doing this (Machin and Vernoit 2011), but the post-2010 academies are less focused on this group of schools.

Teacher quality needs to be improved through better conditions for both *entry* and *exit*. Teacher recruitment and training could be improved in a number of ways.

- Teach First (which is renowned for its outstanding track record in recruiting high-quality graduates) should expand until it becomes one of the main routes into school teaching.
- Mainstream teacher recruitment should become more concentrated in the best universities and schools, following a national recruitment process.
- The probation period for teachers should be extended in length. For example, it could be doubled from two years to four.
- Policies that focus on the grades, qualifications and backgrounds of prospective teachers should be relaxed to encourage a wider range of applications to reflect the fact that teacher effectiveness is not highly correlated with crude background indicators.
- Mechanisms for teachers and schools to share best practice should be more strongly encouraged. The 'London Challenge' programme has shown how successful this can be.

Our proposed measures would, we believe, work together to increase the skills that are needed to make the UK economy a more competitive and dynamic place to do business and they would directly tackle the long-standing problem of poor intermediate and low-level skills. Together they would ensure that fewer of our children leave school ill equipped to work in the competitive international environment that we now face. These proposals would also reduce disadvantage without compromising the achievements of other children.

Other Policies to Support Human Capital

Further Recommendations for Schools

To provide additional support for disadvantaged pupils, the criteria for receiving the Pupil Premium should be expanded to reflect a wider measure of disadvantage than simply free school meals. This need has now been acknowledged by making eligibility for the Pupil Premium dependent on whether a family has ever been eligible for free school meals in the last six years, but available databases could expand the definitions of eligibility further.

The Pupil Premium is planned to increase from £600 to £900 in 2014/15. We recommend that part of the premium should be given in cash to the pupils and their families to provide an individual incentive. This should be conditional on improvements in performance after age 14, such as attendance and grade improvement beyond pre-agreed baseline expectations. This kind of 'conditional cash transfer' programme has proved to be effective in a wide variety of programmes (in welfare reform, for example, re-employment vouchers are usually more effective if the bonus is kept by the job seeker rather than the firm that employs them). The precursor to this approach was the Education Maintenance Allowance, which evaluations show was effective in encouraging children from disadvantaged backgrounds to remain in school. We recommend that the bursary scheme that replaced the Education Maintenance Allowance should be wrapped back into this.

More resources should be made available for programmes that provide better information to children and parents from low-income families on the economic returns to different subjects.

In the spirit of encouraging better teaching, a more flexible system of rewards should be introduced for pay and promotion. This would include ending automatic increments; basing pay on performance and local market conditions; and extra rewards for teachers of core subjects in tough schools. We need swifter action on improved professional development and movement out of the classroom for underperforming teachers. Some of these changes are starting to happen and we expect this process to accelerate under the flexible education system that we are recommending, which should give head teachers the incentives and capabilities to make these reforms.

UK education policy has traditionally lacked rigorous, independent evaluations. Positive steps have been taken in this direction with the creation of the Education Endowment Foundation, but much more could be done. For example, we recommend piloting the release of teacher-level information on performance (in a similar vein to the way that the NHS makes data on surgeons available).

Higher Education

The UK has a world-class system of higher education, home to many of the world's leading universities. For example, the UK is, along with the US, one of only two countries represented in the Shanghai ranking of the world's top ten universities, and it has more major scientific prizes per capita (for example, Nobel prizes) than the US. The benefits from maintaining funding for research and an open environment in which universities can compete for the best students and faculty members cannot be overestimated. The knowledge and understanding created in universities play a central role in building a flexible and adaptable economy. The higher education sector benefits the UK economy as a source of skills, of innovations that raise productivity, and of valuable export earnings in the form of foreign students who choose to study here (an enormous industry of global growth). There are potential advantages to the UK from having the world's future economic, societal and government leaders educated here.

It is essential that the UK continues to attract the best students and faculty from around the world. The current policies on student visas and work visas for non-UK citizens are damaging because of their direct impact on the ability of universities to recruit. We recommend that if the net immigration target itself is not dropped, then students should be removed from the target. These policies send a signal to the world that the UK is becoming insular and they will therefore damage our position in higher education and, if they are sustained for any length of time, they will constrain growth.

One of the main reasons for the UK's success in higher education is a framework of rules and accountability that emphasizes excellence in teaching and research. Universities are largely autonomous in their operational decisions and it is important that this is sustained. There is now a settled institutional framework through the Higher Education Funding Council for England and the other funding councils to channel funds towards centres where research is objectively evaluated. The flexible ecology of higher education allows freedom to build bridges with industry, either in the form of sponsored research or through collaborations in student degree programmes. There is further scope to strengthen and enhance these linkages in undergraduate programmes.

While the system of university fees is controversial, it has the potential to create a more stable funding environment for universities, one that is less dependent on political cycles. This creates a framework for long-term investment in campuses and high-quality programmes.

A future challenge to the mid-tier UK university sector is the delivery of course material and lectures online, such as is done by the Khan Academy, for example. Given the dominance of the English language in science and the flexibility of the higher education sector, this should be an area in which the UK can seize an opportunity.

Vocational Training

Intermediate skills are particularly poorly developed in the UK, as are the transitions between schools and the workplace, hence our relatively high proportion of young people 'not in education, employment or training'. There is now a cross-party consensus that the number of apprenticeships should be increased as they are a vital way to tackle the problem of low/intermediate skills. There has been a significant expansion of apprenticeships since 2010, but unfortunately these have mainly been for the over 25s in relatively low-skilled, low-paying jobs.

Recent reports on apprenticeships by Hilary Steedman, Alison Wolf and Doug Richard have had a common theme. The most important thing is to get employers more involved through a mixture of carrots (devolving more of the skills budget directly to them) and possibly sticks (for example, an industry-specific training levy). Apprenticeships need to be longer, they should pay a training wage (English apprenticeships are relatively highly paid by international standards, which deters many employers), and their administration must be radically simplified. Potential apprentices need accurate information on training and good advice that does not pretend that all types of learning will be equally economically rewarding.

The UK has a long-standing problem of poor basic skills among a large proportion of adults, with particular shortcomings in literacy and numeracy. Many reports (see, for example, Kang *et al.* 2012) estimate that around a fifth of the adult population lack such basic skills. Our suggested policies for improving education and the apprenticeship system will have a long-term effect on reducing this serious problem.

Apprenticeships must be of much higher quality: too much of the expansion of apprenticeships over the last six years has been around low-quality apprenticeships. There should be an element of 'off-the-job' training. Apprenticeships should include an academic component focused on basic skills in English and mathematics, which in the long run would help to tackle the problem of poor adult basic skills. The countries with the most successful apprenticeship programmes concentrate on improving the language and mathematics ability of their post-16 vocational students, and so, belatedly, should the UK.

Pre-school Education

Early years' pre-school education has immense potential to increase skills, since small improvements at an early stage of life will cumulate over an individual's lifetime. Thus, it is far better to intervene early or improve human capital than to wait until someone is struggling fo·

as an adult. Early life experiences can be a source of disadvantage that is later reflected in poor performance in schools. There have been some high-quality randomized controlled trials outside the UK that suggest large returns to intensive interventions: the Perry Preschool project, the Abecedarian Project and Nurse Health Partnerships are good examples.

Given the proven importance of early intervention we support a greater policy focus on improving children's centres as a means of delivering targeted interventions to improve the prospects of children who are most at risk of developing weak cognitive and non-cognitive skills. Children's centres are essentially a scaled-down version of Sure Start, which has also struggled to deliver high-quality services for disadvantaged children (partly because most Sure Start staff are volunteers). The extra resources needed for children's centres need to be concentrated on the disadvantaged, with an emphasis on evaluating best practice and propagating it throughout the system.

Why Have Problems with Human Capital Persisted?

Since the UK's education system has been an area of intense interest and policy reform over the past fifteen years, it may seem surprising that so many problems persist. There have been welcome movements towards greater school autonomy and improved educational standards. Much has been learned about what is effective, but there are factors that are holding back reforms and these problems need to be addressed.

First, publicly available information (such as league tables), school performance targets and Ofsted are all focused on the average pupil rather than on those nearer to the bottom of the distribution. Politicians tend to follow this path because they often target the average voter in elections.

Second, the reforms we discuss threaten a number of vested interests in maintaining the status quo. Some people are understandably fearful of the ideas of changing teachers' contracts, reducing the role of local authorities and allowing greater movement of pupils between schools. Combining the move to a more flexible system with an emphasis on disadvantaged children should help to allay those fears.

Third, because of the high public profile of the education system, there is a tendency for national politicians to tinker with certain areas of human capital policy to give the impression that the government is actively working to improve things. There is also too great a readiness to create the perception of party differentiation for electoral reasons, whether or not that differentiation really exists.

Apprenticeship policy is an example of these problems. The 2011 Wolf review emphasized that the attempted micromanagement of vocational training by central government, with overlapping directives, constant policy reversals and expensive bureaucracy, is at the heart of the problem. As with other areas highlighted by the Commission, the policy uncertainty engendered in this area has been highly counterproductive.

Summary on Human Capital

Growth depends on improving human capital and this starts with higher-quality teaching in schools. We propose a flexible system for education that gives schools greater autonomy and the ability to grow within a national accountability framework that places a premium on radically raising the standards of the bottom ability group. Together with improved choice for parents, better-quality information (across the entire distribution of achievement) and more effective incentives for teachers and schools, this will improve the quality of teaching. The UK's world-class university system must also be sustained and strengthened as a key potential advantage in a rapidly changing world.

1.4 PUBLIC INVESTMENT IN INFRASTRUCTURE[5]

Why Infrastructure Matters

Investments in infrastructure—such as transport, energy, telecoms and housing—are essential inputs into economic growth. They are complementary to many other forms of investment. They also tend to be large scale and long term, requiring high levels of coordination to maximize the wider benefits that they offer. This makes it inevitable that governments will play a vital role in planning, delivering and (to some extent) financing such projects.

Diagnosis: The Problems of Infrastructure in the UK

In the 2012 World Economic Forum report on global competitiveness, the UK was ranked only twenty-fourth for 'quality of overall infrastructure'. In a 2011 infrastructure survey by the Confederation of British Industry, nearly half of respondents rated the UK's transport networks as well

---

[5]For a more detailed discussion see chapters 4 and 5.

below average by international standards. Nowhere are the problems of UK infrastructure better illustrated than by airport capacity in the southeast, where generations of politicians have prevaricated to a point where there is a serious risk to London's position as a major hub.

Improving infrastructure investment requires a radical change: policy must be initiated, decided on and implemented in a much more coherent way. Historically, attempts to overcome market failures in infrastructure investment have led to a mixture of government ownership and provision on the one hand and private sector regulation on the other. This, in turn, has exposed infrastructure investment to important policy risks and decision-making biases that damage investment prospects.

Among the key problems that need addressing in relation to all areas of infrastructure are the following.

- Vulnerability to policy instability—a lack of clarity about strategy, frequent reversals and prevarication over key decisions. For example, it has taken twelve years of reviews, white papers and legislation for government to come forward with a substantial set of energy policy reforms (the most recent being the 2012 Energy Bill).

- Difficulty in basing decisions on sound advice and assessment of policy alternatives built on unbiased appraisals (as opposed to those of lobbyists).

- The limitations of a planning system that does not properly share the benefits of development. This has created chronic Nimbyism (local resistance to new developments on the grounds of 'not in my backyard') because of the incentives for small groups of influential citizens and politicians to veto, or cause egregious delays to, projects with wide economic benefits.

- A series of public sector accounting distortions that have made it difficult to weigh up benefits and costs in a coherent way. In particular, targets for fiscal policy often draw on measures of public debt while failing to account for the value (and depreciation) of public assets.

These problems affect all major public sector capital projects to some degree, but they vary in their severity. The consequences for long-term growth and patterns of development in the UK also vary. We focus mainly on transport and energy, where the problems are well understood and where the potential damage to growth is likely to be more severe, but we also briefly discuss housing and telecoms.

Transport

Transport needs to adapt to a growing population and changing needs in different parts of the country. Underinvestment and inadequate maintenance characterize the provision of roads, railways and airports. There are particular inefficiencies in how transport is priced and how decisions are made and financed. The 2006 Eddington Review[6] cited a potential cost of £22 billion per annum in increased congestion by 2025 if the transport network fails to keep up with demand. The UK lacks a long-term strategic vision based on coherent and transparent criteria.

In terms of usage and economic importance, the *road* network is the most important means of transport. It accounts for three-quarters of passenger travel and two-thirds of freight. UK road congestion is among the worst in Europe, particularly in urban areas, reflecting inadequate investment over several decades. Responsibility for maintaining, operating and improving the network of national roads resides with the Highways Agency, but the remainder of the network is the responsibility of local authorities. This fragmentation means that there is a lack of long-term, strategic thinking. While the government has established a systematic process of five-year plans for railways, with an associated funding commitment, there is nothing comparable for roads.

The *aviation* sector suffers from constrained airport capacity, particularly hub runway capacity in the southeast. UK international gateways have some of the worst delays in Europe: a quarter of Heathrow and Gatwick flights are delayed by over fifteen minutes. Both Heathrow and Gatwick are operating at near full runway utilization. Given that the UK has a comparative advantage in international business services where face-to-face relationships are vital, failure to deal with these issues demonstrates remarkable complacency.

Long-standing failings are also apparent in the management and operation of *railways*. These include a poor reliability record by international standards. There is still insufficient emphasis on implementing long-term plans to reduce carbon intensity or on alleviating problems of passenger crowding at peak times, especially in the southeast. Persistent problems with high costs have also failed to be adequately confronted. We

---

[6]The Eddington Review was commendable in that it (i) looked at a clear, credible forward-thinking framework; (ii) tackled the problems and bottlenecks in terms of their severity and economic and social returns; and (iii) drew on strong academic advice. The fact that it got 'buried' illustrates the problem with UK policymaking and the inadequacies of the one-off review approach.

have committed to long-term funding of rail projects with relatively low benefits in relation to their costs in preference to investment in roads where the benefits are unambiguously greater.

Energy

In common with other OECD countries, the UK faces significant challenges in trying to achieve a balance of *security*, *stability* and *affordability* in energy supply, while at the same time complying with relatively stringent *carbon targets*.

Successive UK governments have failed to deliver stable, credible, long-term policy/regulatory environments that are capable of attracting private investment on the scale and in the manner required to meet these challenges. Investors see policy as unstable either because of ad hoc tinkering or because of major changes in political objectives. For example, uncertainty about the level of subsidy for wind projects means that businesses have lacked long-term clarity on the basis of which to invest. Similarly, in the last decade, North Sea operators have experienced four major changes to the taxes they have had to pay. These changes create inefficiencies, as a windfall tax in one year's budget is followed by tax breaks in a subsequent budget.

This has all occurred at a time when more than a fifth of the UK's electricity-generating capacity is due to be decommissioned within the next ten years. Ofgem, the energy sector regulator, has warned that there could be an imminent drop in spare electricity capacity from a margin of 14% at present to just 4% by 2015 (Ofgem 2012).

The government's Electricity Market Reform programme is geared towards providing a framework for investment. But it will take time to build confidence, which has been dented by constant internal bickering in government resulting in revisions to the framework every few years. The current policy framework assumes big increases in future gas and oil prices, which may not transpire. Technological change is making substitution between different sources of energy easier and creating new sources of energy and new ways of storing it. Revolutionary changes are being brought about by unconventional gas production. In the US, gas extraction from tight formations such as shale and coal ('fracking') has provided the country with enough gas to meet domestic electricity demand for over 500 years at current usage levels. If other countries succeed in commercializing these reserves in the same way as the US has, then gas will fundamentally change the way we think about resource scarcity and

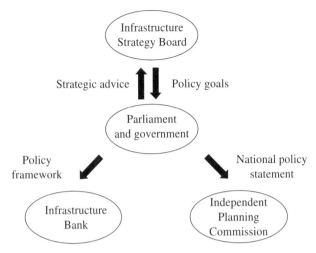

Figure 1.8. Our new institutional architecture for infrastructure.

will provide a cheap, abundant and cleaner fossil fuel to pave the way to a low-carbon economy.

Such changes put a premium on flexibility and diversity of supply rather than becoming locked into a limited number of energy sources. They also mean that plans to reduce greenhouse gas emissions should be developed in a timely way, establishing a predictable framework that can take account of potential changes in markets and technologies.

Core Recommendations on Infrastructure

The persistent failures of infrastructure policy in the UK require us to come up with a new approach. Our main proposal is for a new institutional architecture to govern infrastructure strategy, delivery and financing. A set of complementary institutions is illustrated in figure 1.8.

Our proposal has three core institutions.

An *Infrastructure Strategy Board* (ISB) to provide strategic vision in all areas: its key function would be to provide independent expert advice on infrastructure issues. It would lay the foundation for a well-informed, cross-party consensus to underpin stable long-term policy. The ISB would support evidence gathering from experts and operate thorough transparent and wide-ranging public consultations, engaging interested parties and members of the public in the debate over the costs and benefits of policy options. The ISB would obtain its authority from and be accountable to parliament. Its mandate would be laid down by statute. As a standing body, it would produce regular reports on infrastructure needs and long-term priorities and challenges. The ISB would be governed by a high-profile, independent management board, which would be directly accountable to and appointed by parliament.

An *Infrastructure Planning Commission* (IPC), which would be charged with delivering on the ISB's strategic priorities. This body existed in the recent past, but it has now been replaced by the Infrastructure Planning Unit under the auspices of the Department for Communities and Local Government. This change reintroduced ministerial approval for projects and we believe that independence from ministerial decision making should be restored. The IPC is designed to give predictability and effectiveness to (mostly private) investment that drives implementation of strategy. It must not be misunderstood as a 'central planner'.

An *Infrastructure Bank* (IB) to facilitate the provision of stable, long-term, predictable, mostly private sector finance for infrastructure. There are good theoretical reasons for the creation of such a bank. It can help to overcome key market failures in capital markets in a direct and constructive way. In particular, it can help to reduce policy risk and, through partnerships, to structure finance in a way that mitigates and shares risk efficiently. This will require a whole range of financial instruments, including equity and structured guarantees. There are good practical examples that show the advantages of a bank with this sort of mandate, such as Brazil's BNDES, Germany's Kreditanstalt für Wiederaufbau (KfW), the European Bank for Reconstruction and Development, and to some extent the European Investment Bank. The IB would develop banking and sector-specific skills in new and important areas. Through its partnerships, it would provide powerful examples with catalytic effects on private investment. It could have a very strong multiplicative impact so that its investments have effects much larger than the amount of capital it puts in. The IB would be governed by an independent board with a clearly defined mandate and access to capital markets.

In addition to creating the institutions listed above, we need to institute *generous compensation schemes* to extend the benefits of infrastructure projects to those who might otherwise stand to lose out, either due to disruption caused by the construction phase of a project or by the long-term impact on land and/or property values. The principle is to share the broad value that the implementation of the national strategy will bring. Such compensation schemes should be enshrined in law and built into the thinking of the ISB and the operations of the IPC. At present, the UK does not provide adequate compensation for individuals who bear the costs of development. This contrasts with other countries, where mandatory compensation due to noise, travel or other disruptions is commonplace. The UK's problem arises partly because the level of compensation is low and partly because existing compensation schemes are primarily communal. Both communal and individual schemes are necessary.

Our proposed infrastructure institutions would facilitate long-term planning and reduce policy instability in the planning, delivery and financing of infrastructure projects in the UK. The new institutional architecture would allow governments to choose their priorities and decide on strategy but, crucially, it would ensure that political decisions are taken in the right place; that they do not expand to aspects of strategy and/or implementation where they add little value and can be a costly source of instability (for example, planning); and that they represent credible commitments for current and prospective investors. In addition, the new framework would support a political debate informed by rigorous, independent assessment of policy alternatives, fostering the formation of cross-party consensus where possible, making political procrastination harder and thus generally improving the quality of policymaking.

The projects considered by the Infrastructure Strategy Board, delivered by the Infrastructure Planning Commission and financed by the Infrastructure Bank would be those of greatest national priority, such as road, aviation and energy projects. But the programme of work could also be responsive to large-scale regional project infrastructure proposals from outside parliament. For example, local enterprise partnerships (collaborations of businesses, local authorities and other groups in an economically meaningful unit) may put together a bid for building a cluster of science parks, which would involve spending on transport, buildings, energy and telecoms.

Allowing such sub-national bids would ensure a more bottom-up approach to major regional projects that involve strategic thinking. This would help to use more local initiative and decentralized information than would be available at a national level. The abolition of Regional Development Agencies and regional offices has left a strategic planning vacuum between the national level and the very micro-level (districts). Indeed, the institutions that support regional economic development in England are a classic example of policy instability, being the subject of numerous reforms, often with radical policy swings following national elections.

Box 1.1. An example of how our infrastructure proposals would help the impasse over the shortfall in runway capacity in the southeast.

The Infrastructure Strategy Board would be a permanent, dedicated source of independent and analytically robust advice that would help to align political views. Had it existed, the need to set up the Davies Commission to investigate the runway capacity problem again from scratch would have been avoided. The expansion of Heathrow has already been discussed by numerous other inquiries (the 1968 Roskill Commission, for example). Rigorous information about the costs and benefits of different policy options would have been available from a team of experts long immersed in the strengths and weaknesses of the existing evidence.

The Infrastructure Planning Commission would operate under the rules defined by National Policy Statements like those currently used. It would ensure that planning is not used to reopen political debates at every step in the process while implementing policy. The Infrastructure Planning Commission would deal with the ensuing planning practicalities: namely, reviewing and deciding on specific applications for development consent. It would also decide how to compensate those who stood to lose from the expansion of an existing airport or the building of a new one, following a set of clear rules enshrined in law. This would help to mitigate political bickering and deliver transparent and predictable planning decisions.

Other Policies to Support Infrastructure

Public investment should not be hamstrung by accounting methods that impede a focus on economic returns. Therefore, for fiscal targets to be useful as a strategic management tool, they should incorporate the value of public sector assets rather than concentrating solely on public sector debt. Otherwise there is no distinction between extra borrowing to finance consumption and borrowing to finance investment in new assets or in repairing existing assets. The failure to use proper public accounting methods makes public investment (for example, in road maintenance) look artificially expensive and hampers good decision making. It is like judging a firm solely on the profit and loss account while ignoring the balance sheet. The UK is leading efforts in improving *public sector accounts* (for example, through the publication of 'Whole of Government Accounts'). It is time for government to use these new accounts as the basis for policymaking.

Road pricing is an idea whose time has come. There are no major technological impediments to a system that would manage congestion, be fairer and improve incentives for building and maintenance. To the extent that there are political impediments with moving to comprehensive road pricing, these can be overcome in the longer term. A new regulator should administer the system following a regulatory asset base model: an approach that has proved to be successful in other areas of infrastructure. By creating dedicated revenue streams, this would help to provide a long-term solution to the problem of road investment, maintenance and financing. Road pricing could be made attractive to the electorate by accompanying its introduction with a cut in fuel duty, as a large component of the tax is currently rationalized by the need to limit congestion. In some circumstances, national roads (operated by the Highways Agency) could be auctioned off and shadow tolls introduced in this section of the road network.

The undersupply of *housing*, especially in areas of the country that have experienced high economic growth, has pushed up house prices. The UK has been incapable of building enough houses to keep up with growing demand. Many of the long-term issues of strategic planning and delivery that we have highlighted apply equally to housing investment even though most of the investment is undertaken by private business. The ISB and IPC should also take responsibility for long-term strategy and delivery of housing throughout the UK, where this is naturally complementary with infrastructure goals. Schemes to increase the amount of land available for development need to overcome local resistance. Institutionalizing a flexible system of compensation for those who stand to lose from new developments is important, for example, via funding local amenities, reductions in council tax payments or straightforward cash payments. Appropriately generous compensation schemes should, in particular, help to diminish local opposition to development.

With regards to telecoms, *broadband* plays an increasingly important role in connectivity. But the UK's broadband infrastructure is not outstanding compared with other countries. The UK typically ranks in the middle of the table in terms of raw broadband performance and deployment, including for broadband speed and network coverage. But compared with other advanced economies, we tend to spend more time online, buy more online and the value added generated by internet-related activities represents a larger share of GDP than in almost any other country (OECD 2012b). To continue taking advantage of the extraordinary opportunities that the internet offers, we must continue to be prepared to respond flexibly and promptly to a rapidly changing technological environment. Again, the institutional architecture we propose could help with problems here as they arise.

Why Have Problems with Infrastructure Persisted?

There is nothing new in recognizing that poor infrastructure is a major UK problem with detrimental consequences for growth. Historically, the policy thrust has been away from investment programmes driven by the government because of a suspicion that such projects offer low efficiency and poor value for money. This is understandable, and similar infrastructure problems exist in the even more free market US. It must be recognized, however, that infrastructure investment inevitably requires a long-term government strategy.

In the 1930s and 1940s, infrastructure investments were largely made in the private sector. The private sector subsequently came to be widely regarded as taking too short term a view; its investment record was considered insufficient and so it was forced to give way to government. Privatization in the early 1980s came about while important shifts in the economy were taking place, including economic activity moving from large energy-intensive industries towards services. In addition, the assets built by the public sector in the 1960s and 1970s were still far from the end of their life cycle. The result was that the need for policy frameworks that provide stability to investors was largely overlooked and the lessons of the 1930s and 1940s were forgotten.

Although procrastination is possible for long periods of time as these are long-lived investments, it is now clear that these problems can no longer be avoided as the existing infrastructure grinds to a halt.

The adversarial nature of UK politics means that we have a great deal of policy 'flip-flopping'. In some areas, the costs of such policy instability do not matter too much, but in areas that require investment for the long term—for infrastructure, as well as in the area of skills and innovation—political uncertainty is extremely costly.

Summary on Infrastructure

We propose a new institutional architecture for infrastructure to provide better strategy development and delivery and funding of major infrastructure in transport and energy. Together, the Infrastructure Strategy Board, the Infrastructure Planning Commission and the Infrastructure Bank will unblock projects and share the gains from development. We believe that this will dramatically reduce the policy instability that has led the UK's infrastructure to be poor in comparison with other countries and which is holding back growth.

1.5 Private Investment and Innovation[7]

Why Private Investment and Innovation Matter

Investment in equipment and new ideas (technological and managerial) is a crucial engine of growth. Investing in capital allows existing firms to incorporate new technologies and can be an important part of their strategies to reorganize production processes towards global best practice. The dynamism of innovative new firms that introduce new products and processes is also important for growth via the process of 'creative destruction' that propels economic change.

Fostering a supportive environment for investment and innovation is central to having a dynamic and productive economy. For example, access to finance is essential to support investment, allowing firms to compete effectively in the global marketplace and helping them to anticipate and respond to changing markets and opportunities.

Even though investment and innovation are key processes of the market economy, the policy environment plays an important supporting role. A climate of macroeconomic stability is an important background factor, but many other policies influence investment and innovation, including policies that affect competition, market access, finance, taxation and regulation.

Diagnosis: The Problems of Private Investment and Innovation in the UK

As figure 1.7 shows, UK investment levels as a share of GDP have historically been lower than those of France, Germany and Japan (and similar to those of the US). The *composition* of UK investment is also problematic. It is heavily weighted towards property and buildings and is much lighter on equipment (which embodies newer technologies). UK intangible investment is also weak in certain areas.

- The UK punches above its weight with a strong science base and an internationally dynamic higher education sector with supporting structures through the 'research excellence framework' administered by the Higher Education Funding Council for England. Less than 4% of the world's researchers are based in the UK yet they manage to produce 6.4% of all scientific articles and receive 10.9% of citations. But commercialization of their insights and inventions

---

[7]For a more detailed discussion see chapter 6.

has historically been weak in the UK, with lower R&D and patenting intensity than in other major countries. Whereas most countries have been increasing their R&D intensity, the proportion of GDP spent on business R&D has been declining in the UK since the early 1980s.

- In measures of management quality, the UK is mediocre by international standards, ranked significantly below the 'premier league' of countries, such as Germany, Japan and the US. This gap matters because recent evidence suggests that about a third of international productivity differences can be attributed to management quality.

Low investment and innovation generate lower levels of labour productivity or GDP per hour. There has been a long-standing productivity gap between the UK and three close comparators: France, Germany and the US. Despite the progress discussed above, the UK still has substantially lower GDP per hour than these countries.

The long-term capital investment gap in the UK has become more pressing in recent years. Business investment remains around 15% below its pre-recession peak. Large firms seem to be sitting on cash piles, held back both by low expected demand and by uncertainty. SMEs have smaller reserves but are being held back by banks' reluctance to lend while they rebuild their balance sheets.

The other failures of investment that we have highlighted in this book act as a deterrent to private investment. Firms may be discouraged from investing in the UK by a lack of skilled labour. Thus, efforts to increase human capital are likely to provide a boost to investment by firms. Relatively low levels of public investment in infrastructure are a further impediment. We therefore see increases in private investment as an important further dividend from getting the right skills and infrastructure policies.

But there is a further issue holding back investment and innovation that we believe is equally worrying. There is evidence that UK investment performance has been weakened by a series of problems in the functioning of capital markets.

First, financiers take an excessively short-term outlook when weighing up investment opportunities. Long-term investment is discouraged by investor impatience and a hyperactive mergers and acquisitions market. The 2012 Kay Review concluded that corporate executives and financial intermediaries, such as fund managers and investment analysts, help to foster this short-term approach.

Such 'short-termism' is likely to be particularly acute for funding innovation, which is hard to collateralize and highly risky. Innovation is a public good in terms of the lessons it offers others. The high costs of undertaking due diligence steer private equity investors towards funding a smaller number of larger investments in later-stage businesses at the expense of early-stage venture capital for SMEs with high growth potential.

Second, a sizeable body of evidence suggests that there is a debt financing gap for younger businesses that lack a track record. The gap arises because of the difficulty that investors have in trying to distinguish high-risk entrepreneurs from low-risk ones. Younger firms—mainly SMEs—are often the most innovative and hence this capital market failure has long-term growth effects.

The UK performs well in attracting inward investment but performs poorly in creating leading global firms. Productive entrants do not grow to scale nearly as quickly as they do in the US and this slow 'reallocation' is an important drag on relative productivity. Too often UK firms in high-tech and capital-intensive sectors are acquired by foreign businesses instead of being able to raise growth capital themselves.

Core Recommendations on Private Investment

Addressing these problems is not easy. The Commission welcomes recent short-term measures such as the 'funding for lending' scheme to deal with the lending drought. But this scheme is not designed to deal with structural issues.

One important route with longer-lasting benefits could be through spurring increased *competition* in retail banking. The direction of travel in recent years has been in the opposite direction: the absorption of HBOS by Lloyds TSB in 2008, for example. But there is a mounting case for formulating a plan to reduce concentration in the retail banking sector. This would be a radical intervention, so before taking the step of referring such a proposal to the new Competition and Markets Authority, with a narrow and time-limited remit, we recommend the measures that follow.

Liberalizing entry conditions, including speeding up the process for obtaining a banking license, is essential. The OFT has committed to work with the Prudential Regulation Authority to review the application of prudential requirements to ensure that new entrants and smaller banks are not disproportionately affected, for example, by requirements to hold more capital than incumbents. It is important that the process is completed in a timely fashion.

In addition to the recently introduced automatic redirection service, further measures to reduce switching costs between banks are vital, including greater transparency. It should be as easy to transfer a bank account as it has now become to transfer a mobile phone number across operators.

Increased competition in banking would have a variety of benefits. It would encourage banks to seek out profitable lending opportunities more assiduously. It could also stimulate relationship lending as retail banks focus on more mundane finance rather than 'casino' activities.

The Commission supports, with some provisos, current moves towards the creation of a *Business Bank*. At present, the remit of the mooted bank is to deliver the existing programmes of the Department for Business, Innovation & Skills (BIS) using £1 billion (leveraged up to £10 billion) for additional lending to manufacturers, exporters and high-growth firms. The rationale is that the bank will be able to access funds on more favourable terms than commercial banks (especially those currently saddled with a legacy of poor past investment decisions) and will therefore have a lower cost of capital.

The Business Bank's lower cost of capital and its remit to consider social returns would allow it to make loans that would typically be avoided by commercial banks. In particular, it would be able to take a wider economic view of the benefits of investing in certain sectors, including cases where there are potential long-term social returns from developing new technologies. This would mean a particular focus on lending for innovation investments to new and growing firms, which experience the most acute financial market failures and where the externalities will be greatest. Since this would include green technologies, there would be a case for folding the Green Investment Bank into the Business Bank.

The Business Bank should play an important role in creating a corporate bond market for SMEs. This would require a platform for SME loan securitization along the lines advocated by the 2012 Breedon Review. By removing the requirement for investors to analyse the credit quality of many small issuances from individual SMEs, such a platform would relax SME financing constraints and kick-start institutional investment in these firms.

The Business Bank does carry risks. To be effective, its governance has to be removed from immediate political pressures and it needs to operate on the basis of clearly defined economic objectives. We recommend that it is run by an appointed independent board to oversee operational decisions independently from BIS. It should also operate under a charter that clearly articulates its mission and ensures that the bank is held account-able for delivering that mission.

The proposal for a Business Bank also has to be a long-term commit-ment supported by cross-party consensus to avoid the perennial process of abolition, reinvention and rebranding that has characterized much gov-ernment policy in the past. These features are shared with our proposals for infrastructure institutions (including the Infrastructure Bank), but the skills required for the Business Bank are quite distinct so the institutions should be kept separate.

Other Policies to Support Private Investment and Innovation

Making the Financial System More Stable

The Commission endorses the Vickers Report on banking regulation and encourages the government to implement both the letter and spirit of its recommendations (Independent Commission on Banking 2011). Some LSE Growth Commission commissioners wanted to go further and rec-ommend the structural separation of the investment and retail arms of banks along the lines of the US Glass–Steagall Act, but the consensus was to wait and see how the current set of Vickers and Basel III reforms worked before deciding whether to press ahead with something more rad-ical and potentially disruptive. Although such reforms would help make banking safer and more stable, in the short term, higher capital require-ments will often mean less lending, particularly to risky projects. Recent announcements that suggest a less stringent timetable for implementing the Basel III reforms therefore seem to be a sensible move so long as the delay is not too long.

Holding Assets for Longer

To combat short-termism, the Commission recommends that equity voting rights be linked to investment duration, with rights becoming stronger the longer the holding period. This would follow the spirit of the US Securities and Exchange Commission's proposal for a one-year hold-ing period being a requirement before shareholders are able to amend, or request an amendment to, a firm's governing documents concerning nom-ination procedures for directors. A concern with this is that it could lead to control by insiders or 'tunnelling', as happens in many southern Euro-pean and developing countries. We view this as less likely in the UK, with its strong rule of law, protection of minority investors and transparent contracting environment, but the design of this proposal must clearly be carefully crafted.

Tax Policy and Innovation

Debt finance is less attractive for an innovative firm than an equity stake because of the inherent riskiness of future revenue streams. Our current tax system creates a bias towards debt and against equity that distorts investment incentives generally and investment in innovation in particular.

Following the recommendations of the 2011 Mirrlees Review, we support the introduction of an 'allowance for corporate equity' (ACE). This would offer a tax break for issuing equity, which would ensure equal treatment of equity- and debt-financed investments. There is a range of options under an ACE for creating a level playing field between debt and equity. Any resulting loss of corporate tax revenue could, in principle, be offset elsewhere in the tax system. For example, the Mirrlees Review proposes using a broad-based tax on consumption rather than increasing the corporate tax rate.

The Mirrlees Review estimates that introducing an ACE could boost investment by around 6.1% and GDP by around 1.4%. This is mainly because an ACE lowers the cost of capital. In addition, an ACE would help to rebalance the UK economy away from debt and towards equity finance. A corporate tax system of this kind has now been introduced in several countries. In addition to stimulating investment, an ACE has the potential to increase financial stability by reducing the bias towards debt finance.

The share of GDP devoted to business R&D has been rising in almost all OECD countries since the Second World War, but it started *falling* in the UK in the 1980s. We view the R&D tax credit system introduced in the 2000s as a positive development, and it has certainly helped to arrest this decline. HM Revenue & Customs defines R&D in a fairly narrow and formal way for tax purposes, due to legitimate concerns over tax avoidance. So there need to be ways of supporting investments in innovation directly without further complicating the tax code. One route is through the Business Bank, as it can take a wider view of the social returns to innovative projects. This would help to address weaknesses in the commercialization of inventions from the science base. The Business Bank could also be permitted to use a variety of venture-capital-style financing approaches as well as making standard business loans.

Funding for innovative start-ups often comes from alternative sources, such as venture capital, angel funding and private equity in high-tech sectors. This is welcome and it is well known that clusters like Silicon Valley have a deep seam of such liquidity. Unfortunately, such agglomerations of high-tech activity are extremely hard for governments to manufacture, although it can certainly hold them back through onerous regulations. Finance often follows after high-tech clusters have got going due to other factors, such as the presence of world-class universities like Stanford and Berkeley in California's Bay Area. Finance helps the next stage of development, but it is not the prime mover. Hence, we do not support introducing additional tax breaks for such alternative investments.

Industrial Strategy

Since the late 1970s, industry-specific 'vertical' policies have been unpopular due to fears that the ambition of 'picking winners' turns into an outcome of 'picking losers'. But some recent successes (such as foreign direct investment in the automotive sector) and the need to foster more green industries have caused a rethink of a more activist industrial strategy. The convening power and coordination role of government can help to bring parties together to recognize and solve problems. There is a role for strategic thinking, therefore, especially as the government touches on almost every industry in some way.

Of course, it is vital that industrial strategy does not divert attention from the importance of 'horizontal' policies, such as promoting competition, R&D, infrastructure and skills, which benefit all sectors of the economy. Nevertheless, spotting cases where there is an impediment to the growth of a sector is an important role for the government. Supportive interventions need not take the form of direct subsidies—removing specific regulatory barriers is more important.

Underpinning new thinking on industrial strategy should be a view of where the UK has some actual or latent comparative advantage. Once these sectors or firms are identified, an assessment must be made of whether they are in areas of global growth. This means taking an appropriately dynamic perspective. For example, investment in low-carbon technologies is likely to be an important area in the future. We recommend a tight focus on what factors inhibit the growth of such sectors and what policies could encourage their growth. Moreover, it is important that this thinking is conducted transparently, with the supporting analysis subject to independent scrutiny.

One example of how highly focused government intervention can help would be the relaxation of severe planning restrictions that are inhibiting the expansion of high-tech clusters in some parts of the country (such as Cambridge and Oxford) where the UK has strong comparative advantage in its universities. Planning restrictions on housing for workers, land-use restrictions and slow roll-out of ultra-fast broadband are particular constraints on these dense centres of new economic activity. The infrastructure institutions we propose should help, but additional political attention needs to be focused on relaxing regulations that are impeding growth. Other examples are management training in the creative sectors, visa restrictions harming universities, and the prevarication over expanding airport runway capacity that harms our comparative advantage in international business services.

What kind of institutions can help to develop and deliver a better industrial strategy? We recommend creating an independent National Growth Council, which would bring together expertise across all disciplines to review relevant evidence and to recommend growth-enhancing policy reforms that could be subject to rigorous evaluation. This body should also challenge government on why successful policies are not introduced and/or why unsuccessful ones are not closed down. The National Growth Council would work with BIS on formulating the evidence base needed to underpin a successful industrial strategy.

The lending strategies of the Business Bank and the Infrastructure Bank should be supportive of this type of industrial strategy. This could be important for industries where there is good evidence that access to finance is holding back investment and innovation. This is particularly true where large upfront investments are needed in an emerging area, such as developing low-carbon technologies.

Policies to Improve Management Quality

Policies that encourage good management practices should be pursued. High levels of competition, meritocratic appointment of chief executives, proper management training and foreign direct investment all lead to improved management performance. But additional specific and directed efforts are warranted given the importance of management. For example, while business education is growing, it is still quite limited in the UK and is undermined by tough immigration controls. There is also evidence that family-run businesses suffer from managerial deficits, so targeted support for management training could be useful for this group. The inheritance tax regime, which allows tax breaks on passing business assets between generations, should also be re-evaluated as it discourages real-location of assets away from family ownership.

Why Have Problems with Private Investment Persisted?

The thrust of financial policy prior to the crisis was generally laissez-faire. Charmed by the success of the City, politicians of all stripes lined up behind 'light-touch regulation'. More conservatively run financial institutions, such as building societies, were demutualized to take advantage of market opportunities that were otherwise denied to them. The need for government-led solutions, especially in an area like finance, went distinctly against the grain. Moreover, the concentration of the UK banking sector was often thought to be a source of stability, especially when protection for depositors was quite limited. The success of the City allowed senior financiers to speak with an authority that limited the ability of government to interfere in the activities of the sector. In contrast, our view is that correcting market failures is a pro-market intervention.

The evidence for both rich and poor countries that greater competition in banking (and in other sectors) improves productivity, management and innovation seems to have had little impact on UK policy thinking. The UK's retail banking system is extremely concentrated, and attempts to promote more competition have floundered. In 2010 the four largest banks accounted for 85% of SME current accounts (Independent Commission on Banking 2011).

The UK is also unusual in not having a publicly supported bank to promote lending to small and new businesses. For example, the US has the Small Business Administration, which provided more than $30 billion in lending to over 60,000 small businesses in 2011. The UK has instead relied on private commercial banking to provide finance to SMEs, and commercial lenders rightly look at business funding in terms of profitable opportunities. But if competition is weak, then the high profits of the banks will result in otherwise commercially viable lending opportunities being overlooked.

Summary on Private Investment and Innovation

Low levels of private investment and innovation in the UK are a reflection of capital market failures. Over-reliance on bank finance along with problems of bank concentration and short-termism are constraining firm growth, especially when it comes to dynamic and innovative SMEs. We propose increasing retail banking competition and developing a strategy for a Business Bank to deal with these issues. We have also proposed a range of complementary reforms to support private investment and innovation.

1.6 GDP AND BEYOND[8]

Discussions about economic growth typically focus on GDP, which attempts to measure a country's economic output. But changes in GDP are an inadequate measure of human wellbeing. For example, growth could be generated by damaging the environment with detrimental long-term consequences. More fundamentally, assessing developments in wellbeing also requires looking at the distribution of market outcomes and improvements in public services. At present, however, the focus of public attention is almost exclusively on quarterly GDP releases as the barometer of economic progress.

The Commission does not believe that any single indicator captures all aspects of wellbeing. There will continue to be debates about progress on the environment, inequality, tax policy and public services—and each of these debates uses its own measures. There is an important role for independently produced statistics to support such discussions. Indicators of subjective wellbeing also have a role.

It is crucial that discussions of growth and development are not confined to a single dimension. But given our limited collective attention span, there is some advantage in choosing to promote one additional indicator of how changes in GDP per capita affect average households.

Our preferred measure is median household income. Focusing on household income provides a better way of capturing what people actually receive out of national income. The median is better than the mean since it is reflective of progress in the middle of the income distribution. For example, increases in GDP that go solely to the rich would not increase this measure. Thus, looking at median income would create more focus on inclusive growth that generates wider benefits. It also reminds us to look more deeply into distributional issues, particularly for the poorest parts of society.

It is possible to produce up-to-date measures of the evolution of median household income by making use of household survey data. Thus, median household income could be published on a timely basis alongside GDP. As more accurate information becomes available, the measures could be updated (for example, through so-called nowcasting techniques).

---

[8]For a more detailed discussion see chapter 7.

A new focus on median household income would, we believe, influence debates about growth policy. Median income growth has lagged behind GDP per capita since the early 1980s, in part because of the growth of income inequality, meaning that average income has grown faster than the median. In the years running up to the crisis, GDP per capita grew much faster than median household income, in part because there was a significant increase in government spending on health and education, which is reflected in GDP but not in income. The median is not perfect, of course, because inequality can still widen at other parts of the distribution, but it is better than ignoring distribution entirely and it is easy to communicate to the public.

While the key proposals in this book are geared towards raising GDP, monitoring developments in median household income would be a particularly valuable way of gauging the inclusiveness of the growth that is generated. Progress in improving skills towards the lower end of the distribution would, we believe, create an especially important dividend that could be measured using this indicator. But shifting the public debate towards monitoring median household income as well as GDP would allow us to look more widely at inclusive growth and living standards beyond income, including education, health and a sense of community.

1.7 How to Get to Where We Want to Go

Our core proposals constitute a manifesto for long-term growth that we believe can form the basis of a political consensus. This can provide the kind of stable policy framework that will encourage long-term investment in the UK.

But while cross-party commitment to the policies that are needed would be a good first step, it will not be enough by itself. If such policies are to have a material impact on growth, action must be sustained over several parliaments. The Commission's discussions have highlighted how, in many crucial areas (notably education, infrastructure and financing for innovation), there has been a sustained failure to implement long-term strategic approaches to policy. This weakness has been recognized in many recent reviews.

We must break the familiar cycle of institutional churn and political procrastination to find ways of ensuring that difficult and contentious long-term decisions are based on the best available independent expertise. This is not a plea to take the politics out of long-term investment: apart from its moral imperative, a healthy democracy is vital for keeping policy responsive and government accountable. But politics is best in its right place: making strategic choices, setting objectives and holding executive bodies to account.

Drawing on examples of effective institutional innovation, we have made the following proposals.

- Create a 'flexible ecology' for schools, with a greater institutionalized focus on the performance of disadvantaged children. There is also a need to reduce local authority control and provide a more flexible labour market for teachers, with greater on-the-job performance evaluation.

- Create a new institutional architecture to improve the planning and delivery of infrastructure of national importance. The system needs a body (or bodies) tasked with identifying strategic priorities for infrastructure and helping to create a more stable policy environment that will encourage the provision of long-term private finance for infrastructure investment.

- Increase competition in retail banking and ensure that the Business Bank has an independent board and a remit to support SMEs and innovation.

Implementation of an ambitious long-term growth programme will require sustained effective direction from the centre of government. This is another area where institutional change is overdue. Unlike in many other democracies, the Whitehall machinery for providing strategic advice and overseeing implementation is relatively small scale and informal and has been prone to radical change between one government and the next. This needs to change. The absence of stable machinery at the centre of government makes it more difficult to develop and implement a long-term strategy for promoting economic growth.

Strategy and performance management are vital functions that cannot be left to ad hoc units staffed by a shifting population of short-term, often party political, staff. Without continuity, strategy is overwhelmed by short-term politics and performance management is interrupted and ineffective. Constant flux in Number 10 and the Cabinet Office leaves too much power in the hands of HM Treasury, which is above all a finance ministry. This cycle of 'uncreative destruction' is wasteful and inhibits the evolution of successful institutions.

There have been many proposals for creating a substantive and stable centre of government (as argued for in Lord Heseltine's recent review, for example (Heseltine 2012)). Elements of a system that could win broad-based support include the following.

- There must be a permanent, top-level political mechanism for setting strategic direction and overseeing implementation.
- This mechanism has to be supported by proper planning processes, which directly involve departments, to translate strategic direction into concrete plans and action across government.
- These implementation plans must be underpinned by clear accountability and proper management information to track progress.

The challenge now is to implement these ideas, to support a clearly articulated long-term growth strategy—and to then stick with them across governments.

In the next fifty years the world will change radically—in terms of technology, sustainability and the global balance of economic and political power. Some of these changes may not be benign, causing instability—financial, fiscal, social, political and environmental—and potentially derailing paths to increasing prosperity. We can anticipate some of the emerging patterns, but not others. We must, however, be prepared to respond to all of them.

This means putting a premium on policies and institutions that foster anticipation and flexibility. It also means putting a premium on systems that celebrate and encourage entrepreneurship, innovation, opportunity and discovery. Establishing a strong, stable and credible investment climate for human, physical and innovation capital is a crucial step towards creating this kind of society. We call for a group of people from across society and all the UK's political parties to work on a manifesto for growth such as the one we have championed in this book.

REFERENCES

Breedon Review. 2012. *Boosting Finance Options for Business.* Department for Business, Innovation & Skills.

Card, D., R. Blundell and R. Freeman. 2004. *Seeking a Premier Economy: The Economic Effects of British Economic Reforms, 1980–2000.* Cambridge, MA: National Bureau of Economic Research.

Corry, D., A. Valero and J. Van Reenen. 2011. UK economic performance since 1997: growth, productivity and jobs. Special Paper 24, Centre for Economic Performance.

Crafts, N. 2012. British relative economic decline revisited: the role of competition. *Explorations in Economic History* **49**(1), 17–29.

Eddington Review. 2006. *The Eddington Transport Study. The Case for Action: Sir Rod Eddington's Advice to Government.* Department for Transport.

Heseltine, M. 2012. *No Stone Unturned: In Pursuit of Growth. The Lord Heseltine Review.* Department for Business, Innovation & Skills.

Independent Commission on Banking. 2011. *Final Report: Recommendations.*

Kang, L, M. O'Mahony and F. Peng. 2012. New measures of workforce skills in the EU. *National Institute Economic Review* **220**(1), 17–28.

Kay, J. 2012. *The Kay Review of UK Equity Markets and Long-Term Decision Making.* Department for Business, Innovation & Skills.

Lindley, J., and S. Machin. 2013. Wage inequality in the Labour years. *Oxford Review of Economic Policy* **29**(1), 165–177.

Machin, S., and J. Vernoit. 2011. Changing school autonomy: academy schools and their introduction to England's education. Discussion Paper 123, Centre for the Economics of Education.

Mirrlees Review. 2011. *Mirrlees Review: Reforming the Tax System for the 21st Century.* Institute for Fiscal Studies.

OECD. 2012a. *Going for Growth.* Paris: Organisation for Economic Co-operation and Development.

OECD. 2012b. *OECD Internet Economic Outlook 2012.* Paris: Organisation for Economic Co-operation and Development.

OECD. 2012c. *Factbook 2009: Economic, Environmental and Social Statistics.* Paris: Organisation for Economic Co-operation and Development.

Ofgem. 2012. Electricity capacity assessment, 126/12. Office of the Gas and Electricity Markets.

ONS. 2012. The productivity conundrum, explanations and preliminary analysis (October). Available at www.ons.gov.uk/ons/dcp171766_283259.pdf.

Richard, D. 2012. *The Richard Review of Apprenticeships.* School for Startups.

Roskill Commission. 1971. *Roskill Commission on Third London Airport.* Her Majesty's Stationery Office.

Wolf, A. 2011. *Review of Vocational Education: The Wolf Report.* Department for Education.

UK Economic Performance

By João Paulo Pessoa and John Van Reenen

2.1 UK RELATIVE ECONOMIC PERFORMANCE SINCE 1997: GROWTH, PRODUCTIVITY AND JOBS

2.1.1 *Introduction*

Although the British people have consistently seen improvements in their material wellbeing over many centuries, British per capita GDP was in relative decline compared with that in the US, Germany and France from at least 1870 to 1979. Since then, this pattern has reversed and the UK has been catching up with these countries. British economic performance from 1997 to 2007 was strong, with GDP per capita growing faster than in any other G6 country. This broadly continued the post-1979 trend: market sector output per hour grew at 2.7% per annum between 1979 and 1997 and at 2.8% per annum between 1997 and 2007.

In this chapter we will show that UK performance in terms of GDP per capita (adult) has been better since 1980 than in many other countries. The post-2008 crisis took a severe toll on all OECD countries, though, with the UK faring somewhat worse than average. If we look at the period 1997–2011, however, UK productivity growth was second only to that in the US, and growth in GDP per worker was as good as in other countries. The employment rate in the UK is higher than in continental EU countries and similar to that in the US. However, UK productivity levels (GDP per hour) still lag behind those in the US, Germany and France.

This is an update of sections 1 and 2 of Corry *et al.* (2011), which was prepared for the LSE Growth Commission. We thank Higher Education Innovation Funding and the Economic and Social Research Council for financial support through the Centre for Economic Performance. Many people have kindly given us data and have commented on our work including Chris Giles, Jonathan Haskel, Bill Martin, Nick Oulton, Jonathon Portes, Ray Barrell and Ana Rincon-Aznar. Neither the Centre for Economic Performance nor the Economic and Social Research Council have any political affiliation or institutional view and both authors write only in a personal capacity.

Contrary to popular belief, we show that productivity growth between 1997 and 2007 was not mainly due to sectors such as finance, property, government and oil. Finance accounted for only 0.4% of the 2.8% annual productivity growth in the market economy between 1997 and 2007 (up from 0.2% in the 1979–97 period). Distribution and business services were much more important contributors to productivity growth. Rates of total factor productivity (TFP: a measure of technical change) growth were about 1% per annum between 1979 and 2007. They were similar before and after 1979, but information and communications technology (ICT) and skills made a larger contribution after 1997 (more similar to the picture in the US than that in the EU).

We begin the chapter by laying out some facts about economic performance since 1997, but we put them in an international and historical context. First we look at the aggregate trends in GDP, productivity and jobs (section 2.1.2). After showing that the UK has performed surprisingly strongly overall we look in more detail at where productivity growth has come from in terms of the contribution of different sectors, such as finance, and in terms of different factor inputs, such as capital and skills (section 2.1.3).

Overall, we find that UK performance was impressive between 1997 and 2011 compared with other major countries, in terms of both productivity and the labour market. The productivity performance was not primarily driven by the 'bubble' sectors of finance, property or government services (at least in an accounting sense). Rather, human capital, ICT and efficiency improvements were the dominant forces, especially in the business services and distribution sectors.

2.1.2 Analysis of Aggregate Trends in National Income and Productivity

We begin by comparing the macro-level economic performance of the UK with its major peers. We look at the period up to 2008, i.e. the period leading up to the global shock of the Great Recession, and we use the most recently available internationally comparable data at the time of writing (that is, data for 2011). In table 2.1, the first three columns examine the 1997–2011 period and the last three the 1997–2007 period.

We use data from the Conference Board, which collects internationally comparable data on output, employment, hours and other items to estimate economic performance. This is similar to the OECD data used previously in Corry *et al.* (2011). Tables 2.1 shows that during the 1997–2011 period UK GDP growth was second only to that in the US (1.84% per

Table 2.1. Growth of GDP, GDP per person and GDP per adult, 1997—2011.

	1997–2011			1997–2007		
	GDP	GDP per capita (person)	GDP per capita (adult)	GDP	GDP per capita (person)	GDP per capita (adult)
UK	1.84	1.33	1.12	2.89	2.42	2.20
US	2.18	1.23	0.99	2.98	1.95	1.63
Germany	1.36	1.41	1.13	1.67	1.64	1.35
France	1.66	1.10	0.93	2.31	1.75	1.51
Japan	0.49	0.41	0.20	0.98	0.84	0.63
Italy	0.68	0.25	0.14	1.45	1.08	0.94

Notes. Cumulative annual growth rates (in %). Analysis based on Conference Board data (extracted on 8 June 2012). GDP is measured in US dollars, at constant prices and constant purchasing power parity, with a Conference Board base year of 2011. 'Adult' refers to working age adults; data obtained from US Bureau of Labor Force Statistics and includes the civilian population aged over 16. Data for unified Germany from 1991.

annum versus 2.18% per annum). Of course, absolute economic growth is not as important for welfare as national income per person, as this will ultimately determine wages and consumption. In terms of GDP per capita growth (in terms of the total population), which is a key measure of material economic welfare, only Germany outperformed the UK (1.33% per annum versus 1.41% per annum).

Could some of these patterns be driven simply by different demographic trends? To partially control for this, the third column of table 2.1 presents GDP per adult (this is the main measure of overall economic performance that we use in this chapter). Here again, the UK was outperformed only by Germany, and even then only very marginally. Although data from the most recent years are likely to be revised, even if the UK's 2008-11 growth was much worse than recorded, its relative position over the entire post-1997 period is unlikely to dramatically change as other countries will also have their data revised.

We also analyse the net domestic product (NDP), which is defined by the OECD as GDP minus consumption of fixed capital.[1] Stiglitz *et al.* (2009), among others, recommend net measures as they better reflect welfare changes. If the depreciation rate in a given country is large, it means that a significant amount of GDP is set aside to replace capital, which significantly diminishes what the society can potentially consume. Table 2.2 is

---

[1] Consumption of fixed capital represents the reduction in the value of the fixed assets used in production during the accounting period that is a result of physical deterioration, normal obsolescence or normal accidental damage.

Table 2.2. Growth of NDP, NDP per person and NDP per adult, 1997—2011.

	1997–2011			1997–2007		
	NDP	NDP per capita (person)	NDP per capita (adult)	NDP	NDP per capita (person)	NDP per capita (adult)
UK	1.84	1.43	1.13	2.95	2.63	2.25
US	2.07	1.10	0.87	2.84	1.82	1.49
Germany	1.31	1.33	1.08	1.66	1.63	1.34
France	1.48	0.88	0.76	2.19	1.55	1.39
Japan	0.15	0.06	0.15	0.75	0.62	0.39
Italy	0.42	0.00	0.12	1.30	0.96	0.78

Notes. Cumulative annual growth rates (in %). Analysis based on Conference Board data (extracted on 8 June 2012) and NDP obtained using OECD capital use data as a percentage of GDP. 'Adult' refers to working age adults; data obtained from US Bureau of Labour Force Statistics and includes the civilian population aged over 16. Data for unified Germany from 1991.

very similar to table 2.1 except it lists NDP figures instead of GDP ones. In fact, the UK performs even better on this measure than on GDP, outstripping all countries (including Germany) on a per capita basis and on a per adult basis.

Following the approach of Card and Freeman (2004) we focus on GDP per adult as our preferred measure of GDP per capita (see columns 3 and 6 of table 2.1). The denominator is defined as adults in the civilian, non-institutional population over the age of 16 (for most countries).[2] Output per capita can be decomposed into its constituent elements: output per labour input (or 'productivity') and labour input per capita (a measure of labour market performance). Two alternative measures of labour input are considered: number of workers and total hours worked.[3] This type of decomposition allows us to determine how much of a country's growth performance is due to working 'smarter' (i.e. productivity gains) and how

[2]Data on 'working age adults' are obtained from the US Bureau of Labor Statistics (www.bls.gov/fls/flscomparelf/population.htm). Card and Freeman (2004) used Bureau of Labor Statistics data for civilian, non-institutional working-age adults for 15–64-year-olds, but the current Bureau of Labor Statistics data that we used is defined as the civilian, non-institutional population over the age at which compulsory schooling ends (16 for most countries), and no upper limit is specified. It is noted that the German data includes the institutional population. OECD data on 15–64-year-olds is currently unavailable for 2010 for all four countries considered here, but we obtain qualitatively similar results to those reported here when using this data over the shorter time period.

[3]As defined by the Conference Board at www.conference-board.org/data/economy database/: 'Total hours worked represent the aggregate number of hours actually worked as an employee or a self-employed person during the accounting period and when their output is within the production boundary'.

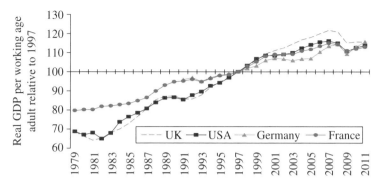

Figure 2.1. Trends in real GDP per capita (adult) relative to 1997.

Notes. Analysis based on Conference Board data (extracted on 8 June 2012). GDP is measured in US dollars, at constant prices and constant purchasing power parity, with a Conference Board base year of 2011. 'Adult' refers to working age adults; data obtained from US Bureau of Labor Force Statistics and includes the civilian population aged over 16. Data for unified Germany from 1991. For each country the logged series is set to 100 in 1997, so the level of the line in any year indicates the cumulative growth rate (for example, a value of 110 in 2001 indicates that the series has grown by $\exp(10/100) - 1 = 11\%$ between 1997 and 2001). The steeper the slope of the line, the faster growth has been over that period.

much is due to working 'harder' (i.e. higher employment rates or more hours worked per average adult).

The results are contained in figures 2.1 (GDP per capita), 2.2 (GDP per worker) and 2.3 (GDP per hour). We set the baseline for each series as 1997 to show the cumulative performance of the UK and other countries before and after the 1997 election.

We plot GDP per capita in figure 2.1. The fact that the UK line ends up above those for every other country shows in graphical form what was already revealed by the numbers in table 2.1. The fall in GDP per capita during the Great Recession is evident in all countries, but appears to be particularly large for the UK. Figure 2.1 also shows that the UK grew faster than its peers in the 1979–97 period. During this period under a Conservative government, growth in UK per capita GDP was similar to that in the US and significantly stronger than that in France (we do not have a consistent series for Germany because of re-unification in 1989).

As discussed earlier, GDP per capita can be decomposed into productivity growth and labour market performance. As an accounting identity, GDP per capita is equal to the product of GDP per employee (productivity) and employees per capita (the employment rate). An alternative decomposition is that GDP per capita is equal to the product of GDP per hour and hours worked per capita. GDP per hour is a better measure

55

of productivity than hours worked per worker because it accounts for part-time work, for the fact that some workers may hold multiple jobs and for differences in hours worked due to holidays, sickness, maternity leave, etc. (although hours are harder to measure accurately). Higher employment rates are easier to interpret as a desirable social outcome than higher hours worked per capita, however, as (all else equal) workers would prefer more annual leave and a shorter working day. Given the ambiguity of which decomposition is better, we present both.

Figure 2.2 presents the first decomposition using GDP per worker as a measure of productivity. Part (a) shows that growth in the UK's GDP per worker was as fast as that in the US between 1997 and 2008; this is impressive because this period is that of the US 'productivity miracle' (Jorgenson 2001). The UK managed, therefore, to hold onto the tail of the US tiger. US productivity outstripped that in the UK through the Great Recession, which reflects the much more aggressive job shedding that occurred in the US in response to the downturn. UK productivity growth was better than it was in Continental Europe, however. Again, productivity performance was strong in the UK in the pre-1997 period; in fact, during the 1979–97 period, under Conservative governments, GDP per worker grew faster in the UK than it did in both the US and France.

Figure 2.2 (b) shows employment rates. Over the period 1997–2007 the growth in the employment rate in the UK was similar to that in France and Germany. The US, by contrast, showed very poor jobs performance, with the employment rate falling by nearly 5% up to 2008 and then plummeting during the Great Recession. This can be seen if we consider the fact that the US unemployment rate rose from 5% to almost 10% during this period, whereas in the UK the increase in unemployment was more modest (currently around 8%) despite a larger fall in GDP. In Germany unemployment has hardly risen at all. The UK's employment rate at the end of the period of Conservative government was similar to that at its beginning: it did not rise, as it did in the US during the same period, but it did not fall either, as it did in France. What is more striking is how volatile the jobs market was, with a huge boom in the late 1980s and busts in the early 1980s and early 1990s.

Figure 2.3 repeats the analysis of figure 2.2 but for productivity measured in hours instead of workers; it shows broadly similar trends. In general, the UK productivity position looks weaker compared to the EU countries on a per hour basis as UK hours per worker are higher. For example, while figure 2.2 showed that UK GDP per worker growth was faster than in France both before and after 1997, figure 2.3 shows that

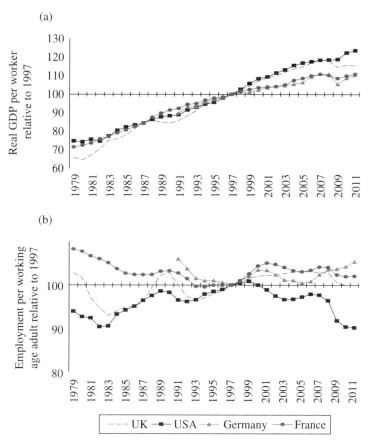

Figure 2.2. Trends in (a) real GDP per worker and
(b) employment per capita (adult) relative to 1997.

Notes. Analysis based on Conference Board data (extracted on 8 June 2012). GDP is measured in US dollars, at constant prices and constant purchasing power parity, with a Conference Board base year of 2011. 'Adult' refers to working age adults; data obtained from US Bureau of Labor Force Statistics and includes the civilian population aged over 16. Data for unified Germany from 1991. For each country the logged series is set to 100 in 1997, so the level of the line in any year indicates the cumulative growth rate (for example, a value of 110 in 2001 indicates that the series has grown by $\exp(10/100) - 1 = 11\%$ between 1997 and 2001). The steeper the slope of the line, the faster growth has been over that period.

France's growth in terms of GDP per hour was similar to that in the UK during the 1979–97 period.

This analysis gives a fairly clear picture of Britain's performance under the Labour governments of 1997–2010. GDP per capita outstripped that in the other major economies because the UK did well in terms of both

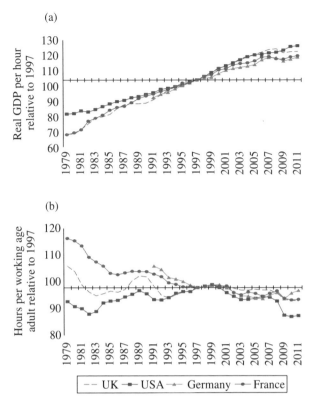

(a)

(b)

-- UK --■-- USA --▲-- Germany --●-- France

Figure 2.3. Trends in (a) real GDP per hour and
(b) hours per capita (adult) relative to 1997.

Notes. Analysis based on Conference Board data (extracted on 8 June 2012). GDP is measured in US dollars, at constant prices and constant purchasing power parity, with a Conference Board base year of 2011. 'Adult' refers to working age adults; data obtained from US Bureau of Labor Force Statistics and includes the civilian population aged over 16. Data for unified Germany from 1991. For each country the logged series is set to 100 in 1997, so the level of the line in any year indicates the cumulative growth rate (for example, a value of 110 in 2001 indicates that the series has grown by $\exp(10/100) - 1 = 11\%$ between 1997 and 2001). The steeper the slope of the line, the faster growth has been over that period.

productivity (faring only a little worse than the US and better than the EU on this measure) and the labour market (faring better than the US and only a little worse than the EU). This was a solid performance, contrary to the general perception of the period. However, it is also true that the UK did well in terms of productivity in the Conservative years of 1979–97, so recent UK performance is more likely to be a continuation of a post-1979 trend, rather than a sharp break with the past.

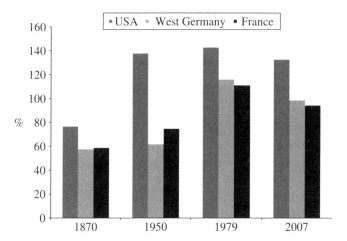

Figure 2.4. Real GDP per capita (UK = 100 in each year).

Notes. Reproduced from Crafts (2010). Analysis based on data sourced from the Angus Maddison historical database, with the data for West Germany in 2007 coming from Statistiches Bundesamt Deutschland 2010. Note that estimates refer to Germany from 1870 to 1937.

Taking an even longer-run perspective, we see in figure 2.4 that there appears to be a break in the UK's declining relative performance in 1979. For example, in 1870 German GDP per head was 58% of that in the UK, while in America it stood at around three-quarters of the UK level (77%). Just over a century later, in 1979, Germany's GDP per capita was 16% higher and the US's was 43% higher than that of the UK. By 2007, however, the UK had closed the gap with Germany and was only 33% behind the US. This pattern can also be observed in figure 2.5, which shows UK per capita GDP growth relative to other developed economies since 1950. UK per capita GDP grew more slowly up to the 1970s, becoming faster in the 1980s and afterwards.

We also study how mean and median household income (as defined by the OECD in its Social Welfare Statistics, Income Distribution–Inequality database) evolve over time. In figure 2.6[4] we can see the growth of these

---

[4]Equivalized income (in national currency in constant late 2000s prices) refers to cash income, excluding imputed components. Data refer to market income (i.e. before transfers and taxes) and disposable income (i.e. after transfers and taxes) and their components. The income attributed to each person is 'adjusted' for the square root of household size. 'Mid 1980s' corresponds to 1984 in France and the US and to 1985 in Germany and the UK. 'Mid 1990s' corresponds to 1996 in France, to 1995 in the US and Germany, and to 1994/95 in the UK. 'Mid 2000s' corresponds to 2005 in France and the US, to 2004 in Germany, and to 2004/5 in the UK. 'Late 2000s' corresponds to 2008 in France, Germany and the US, and to 2004/5 in the UK.

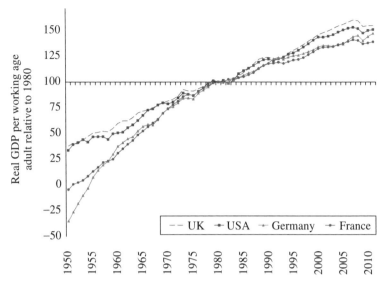

Figure 2.5. Trends in real GDP per capita since 1950.

Notes. Analysis based on Conference Board data (extracted on 8 June 2012). GDP is measured in US dollars, at constant prices and constant purchasing power parity, with a Conference Board base year of 2011. For each country the logged series is set to 100 in 1980, so the level of the line in any year indicates the cumulative growth rate (for example, a value of 110 in 2001 indicates that the series has grown by $\exp(10/100) - 1 = 11\%$ between 1980 and 2001). The steeper the slope of the line, the faster growth has been over that period.

series in the UK, the US, Germany and France. Clearly, mean income increased by significantly more in the UK than it did in other countries, while the median grew slower up until 2000 but recovered after this.[5] Unfortunately, the available data do not give us information about the period after the Great Recession. Median income increased less than mean income did in all countries, indicating that inequality was generally rising over this period.

The rise in UK inequality can be seen from another perspective. Lindley and Machin (2011) show that the ratio of workers at the 90th percentile to those at the 10th percentile of the income distribution (i.e. the richest tenth of the population versus the poorest tenth) grew significantly in the UK in the past three decades, especially during the 1980s. This is shown in figure 2.7 for both men and women.

---

[5]Due to a change in source in 2000 for the UK, data prior to around 2000 have been interpolated for the OECD's current income definition.

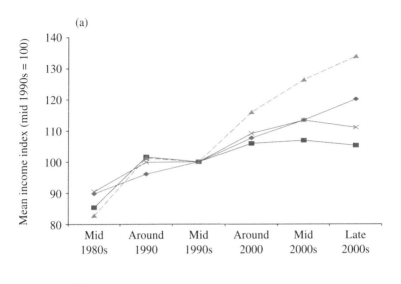

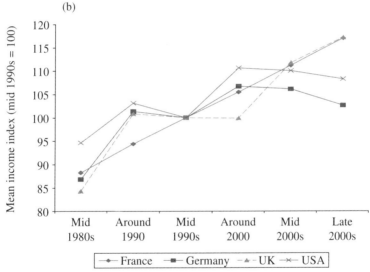

Figure 2.6. Trends in real (a) mean household income and (b) median household income relative to the mid 1990s.

Notes. Analysis based on OECD Social Welfare Statistics data. For each country the series is set to 100 in the mid 1990s, so the level of the line in any year indicates the cumulative growth rate (e.g. a value of 110 in 2001 indicates that the series has grown by 10% between 1997 and 2001). The steeper the slope of the line, the faster growth has been over that period.

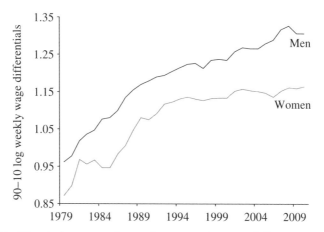

Figure 2.7. Ninetieth percentile–tenth percentile wage differential by gender.

Notes. Reproduced from Lindley and Machin (2011), using data from the New Earnings Survey (NES) and the Annual Survey of Hours and Earnings (ASHE). The difference in the natural logarithm of weekly wages of full-time workers at the 90th percentile (the richest tenth) and the 10th percentile (the poorest tenth).

2.1.3 *Where Did the Growth in UK Productivity Come From?*

Introduction

We now turn to the exercise of accounting for what lies beneath these aggregate trends in UK productivity. Rigorous and comparable cross-national data at the industry level is not currently available for the years after 2008, so we initially focus on the period leading up to the Great Recession. We use the KLEMS database (O'Mahony and Timmer 2007), which is the best available source of harmonized productivity data (at the time of writing in June 2012) for the major countries that we want to look at.[6] It is consistent with national accounts, describes all assumptions made and contains comparable data on education for each industry (which is important for labour quality measurement).

We consider two ways of decomposing growth. First, we look at the contributions of the 'factor inputs' to growth, i.e. the quantity and quality of capital and labour. Second, we examine the contributions of various industries to the aggregate productivity performance of the UK and its key comparators. Broadly, we find that during the period of the last Labour government overall labour productivity growth was similar to that in the previous Conservative period, but its composition changed: human capital and ICT accounted for a greater proportion of growth. Low-tech

---

[6]The KLEMS database is available at www.euklems.net.

capital became less important and overall efficiency growth (called 'total factor productivity' or TFP) remained at about 1% throughout. Perhaps the most striking fact is that, looking at the different sectors, finance was *not* responsible for much of the productivity growth (around 14%), implying that finance is unlikely to have been the main cause of the strong productivity performance.[7]

Decomposing Growth into Factor Inputs: The Growing Importance of Skills and Computer Technologies

In this subsection we describe an accounting exercise that primarily focuses on the 'market economy' as defined by KLEMS, which strips out the public sector and real estate. For the public sector, value added is particularly hard to measure (we discuss these non-market economy sectors below), and international comparisons are therefore problematic. Real estate is excluded because output in this industry mostly reflects imputed housing rents rather than the sales of firms; consequently, residential buildings are also excluded from the market economy capital stock (Timmer *et al.* 2010). The market economy makes up around three-quarters of the total economy in the UK, and slightly less than that in the comparator countries (see figure 2.8). Carrying out this analysis for gross value added (gross value added (GVA) plus taxes on products minus subsidies on products equals GDP) as our measure of output, we find that a picture of strong UK performance emerges, as it does using the GDP numbers in table 2.1.

Figure 2.8 shows the way in which aggregate value added has been split between different sectors since 1979. In all countries, there has been a strong trend away from manufacturing and other goods-producing sectors and towards services. But this trend is particularly strong in the UK, with a shift towards business services, whose share of aggregate value added rises from 7% to 13% during the period.

Significantly, figure 2.8 shows that growth in the public sector and in the finance and real estate sectors from the period of Conservative

---

[7]Furthermore, it is worth noting that the aggregate GDP growth numbers are not affected by mis-measurement of the output of the investment bank's 'toxic assets' (such as mortgage-backed securities, CDO-squareds, etc.). This is because national accounts look at annual growth using an expenditure-based GDP measure rather than the output-based measure of GDP. The 'toxic rubbish' parts of the banking sector are all classified as intermediate inputs sold to non-financial businesses, so they do not really show up as GDP. The exception is net exports, where 'toxic rubbish' could show up. But net exports accounts for only 1.5% of GDP in total and it would therefore make only a minor contribution to growth even if all net exports could be placed in the 'toxic rubbish' category. The contribution of finance to GDP is from plain vanilla banking services sold to households.

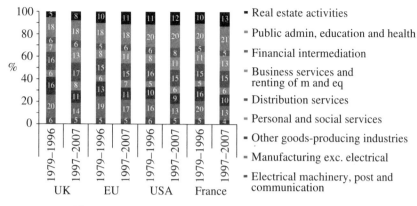

Figure 2.8. Sector shares of market economy GVA.

Notes. Data come from the KLEMS database. 'EU' represents all EU-15 countries for which growth accounting could be performed, i.e. Austria, Belgium, Denmark, Finland, France, Germany, Italy, the Netherlands, Spain and the UK. Data for France and for the EU are available from 1981 onwards.

government to the subsequent Labour period has been lower than often imagined. Financial intermediation is about 6% of aggregate value added in both periods, and the contribution of the public sector (public administration, health and education) also remains constant, at 18% of value added. The contribution of real estate activity has grown, but only from 5% to 8%. According to figure 2.8 the size of the market economy was only 3% smaller under Labour than it was in the previous period. This fall was less than that seen in France (a 4% fall) but more than was seen in the US and the EU as a whole (1% falls).

We now focus on the market economy. Table 2.3 shows a decomposition of average annual growth in value added, showing that the UK enjoyed overall growth of 3.2% per annum over the 1997–2007 period, only slightly behind the US (3.4%) and considerably ahead of the EU average (2.5%) as well as France (2.6%). In addition, this growth figure is higher than that in the pre-1997 period, when the average annual growth rate was 2.3%. However, this performance was largely due to the contribution of total hours worked (driven by rising employment). If we strip out the contribution of hours to UK growth of 0.4%, we are left with labour productivity growth of 2.8% per annum, very similar to the 2.7% figure seen in the pre-1997 period.

Despite this constancy on the surface, the composition of UK productivity growth did change between the two periods. The contribution of each factor input is the product of growth in that input and its share in value added, while the contribution of TFP (a measure of technical

Table 2.3. Decomposition of market economy growth in value added.

	UK		EU		US		France	
	1979–1997	1997–2007	1979–1997	1997–2007	1979–1997	1997–2007	1979–1997	1997–2007
1 Market economy output (2 + 3)	2.3	3.2	2.1	2.5	3.2	3.4	1.8	2.6
2 Hours worked	−0.4	0.4	−0.2	0.5	0.9	0.5	−0.4	0.4
3 Labour productivity (4 + 5 + 6 + 7)	2.7	2.8	2.3	2.0	2.2	2.9	2.2	2.2
Contributions from								
4 Labour composition	0.3	0.5	0.3	0.2	0.2	0.3	0.4	0.3
5 ICT capital per hour	0.6	0.8	0.4	0.5	0.8	0.9	0.3	0.4
6 Non-ICT capital per hour	0.7	0.5	0.7	0.6	0.7	0.5	0.4	0.5
7 TFP	1.1	1.0	0.9	0.7	0.4	1.2	1.1	1.0
8 Contribution from knowledge economy (4 + 5 + 7)	2.0	2.3	1.6	1.4	1.5	2.5	1.8	1.6

Notes. Data come from the KLEMS database. 'EU' represents all EU-15 countries for which growth accounting could be performed, i.e. Austria, Belgium, Denmark, Finland, France, Germany, Italy, the Netherlands, Spain and the UK. Data for France and the EU are available from 1981 onwards.

change) is calculated as a residual. The labour composition index takes into account differences in the composition of the workforce in terms of skills, gender and age.[8]

The numbers are detailed in table 2.3 and shown graphically in figure 2.9. Although TFP growth was similar, at about 1% per annum, in both periods, the contribution of labour composition and ICT capital increased in importance after 1997, while the contribution of non-ICT capital has fallen. Overall, the contribution from the 'knowledge economy' (labour composition, ICT capital and TFP) increased in the UK from 2% to 2.3%,

---

[8]See O'Mahony and Timmer (2009), which explains the construction of the labour composition component in the KLEMS database, depending as it does on skills (measured by educational attainment), age and sex of the workforce. Timmer *et al.* (2010) explain that the impact of an ageing population (which implies higher-wage workers) and the increasing employment of females (who tend to be paid less) tend to counterbalance each other. Hence trends in labour composition tend to be dominated by changes in skill composition.

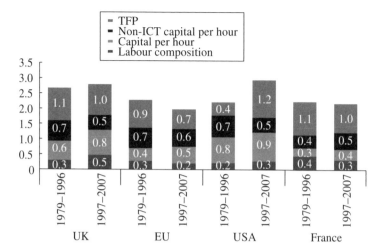

Figure 2.9. Sources of market economy labour productivity growth.

Notes. Data come from the KLEMS database. 'EU' represents all EU-15 countries for which growth accounting could be performed, i.e. Austria, Belgium, Denmark, Finland, France, Germany, Italy, the Netherlands, Spain and the UK. Data for France and for the EU are available from 1981 onwards.

while in the EU it fell and in the US a larger increase, mainly driven by higher TFP growth, was seen.[9]

Which Sectors Are Responsible for Productivity Growth? It Wasn't All a Financial Bubble

The second growth decomposition that we implement is to look at the contribution of different sectors to aggregate productivity. This shows that the highest productivity growth sectors over the 1997–2007 period were electrical machinery, post and communication, financial intermediation, business services and distribution (in descending order). These sectors saw high contributions both from ICT capital per hour and from TFP.

However, a sector's contribution to overall market economy productivity growth depends on both its productivity growth and its size (its share of total market economy GVA). Nationwide aggregate productivity growth can increase either because a sector increases productivity (a 'within effect') or because a high-productivity sector grows in size at

---

[9]Timmer *et al.* (2007) note that while the use of educational attainment as a measure of skill may lead to difficulties with cross-country comparisons (since educational systems, classifications and quality vary between countries), it is useful for tracking developments over time within the same country.

the expense of a low-productivity sector (a 'between effect'). Figure 2.10 shows the breakdown by broad sector, calculated by multiplying the average productivity growth of a sector by its average share in GVA over the corresponding period.[10] Interestingly, financial intermediation was responsible for only 0.4% of the 2.8% annual growth in productivity under Labour. Accounting for 14% ($100 \times \frac{0.4}{2.8}$) of productivity growth with only 9% of the market economy value added is no small achievement, but this sector *already* accounted for 0.2 percentage points of the growth under the Conservatives (when it constituted 8% of market economy value added). And this leaves 86% of aggregate market economy growth due to other sectors. Furthermore, the contribution of finance also increased in other economies: its contribution more than doubled in the US over the same period (from 0.2 percentage points to 0.5 percentage points) and it doubled in the EU as a whole as well (0.1 percentage points to 0.2 percentage points). So the idea that all of the productivity growth in the UK was due to a bubble in finance does not seem to square with the evidence. Furthermore, if we exclude the effect of finance altogether, productivity growth in the UK would have been broadly constant at around 2.5% per annum during the pre- and post-1997 periods.[11]

Although the productivity growth performance does not seem to be directly attributable to the 'bubble' sectors of finance, property and the public sector, there could be some other indirect mechanism. Could productivity in business services, for example, all be driven by the demand from financial services? This seems somewhat unlikely, as many parts of business services (e.g. consultancy and legal) serve primarily non-financial firms. A more subtle argument is that the financial bubble created a kind of unsustainable excess consumption demand that was propping up fundamentally inefficient companies.

However, Giles (2011) shows that the data do not support the assertion that there was a great consumer boom before the financial crisis. In

---

[10]We note that we are using a methodology that is consistent with the use of KLEMS data in Timmer *et al.* (2010), Van Ark (2010) and Timmer (2007), who look at the periods 1980–95 and 1995–2004 or 2005. Using a different approach, and apportioning GVA growth to sectors over 2000–2007, Dal Borgo *et al.* (2011) find similar results in terms of the relative contributions of the different sectors to aggregate value added growth. Of the total growth of 2.83%, 0.31% relates to financial services, with larger contributions coming from distribution (0.88%) and Business Services (0.55%).

[11]Note that we weight the sector contributions to productivity growth using nominal GVA to be consistent with the KLEMS growth-accounting methodology. We also experimented with weighting by GVA share in constant prices, and by share of employment (see Corry *et al.* 2011). The picture does not change much and business services remains the sector with the largest increase in contribution between the two periods.

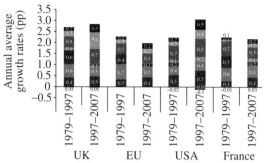

Figure 2.10. Sector contributions to market economy productivity growth.

Notes. Analysis based on KLEMS data. 'EU' represents all EU-15 countries for which growth accounting could be performed, i.e. Austria, Belgium, Denmark, Finland, France, Germany, Italy, the Netherlands, Spain and the UK. Data for France and the EU are available from 1981 onwards. Average sectoral growth rates for the periods 1979–97 and 1997–2007 are weighted by each sector's average share in market economy nominal GVA over the relevant period. The reallocation effect refers to the labour productivity effects of reallocations of labour between sectors that have different productivity levels.

fact, there was a drop in household consumption as a share of national income, from 63.3% in 2002 to 61.3% in 2007. Furthermore, even if this consumption bubble story were true, it is unlikely that this would artificially inflate productivity. A general bubble would increase output and employment hours (temporarily) above their sustainable levels. But it is unclear why this would flatter the productivity numbers. In fact, if generally unproductive activities were being drawn in, this would be more likely to lower measured productivity.

The Role of Non-market Sectors

Our focus has been on the market economy, but one could also perform a growth-accounting exercise for health, education, public administration activities and real estate. This is unlikely to be very reliable because output is extremely hard to measure in these primarily public service activities (Timmer *et al.* 2010), with productivity growth assumed to be zero in most sectors and in most countries. Nevertheless, taking this at face value for a moment, we find that UK output growth in the non-market sectors was greater during the Labour period than it was under the Conservatives, but that labour productivity growth fell from 0.6% per annum to zero. Other EU countries (but not the US) also experienced a decline. This appears to be largely due to negative TFP growth, which affected all countries but was strongest in the UK (see table 2.4).

Table 2.4. Decomposition of growth in value added for
public administration, education and health.

	UK		EU		US		France	
	1979–1997	1997–2007	1979–1997	1997–2007	1979–1997	1997–2007	1979–1997	1997–2007
1 Output (2 + 3)	0.9	1.5	1.8	1.5	1.4	1.7	2.2	0.8
2 Hours worked	0.3	1.5	0.8	0.8	1.5	1.4	1.0	0.4
3 Labour productivity (4 + 5 + 6 + 7)	0.6	0.0	1.0	0.7	−0.1	0.3	1.2	0.4
4 Labour composition	0.6	0.6	0.3	0.3	0.3	0.3	0.4	0.2
5 ICT capital per hour	0.3	0.2	0.2	0.2	0.3	0.4	0.1	0.2
6 Non-ICT capital per hour	0.2	0.1	0.3	0.3	0.6	0.5	0.3	0.3
7 TFP	−0.5	−0.9	0.2	−0.1	−1.4	−0.9	0.4	−0.3
8 Contribution from knowledge economy	0.4	−0.1	0.7	0.4	−0.8	−0.2	0.9	0.1

Notes. Data come from the KLEMS database. 'EU' represents all EU-15 countries for which growth accounting could be performed, i.e. Austria, Belgium, Denmark, Finland, France, Germany, Italy, the Netherlands, Spain and the UK. Data for France and the EU are available from 1981 onwards.

This is consistent with the story that the large increase in public services expenditure after Labour's election victory in 1997 led to a fall in productivity in these sectors. For example, even after improvements in measurement following the Atkinson Review (Atkinson 2005), NHS productivity appears to be flat at best. Undoubtedly, low productivity in the public sector is a major problem and there is much debate over whether Labour's much-delayed reforms to public services had any effect on efficiency.

Productivity Levels

Although the UK's overall productivity growth has been strong, it is worth recalling that productivity in terms of overall level still lags behind other countries despite the gap narrowing since the early 1990s. UK GDP per hour worked was 25% below that in the US in 2011, 20% below that in France and 12% below that in Germany (see figure 2.11).

The productivity gap between the UK and other developed economies increased during the Great Recession. This can be seen more clearly in

69

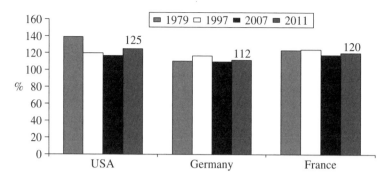

Figure 2.11. Labour productivity levels, GDP per hour.

Notes. Analysis based on Conference Board data (2012). GDP is measured in US dollars, at constant prices and constant purchasing power parity, with a base year of 2011.

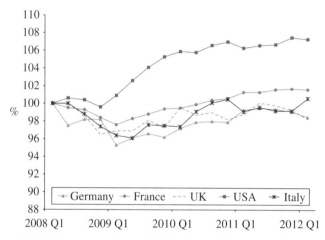

Figure 2.12. Output per hour (2008 Q1 = 100), seasonally adjusted.

Notes. Reproduced from ONS (2012). For the US, real productivity per hour only covers the business sector, as no total productivity measure is publicly available.

figure 2.12. The fall in productivity in the UK was greater than it was in other developed economies, especially the US, where there was considerably more job churn during the crisis.

2.1.4 *Summary of Overall UK Economic Performance Since 1997*

Since 1997 UK economic performance has been strong compared with other countries, and this continues a historical trend that began around 1979. NDP per capita grew faster than in all other G6 nations between 1997 and 2011, with productivity growth in the UK second only to the

American 'productivity miracle'. This UK performance was due to a continued rapid rate of TFP growth and an increasingly important role for skills and ICT. Importantly, the performance was *not* primarily driven by finance, which contributed only around 0.4% of the 2.8% productivity growth in the market sector between 1997 and 2007 (compared to 0.2% of the 2.7% productivity growth in the 1979–97 period). Business services and distribution were much more important sectors. The growth in hours in the non-market sector due to rising government expenditure and a property boom held aggregate productivity back, but not enough to make much of a change in Britain's relative growth position.

2.2 OTHER MEASURES OF BUSINESS PERFORMANCE

2.2.1 *Introduction*

We have focused on productivity because, for economists, this is the key measure of long-run performance. In this section we present a short tour of other indicators of business performance (including regional inequality). This is more of a mixed bag, but overall our sense is that these alternative indicators support the idea that there has been a continuation of the positive trends in business performance since 1997, but with many remaining problems when it comes to the level of UK performance relative to other countries. We investigate investment (domestic and foreign direct), innovation, management, skills, entrepreneurship, exports, profits and regional differences. Data constraints prevent us from implementing the fully consistent analysis of all of these performance measures for the UK relative to other countries before and after Labour's election victory in 1997, but we use the data available where we can.

2.2.2 *Analysis of Key Indicators*

Investment

In section 2.1.3 we showed how important investment in ICT and non-ICT capital is to productivity growth. The contribution of ICT capital to growth was nearly as high in the UK as it was in the US (and was higher than in the EU), and the contribution of non-ICT capital in the UK was the same as it was in the US in both the pre- and post-1997 periods. However, when we look at the levels of total investment, standardized as a percentage of GDP, UK levels are consistently lower than those in France and Germany but similar to those in the US (figure 2.13). In the post-1997

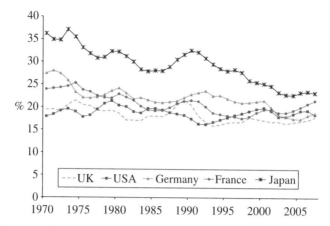

Figure 2.13. Total economy investment as a share of GDP (%).

Notes. OECD STAN database. Investment intensity is calculated as the ratio of gross fixed capital formation to GDP.

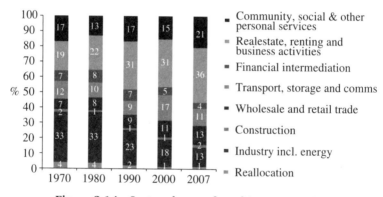

Figure 2.14. Sector shares of total investment (%).

Notes. OECD STAN database. Investment share represents investment composition of the total economy. It is calculated by dividing each industry's gross fixed capital formation by gross fixed capital formation for the total economy.

period, average UK investment was 17% of GDP, compared with 18.9% in the US, 19.3% in France and in Germany, and 24.3% in Japan.

The more favourable performance of the UK in the late 1980s was mainly driven by real estate during the Lawson boom, as shown by figure 2.14, which gives the sector breakdown of total investment. Indeed, the largest share has, for the most part, been related to real estate.[12]

---

[12]The split between real estate and renting and business activities is only available from the early 1990s, but most of this overall investment consists of real estate activity.

The classic interpretation problem with investment is whether it is 'too low' in the Anglo-Saxon countries because of access to finance, short-termism and low public investment, or 'too high' in Continental Europe due to (for example) high minimum wages and union bargaining power. In either case, things have not changed much over time.

Foreign Direct Investment

Foreign direct investment (FDI) may be important for two reasons. First, it is a signal of the success of a country in attracting overseas firms. Second, FDI may bring with it new technologies and modern management practices, as well as stimulating greater competition (Bloom *et al.* 2011). These mechanisms mean that FDI may create positive spillovers, raising the productivity of domestic firms.[13]

The UK has been successful at attracting FDI, with inward FDI stocks higher than comparators both pre- and post-1997, as shown in figure 2.15 (unfortunately, OECD data is not available on a consistent basis for the period before 1990). All countries show growth in FDI between 1997 and 2010, with Germany showing the highest cumulative annual growth rate of 10%, compared with 7% for the UK. The relative acceleration witnessed in the UK, France and Germany may be due to the effects of European integration since the mid 1990s (the growth in US FDI stocks has been constant). UK FDI inflows appeared to be strongly pro-cyclical, picking up from 1997, reaching a peak of 8% of GDP in 2000 during the 'dot com boom', and then falling back to pre-1997 levels before another peak is seen in the mid 2000s (see figure 2.16).[14]

Innovation

A standard measure of innovative inputs is R&D (business-financed R&D makes up 62% of total R&D in the UK (BIS 2010a)). R&D increased slightly as a proportion of GDP between 1997 and 2008, having been falling steadily since the late 1970s (Van Reenen 1997). At 1.8% the ratio is still lower than in other major developed countries (see figure 2.17). Similarly, the UK lags behind the US and Germany with respect to patents granted,

---

[13] The evidence on FDI spillovers is mixed: see Haskel *et al.* (2007).

[14] Outward FDI followed a similar pattern to inward FDI. The UK has had higher outward FDI stocks than its comparators since the early 1990s, but these began to accelerate for the European countries later in the same decade. France has seen the highest compound annual growth rate since 1997: 10%. This compares with 8% for the UK. FDI outflows follow a pro-cyclical pattern, with a peak of 16% of GDP seen in 2000, and another one of nearly 12% of GDP seen just before the Great Recession started.

73

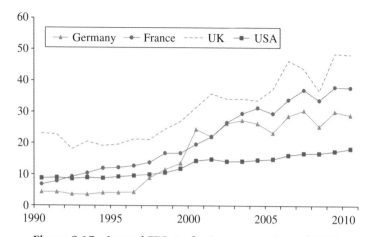

Figure 2.15. Inward FDI stocks (as a percentage of GDP).
Notes. Analysis based on OECD data sourced from www.oecd.org/investment/statistics.

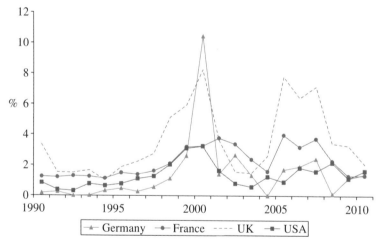

Figure 2.16. FDI inflows (as a percentage of GDP).
Notes. Analysis based on OECD data sourced from www.oecd.org/investment/statistics.

though it has been tracking France on this measure since the 1990s (see figure 2.18).

A wider view of intangibles should also be considered. These are difficult to measure and to compare across countries. According to one set of recent data, the UK had a higher share of value added in intangibles than all other G7 nations (BIS 2010c). In addition to 'traditional innovation', which refers to R&D, design and intellectual property, 'software

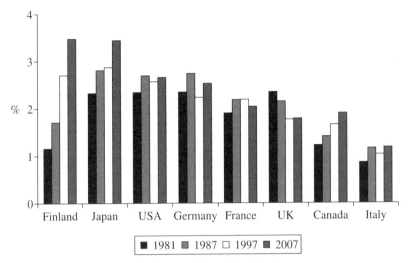

Figure 2.17. Gross domestic expenditure on R&D (as a percentage of GDP).
Notes. Analysis based on OECD Main Science and Technology Indicators, June 2010 (data not available on a consistent basis prior to 1981).

development' and 'economic competencies' are included (the latter comprises training, organizational development, marketing and branding). Capturing the intangibles gives a better view of the service sector's investment in innovation, which is probably understated in the traditional Frascati-based measures of R&D. Other sources of data on intangibles, however, show the UK in a less favourable light compared with other countries (e.g. some OECD data).

Consideration of the time series dimension shows that investment in intangibles has been increasing over time. Nominal investments in intangibles have increased faster than investments in tangible assets: the gap between these different types of investment has widened since 1998, so that by 2008 investments in intangibles were £34 billion higher than those in tangibles (figure 2.19). We note, however, that intangible investment as a share of market output (excluding government) has remained broadly stable in recent years, as has its composition (figure 2.20).

Management

Management is believed to be an important factor in raising productivity and the UK is generally perceived to have a deficit of quality in this area compared with some other leading nations. This perception may, of course, be based simply on the popularity of British exports of television shows that showcase poor managers: *The Office* and *Fawlty Towers*, for

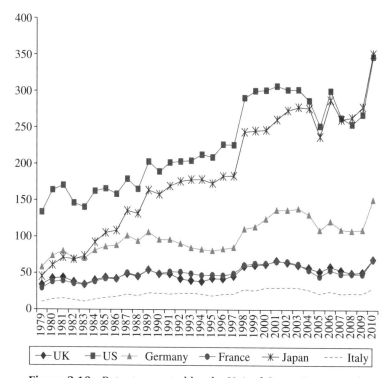

Figure 2.18. Patents granted by the United States Patent and Trademark Office (USPTO), per million of the population.

Notes. Patents data obtained from the USPTO; population data from the OECD.

example. It is very difficult to credibly measure management practices, but Bloom and Van Reenen (2007, 2010) have recently developed techniques to gauge some important aspects of them related to monitoring, targets and incentives. The latest version of their database covers twenty countries, including the UK.

In terms of average management scores, the UK is in the middle of the pack, close to Italy and France but significantly below the 'Premier League' of nations, led by the US but also including Japan and Germany (figure 2.21). Bloom and Van Reenen (2007) show that the UK's management gap with the US is accounted for by the preponderance of family firms, lower human capital and weaker competition.

Unfortunately, the time series of their management data is too short to examine the whole of the 1997–2010 period. However, the UK did appear to be catching up with the US a little on management scores over the 2004–10 period (Bloom and Van Reenen 2010).

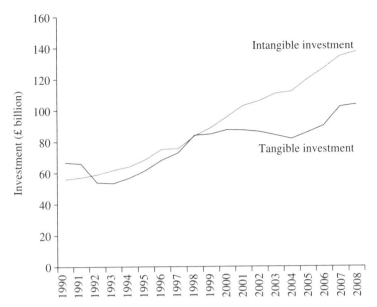

Figure 2.19. Investment by UK firms in intangible
and tangible assets, 1990–2008.

Source: NESTA/BIS Annual Innovation Report 2010.

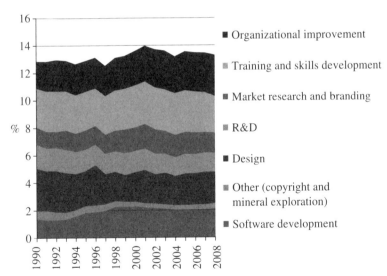

Figure 2.20. Investment by UK firms in intangible assets by
category—share of market sector GVA, 1990–2008.

Source: NESTA/BIS Annual Innovation Report 2010.

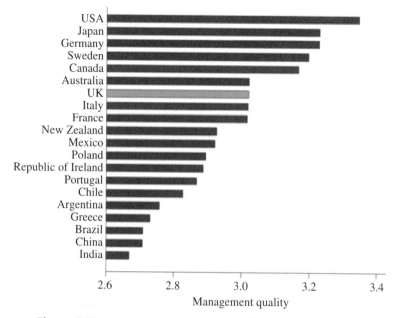

Figure 2.21. Average management quality across countries.

Notes. Analysis from Bloom and Van Reenen (2010). Average score across eighteen questions.

Table 2.5. Public expenditure on education as a percentage of total GDP(% total public expenditure).

	1995		2000		2007	
UK	5.0	(11.4)	4.3	(11.0)	5.4	(11.7)
US	4.7	(12.6)	4.9	(14.4)	5.3	(14.1)
Germany	4.6	(8.5)	4.4	(9.8)	4.5	(10.3)
France	6.3	(11.0)	6.0	(12.5)	5.6	(12.5)

Notes. Expenditure on educational institutions as a percentage of GDP, reproduced from Lent and Nash (2011), based on OECD 'Education at a Glance' data. Note that public expenditure presented here includes subsidies to households for living costs (scholarships and grants to students/households and students loans).

Education and Skills

Public investment in education increased in the UK between 1995 and 2007, from 5% of GDP to 5.4% (see table 2.5). In 2007, public expenditure on education in the UK exceeded that in the US (5.3%) and Germany (4.5%) and was just below France (5.6%).

Since 1997, the proportion of tertiary (or post-secondary school) educated adults rose from 23% to 33% in the UK, representing an average annual growth rate of 3.2%, which is higher than its comparators. In terms of overall level, the UK does better than Germany and France, with 25% and 27%, respectively, in 2008; however, it still lags behind the US, where 41% of those aged 25–64 have a tertiary education (see table 2.6).

The UK does more poorly when it comes to upper secondary and post-secondary, non-tertiary education (which tends to represent vocational courses). Only 37% of those aged 25–64 in the UK have been educated to this level, compared with 43%, 48% and 60% in France, the US and Germany, respectively. However, this proportion has risen since 1997, with an average annual growth rate of 0.2% (compared with a decline in the US and Germany but a greater rise in France).

Finally, the percentage of those aged 25–64 with below upper secondary education was 30% in the UK in 2008 (table 2.6). This has fallen from 41% in 1997, at an average annual rate of 2.7%, representing a faster decline than its comparators. In 2008 the unskilled proportion of the workforce in the UK was at a similar level to France but much higher than in Germany (15%) and the US (11%).

It appears, therefore, that since 1997 progress has been made, and at faster rates than in comparator countries. However, given the gap at the beginning of the period, the UK continues to lag behind its comparators in overall levels, apart from when it comes to tertiary education, where the UK is beaten only by the US.

In terms of vocational skills, it is well known that the UK has problems when it comes to apprenticeships compared with some European countries, such as Germany, Austria and Switzerland (Steedman 2010).

Entrepreneurship

A crude measure of entrepreneurial activity is the number of new firms being registered for VAT. Of course, many companies are registered but are actually non-trading entities (e.g. for tax purposes), so this measure is imperfect. In aggregate there has been an overall rise in registrations, from around 170,000 in 1994 to over 200,000 in 2007 (see figure 2.22).

Disaggregating total VAT registrations by sector, much of the aggregate rise appears to have been driven by 'renting and business activities', the same sector that has made the largest contribution to productivity gains since 1997. Within this category, further investigation (not reported here) shows that the largest sub-sectors were legal and accounting services,

Table 2.6. Percentage of those aged 25–64 by educational level.

		1997	1998	1999	2000	2001	2002	2003	2004	2005	2006	2007	2008	Av. growth
UK	Below upper secondary	41	40	38	37	37	36	35	34	33	32	32	30	−2.7
	Upper secondary and post secondary non-tertiary	37	36	37	37	37	37	37	37	37	38	37	37	0.2
	Tertiary education	23	24	25	26	26	27	28	29	30	31	32	33	3.2
US	Below upper secondary	14	14	13	13	12	13	12	12	12	12	12	11	−1.8
	Upper secondary and post secondary non-tertiary	52	52	51	51	50	49	49	49	49	48	48	48	−0.8
	Tertiary education	34	35	36	36	37	38	38	39	39	39	40	41	1.7
Germany	Below upper secondary	17	16	19	18	17	17	17	16	17	17	16	15	−1.0
	Upper secondary and post secondary non-tertiary	61	61	58	58	59	60	59	59	59	59	60	60	−0.1
	Tertiary education	23	23	23	23	23	23	24	25	25	24	24	25	1.0
France	Below upper secondary	41	39	38	37	36	35	35	34	33	33	31	30	−2.6
	Upper secondary and post secondary non-tertiary	39	40	40	41	41	41	41	41	41	41	42	43	0.6
	Tertiary education	20	21	21	22	23	24	24	24	25	26	27	27	2.9

Notes. OECD 'Education at a Glance' data: see Annex 3 for notes (www.oecd.org/edu/eag2010).

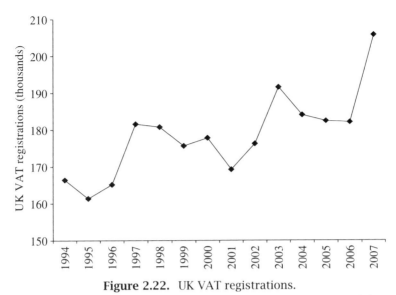

Figure 2.22. UK VAT registrations.

Source: OECD 'Education at a Glance' data: see Corry *et al.* (2011, Annex 3) for notes (www.oecd.org/edu/eag2010).

which grew consistently over the period, and IT/data services, for which registrations were also high.

A measure based on survey data, collected by Global Entrepreneurship Monitor, is Total Early-Stage Entrepreneurial Activity (TEA). This measures the prevalence of working-age adults who are either nascent entrepreneurs (about to start up a business) or are working in a new firm (a new firm is defined as one that has been running for less than forty-two months). According to this data, the UK ranks above average, and above Germany and France (but below the US), with just over 6% of working-age adults involved in entrepreneurial activity (see figure 2.23).

Exports

Since the early 1990s, exports as a proportion of GDP have remained around 25–28% in the UK—a similar level to that found in France (see figure 2.24). Exports make up a lower proportion of GDP in the US, at around 10–11%. All three countries have seen relatively flat trends. However, Germany's exports increased from around 25% of GDP to nearly 50% before the Great Recession, falling back to 40% in 2009.

In terms of export mix, 41% of UK exports were related to services in 2009 (BIS 2010b). The UK's share of the world goods export market has declined in recent years, falling from 4% in 2000 to 3% in 2009 (BIS

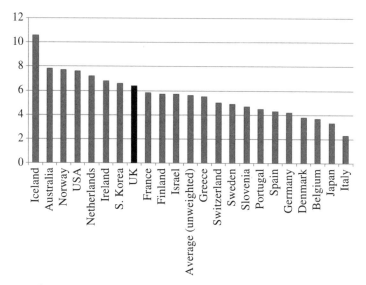

Figure 2.23. Total Early-Stage Entrepreneurial Activity.

Notes. Data sourced from Global Entrepreneurship Monitor's *2010 Global Report*, based on a 2009 survey. Total Early-Stage Entrepreneurial Activity refers to the proportion of the working-age population that is involved in starting or growing a new business.

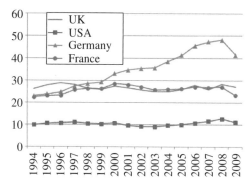

Figure 2.24. Exports of goods and services as a percentage of GDP.

Notes. Data sourced from IMF data mapper, balance of payments statistics (www.imf.org/external/datamapper/index.php).

2010b). With the exception of Germany (whose share increased during the same period), other major industrial economies have experienced a similar trend, due to the rising shares of emerging economies. However, the UK has increased its share of world services exports since 1990, reaching 7% in 2009 (one of the few developed countries to see an increase), and it has remained the second largest exporter of services (after the US).

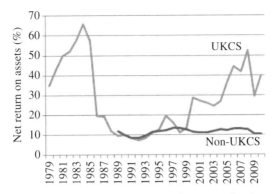

Figure 2.25. Annual net rates of return of private non-financial corporations; UKCS and non-UKCS split.

Notes. Analysis based on ONS data. UKCS refers to UK Continental Shelf, North Sea oil production. Non-UKCS consists of manufacturing, services, construction, electricity and gas, agriculture, mining, quarrying, etc.

The UK's export and import performance has been rather poor since 2008, despite a huge devaluation of sterling (see Corry *et al.* 2011).

Profitability

While economists and policymakers focus on productivity, businesses themselves naturally focus on their bottom line. Profitability is rather an ambiguous indicator from a welfare point of view as it might rise for positive reasons (e.g. innovation) or negative ones (e.g. monopoly power).

Data from the ONS give a time series of profitability measured as net operating profits divided by net capital employed. Figure 2.25 splits UK Continental Shelf (UKCS), which refers to North Sea oil, from all other private non-financial institutions. While UKCS profitability has tended to track the oil price, non-UKCS profits have been relatively flat, at around 10–15%, over the period. There is no evidence of any systematic decline under Labour.

The ONS splits non-UKCS companies between services and manufacturing, as shown in figure 2.26. Here we see that profitability in both services and manufacturing appeared to peak around 1997. Interestingly, the decline in manufacturing margins after 1997 coincided with a period when sterling was strong and when there was increasing competition from globalization, putting downwards pressure on margins. The margin seems to have settled, at around 10%, from the early 2000s until the Great Recession. Services margins fluctuated at a higher level, with an

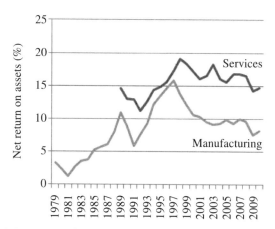

Figure 2.26. Annual net rates of return of private non-financial corporations; services and manufacturing split.

Notes. Analysis based on ONS data: net operating surplus divided by net average capital employed.

average of 17% over the period 1997–2008, but dropped off again during the recession.

Analysis of the share of profits in national income also shows considerable stability in the UK over time (Pessoa and Van Reenen 2011).

2.2.3 *Regional Disparities*

Regional disparities are often said to be a major problem for the UK and a cause not only of social concern but of worse overall performance. In particular, it is thought that London's dominance over the rest of England and the UK's other three countries 'holds back' the UK. These claims need to be given some thought. Inequality can certainly be a moral concern, especially as it has grown dramatically since 1979 (Machin and Van Reenen 2010). But it is ultimately inequality between individuals or households that is the main concern, not between areas per se. Since only a very small amount of the inequality between people appears to be accounted for by their region, it is hard to see why spatial inequalities should get as high a weight vis-à-vis individual and household inequality as they do (except when it comes to politicians, whose constituencies are geographically based).

Since our focus in this chapter is on aggregate performance rather than distribution, a regional analysis would be relevant if it were the case that regional inequality was a causal influence on slower growth. But the evidence is that greater equality across places is consistent with both faster and slower aggregate growth: there is no well-founded empirical or theoretical relationship. On the other hand, if growth is exclusively in one area (London and the southeast), we can get situations of excess demand for labour and assets, which can push up equilibrium unemployment. In addition, much of the literature on the benefits of agglomeration show that cities should be the engines of growth, and the UK's failure—especially in the 1980s—to have strongly growing cities outside London cannot have helped in efforts to secure growth and productivity.

With this in mind, what are the facts?

UK Regions Are Unequal

UK regions, cities and neighbourhoods appear unequal according to a number of measures: average earnings, employment, and many other socioeconomic outcomes. In terms of GVA per head, the top-ranked 10% of UK (NUTS 3 level[15]) regions have value added at least 50% higher than the bottom-ranked 10% (Gibbons *et al.* 2010). Similarly, value added per hour in 2008 was over 50% higher in London than in Wales.

Figure 2.27 presents value added per head, per filled job and per hour at the level of the more aggregated (NUTS 1) regions. Value added per head shows larger variation due to commuting patterns: commuters contribute to London's output, which is then shared between Londoners. Therefore, productivity measures give a clearer picture. Value added per hour worked in London was 32% higher the UK average in 2009.

Regional Inequality Persists Over Time

Regional inequality in the UK (as measured by wages or productivity) has been very stable since 1997. Overman (2010) analyses regional wages (rather than productivity) because (i) wages are linked to productivity and (ii) good individual-level (micro) data on wages are available. The regions analysed are 157 'labour market areas', of which 79 are single 'urban' travel to work areas and 78 are 'rural areas', over the period 1998–2008.

---

[15]The NUTS classification is a hierarchical system for dividing up the economic territory of the EU for the purpose of regional analysis and policy. NUTS 1 regions are the major socioeconomic regions. NUTS 2 regions are the basic regions for the application of regional policies. NUTS 3 regions are small regions for specific diagnoses. For further detail see http://epp.eurostat.ec.europa.eu/portal/page/portal/nuts_nomen clature/introduction.

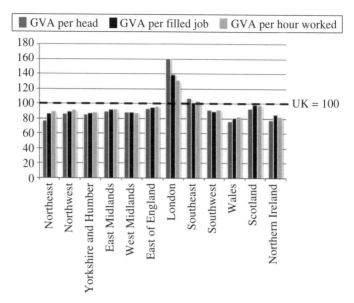

Figure 2.27. Regional economic indicators by NUTS 1 region, 2009.
Notes. Data sourced from BIS regional economic performance indicators, based on ONS data.

The overall level of between-area wage disparities has remained roughly constant during the period. Figure 2.28 shows average wages in 2008 plotted against average wages in 1998. Wages are normalized by dividing by the year average.

If relative average area wages were completely persistent across time, the dots would sit on the 45° line. The dashed line (which shows the results from regressing 2008 normalized wages on 1998 normalized wages) shows this is not quite the case. On average, the areas with the lowest wages have caught up slightly while the areas with the highest wages have fallen back, although the effect is not very pronounced. Furthermore, it appears that this 'churning' tendency among the rankings is not being driven by the highest-wage areas, which tend, if anything, to have seen their position improve (as they mainly sit above the 45° line).

To what extent do these disparities arise because of differences in the types of worker in different areas (sorting effects) or because of different outcomes for the same types of worker in different areas (area effects)? Empirically, most of this wage disparity across areas is due to individual characteristics, i.e. who you are turns out to be more important than where you live.

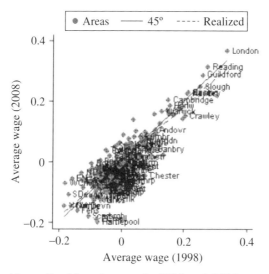

Figure 2.28. Normalized hourly wage in 1998 and 2008 across 157 areas.

Source: Gibbons *et al.* (2010). *Notes.* The graph plots the average area wage in 1998 against the average area wage in 2008 (expressed as a ratio to the UK average).

Regional Disparities in the UK Are Larger than in Other EU Countries

The UK does seem to have somewhat greater inequality between regions than other countries, primarily because of the success of London. This is shown in figure 2.29: compared with other EU15 countries, the UK is second only to Ireland in terms of the average regional difference from national GDP per capita.

Summary on Regional Differences

London has higher productivity and wages than other UK regions and this regional disparity is greater than in most other countries. Most spatial wage inequality is between individuals rather than regions (or more disaggregated areas), and most of this is due to individual characteristics rather than space-based 'agglomeration' effects. In other words, the higher wages in London are mainly because more productive people live and work in London rather than because London somehow makes everyone who works there more productive.

The spatial distribution has been reasonably stable despite many policies since 1997 that have tried to get other regions to grow faster than London. How much this regional disparity is an economic or ethical problem of an 'unbalanced' economy is unclear.

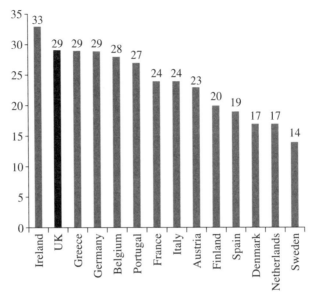

Figure 2.29. Dispersion of regional GVA per capita (average regional difference from national GDP per capita (%) in 2007).

Notes. Eurostat data on EU15 minus Luxembourg.

2.2.4 *Summary on Indicators of Business Performance*

The UK's economy shows some long-standing problems in terms of the level of business performance (e.g. in productivity, innovation and inter-mediate skills), but it has also shown some signs of improvement in recent years, mirroring productivity improvement. Skills, especially at the level of college education, have grown rapidly, as has ICT investment. R&D intensity remains low, but it has stopped falling and intangible investment and entrepreneurship seem impressive. Investment is lower than in Continental European countries, but FDI remains strong. Taken as a whole, these indicators certainly do not suggest that business performance and the underpinning requirements for productivity growth have deteriorated since 1997, and there has clearly been some movement in the right direction, especially when it comes to human capital and innovation.

REFERENCES

Atkinson, A. B. 2005. *The Atkinson Review: Final Report. Measurement of Government Output and Productivity for the National Accounts.* Palgrave Macmillan.
BIS. 2010a. Economic growth. BIS Economics Paper 9.

BIS. 2010b. UK trade performance: patterns in UK and global trade growth. BIS Economics Paper 8.

BIS. 2010c. *Annual Innovation Report*. Available at www.bis.gov.uk/assets/BISCore/innovation/docs/A/11-p188-annual-innovation-report-2010.pdf.

Bloom, N., and J. Van Reenen, 2007. Measuring and explaining management practices across firms and countries. *Quarterly Journal of Economics* **122**, 1351–1408.

Bloom, N., and Van Reenen, J. 2010. Why do management practices differ across firms and countries? *Journal of Economic Perspectives* **24**, 203–224.

Bloom, N., R. Sadun and J. Van Reenen. 2011. Americans do IT better: US multinationals and the productivity miracle. *American Economic Review* **102**(1), 167–201.

Card, D., and R. B. Freeman. 2004. What have two decades of British economic reform delivered? In *Seeking a Premier League Economy: The Economic Effects of British Economic Reforms, 1980–2000* (ed. D. Card, R. Blundell and R. B. Freeman). University of Chicago Press.

Corry, D., A. Valero and J. Van Reenen. 2011. UK economic performance since 1997: growth, productivity and jobs. Special Paper 24, Centre for Economic Performance. Available at http://cep.lse.ac.uk/conference_papers/15b_11_2011/CEP_Report_UK_Business_15112011.pdf.

Dal Borgo, M., P. Goodridge, J. E. Haskel and A. Pesole. 2011. Productivity and growth in UK industries: an intangible investment approach. Imperial College.

Giles, C. 2011. Busting the myths on the economy. *Financial Times*. Available at www.ft.com/cms/s/0/cc5d60d0-fefa-11e0-9769-00144feabdc0.html#axzz2YSlX51la.

Haskel, J. E., S. C. Pereira and M. J. Slaughter. 2007. Does inward foreign direct investment boost the productivity of domestic firms? *Review of Economics and Statistics* **89**, 482–496.

Jorgenson, D. W. 2001. Information technology and the US economy. *American Economic Review* **91**, 1–32.

Lent, A., and D. Nash. 2011. Surviving the Asian Century. New Era Economics Report, Institute for Public Policy Research.

Lindley, J., and S. Machin. 2011. Rising wage inequality and postgraduate education. Discussion Paper, Centre for the Economics of Education.

Machin, S., and J. Van Reenen. 2010. Inequality. CEP Election Analysis.

O'Mahony, M., and M. P. Timmer. 2009. Output, input and productivity measures at the industry level: the EU KLEMS database. *Economic Journal* **119**, F374–F403.

ONS. 2012. The productivity conundrum, explanations and preliminary analysis. Available at www.ons.gov.uk/ons/dcp171766_283259.pdf.

Overman, H. 2010. Urban renewal and regional growth: muddled objectives and mixed progress. CEP Election Analysis.

Pessoa, J., and J. Van Reenen. 2011. The decoupling of wages and productivity: myth and reality. LSE Mimeo.

Steedman, H. 2010. The state of apprenticeships. *CentrePiece* **15**(2), 19–21.

Timmer, M. P. 2007. EU KLEMS growth and productivity accounts: an overview. *National Institute Economic Review* **200**, 64.

Timmer, M. P., R. Inklaar, M. O'Mahony and B. van Ark. 2010. *Economic Growth in Europe: A Comparative Industry Perspective.* Cambridge University Press.

van Ark, B. 2010. Productivity, sources of growth and potential output in the Euro Area and the United States. *Intereconomics* **2010**(1), 17-20.

Van Reenen, J. 1997. Why has Britain had slower R&D growth? *Research Policy* **26**, 493-507.

Human Capital and Growth: A Focus on Primary and Secondary Education in the UK

By Nitika Bagaria, Novella Bottini and Miguel Coelho

3.1 Human Capital in the UK

Both economic theory and empirical evidence show that, in the long run, human capital is a critical input for growth. Increasing the quality and quantity of skills of those at the lower end of the ability distribution will raise both growth and equity, making it a particularly desirable policy.

School spending per UK pupil has risen sharply over the last ten years. While national indicators of average educational outcomes show significant improvements, these indicators mask the fact that the UK is performing poorly at the lower end of the educational distribution.

In this chapter we propose a flexible system for education—one that gives schools greater autonomy and the ability to grow within a national accountability framework that places a premium on radically raising the standards of the bottom ability group. Together with improved choice for parents, better performance information (across the entire distribution of achievement) and more effective incentives for teachers and schools, this will improve the quality of teaching.

3.1.1 *Educational Expenditure in the UK*

Figure 3.1 tracks education spending per pupil in real terms in the UK since 1950. Real spending levels increased steadily from the early 1950s

We are grateful to a large number of people for kindly submitting written or oral evidence to the Secretariat and the LSE Growth Commission. We are particularly grateful to Simon Burgess, Oliver Clifton-Moore, officials at the Department for Business, Innovation & Skills, Peter Dolton, Eric Hanushek Stephen Machin, David Mardsen, Sandra McNally, Richard Murphy, the OECD, Olmo Silva, Anna Vignoles, Dylan Wiliam, Ludger Wößmann and Gil Wyness. We are also thankful to Anna Valero for providing useful comments on previous versions of this paper, and to Jo Cantlay and Linda Cleavely for logistical support. The views expressed in this chapter do not necessarily reflect the views of the individuals or institutions mentioned above.

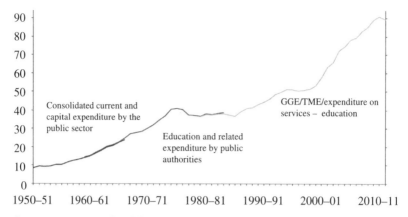

Figure 3.1. UK real public expenditure on education (2011–12 prices, £).

Source: www.parliament.uk/briefing-papers/SN01078. *Notes.* Between 1950 and 1966 the series used is the 'Consolidated current and capital expenditure by the public sector'. It excludes spending on school meals and milk. Between 1960 and 1986 the series used is the Education in the UK series called 'Education and related expenditure by public authorities'. This series includes expenditure on teacher training and the youth service. Between 1980 and the present day the series used are General Government Expenditure (until 1982/83) and Total Managed Expenditure (until 1987/88); expenditure is calculated on a resource basis from 2000/1.

to the mid 1970s. After this period of continuous increase—the longest on record—spending fell during the 1976–77 period and the 1979–80 period. The first half of the 1980s was characterized by flat levels of real spending, and expenditure only returned to mid 1970s levels in the late 1980s. As figure 3.1 shows, the largest annual increases occurred during the 2000s. The real increase in the eleven years to 2010–11 was just over two-thirds (Bolton 2012).

Looking closely at the primary and secondary school sectors, we find that real spending per pupil in these sectors in the UK increased by 4.8% per annum between 1997–98 and 2009–10, leaving spending per pupil significantly above the OECD average. As figure 3.2 shows, total real school spending has increased by about 40% in real terms since 2000, for both primary and secondary schools.

The increase in expenditure has partly been used to bring pupil–teacher ratios down. Pupil–teacher ratios fell from 18.6 in 1997 (for all schools) to 16.9 in 2008, and yet the UK still has high primary class sizes compared with other OECD countries (McNally 2010). Teachers' salaries are the other large determinants of variations in education expenditure.

3.1.2 *Educational Outcomes in the UK*

In this section we document the level of educational attainment in the UK in the recent years. Further, outcomes of different groups within the UK are compared—specifically, the educational attainment of disadvantaged children is compared with that of their wealthier counterparts. In addition, we benchmark to international comparators where possible.

Education performance in the UK is commonly measured by the percentage of pupils attaining five or more GCSEs (Key Stage 4) at grades A*–C at the end of compulsory schooling. Taken at face value, national indicators suggest that performance in GCSEs has been improving. However, there is a concern that at least some of this could be due to students taking easier subjects, grade inflation or 'teaching to the test'. This prompts us to look at how the UK performs internationally.

There are three international tests for evaluating performance in education:[1]

- the Progress International Reading Literacy Study (PIRLS), which is available for the years 2001 and 2006 for pupils of around 10 years old;

- the Programme for International Student Assessment (PISA), which measures the cognitive skills of pupils aged fifteen, was conducted in 2000, 2003, 2006 and 2009; and

- the Trends in International Mathematics and Science Study (TIMSS), which is available for 1999, 2003 and 2007 for pupils aged around 10 and pupils aged around 14 (that is, years 5 and 9 in England).

The latest PIRLS results put England significantly above the international average for 10-year-olds in terms of their reading abilities, but the country's performance is below some other major European countries

---

[1] A new indicator has recently been published by the Economist Intelligence Unit: 'The Learning Curve'. This measure is based on the existing indexes but adopts a wider perspective by adding new criteria such as graduation rates, adult literacy and the effect of years in school on productivity. The new results do not change the ranking at the top: Finland, South Korea and Hong Kong are the best-performing countries, followed by Japan and Singapore. But the ranking positions of some other countries changed sharply. Britain, for example, was placed sixth, much higher than its PISA 2011 classification. As argued by the authors, this improvement is due to the fact that the new index also includes university education, where the UK is a high-performing country. At the same time, this result brings into focus the large quality gap between compulsory and higher education in the UK and the potential negative effect that that has for students that do not attend university ('Pisa envy', *The Economist* (19 January 2013)).

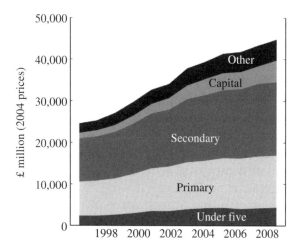

Figure 3.2. Education expenditure by sector in England.
Source: OECD (2012).

(including Italy and Germany) and it has worsened since 2001. The PISA study places the UK close to the OECD average, behind strong performers such as Finland and the Netherlands, in 2009. There was also a small decline in UK performance between 2006 and 2009 according to PISA (McNally 2010).[2]

With regards to measures of secondary school performance, the results from TIMSS match more closely what is found in national key stage tests and more curriculum-based tests, while PISA measures the application of knowledge in everyday situations. According to TIMSS, England is one of the highest performers internationally, and an increase in test scores over time is evident. Thus, international tests confirm that overall performance at the secondary school level has improved in the UK in recent years.

3.1.2.1 *The UK's Long Tail of Poor Achievement*

One of the most striking features of educational outcomes in the UK is the high share of low performers. GCSE results (Key Stage 4) show a 'long tail' of low achievement among 16-year-olds (figure 3.3). This has been a persistent feature of the UK education system and a continuing policy concern. The UK also does worse than other countries when it comes

---

[2]Unfortunately, PISA is not well suited to comparing trends over time because of problems with the English entries in 2000 and 2003.

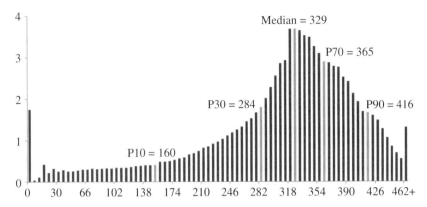

Figure 3.3. Key Stage 4 (GCSE) results (England, 2008): percentage of pupils with results in each band of total GCSE points.

Source: Department for Education. *Notes*. Results are for maintained (state) schools only. Total points are 'capped' by the Department for Children, Schools and Families to show those points gained from a pupil's eight best GCSE (or equivalent) passes at age 16. The system awards 16 points for a pass at G, 22 for an F, up to 52 for an A and 56 for an A*.

to the proportion of the population aged 24–35 that have upper-level secondary qualifications (equivalent to GCSE passes at A*–C or higher qualifications (McNally 2012)).

This result is confirmed by the PISA data, which show significant performance variability within the UK (OECD 2010). Table 3.1 shows the proportion of pupils at each level of performance compared with other countries. High-performing countries such as South Korea and Finland have a narrower range of scores overall. The OECD finds that the gap between the bottom performers and the middle performers is bigger in the UK than the gap between the middle performers and the top performers (OECD 2010).[3] In this respect, the UK closely mirrors the OECD average. In other words, there is a bigger gap created by students falling behind the average score than there is by students pulling away at the top.

Of particular note in this table is the sheer volume of UK students failing to achieve basic proficiency (level 2). Around a fifth of students failed to reach basic proficiency in reading and mathematics, which translates to around 113,000 students in England. This group is more than twice as big as the group of students that reached the top two performance levels. Unsurprisingly, high-performing countries not only have lots of

---

[3] The gap between the 10th percentile and the median is larger than the gap between the median and the 90th percentile.

Table 3.1. Percentage of students at each level of the
PISA proficiency scale for reading, 2009.

	Level					
	< 2	2	3	4	5	6
UK	18	25	29	20	7	1
Key competitors average*	10	18	30	28	12	2
OECD average	19	24	30	21	7	1

*Key competitors defined as Australia, Canada, Finland, South Korea and Singapore. These were chosen as countries that traditionally score well on PISA and are frequently cited in comparison to UK performance. *Source*: Clifton and Cook (2012) using data from OECD (2010).

students at the highest levels, but they also have relatively few students at the lower levels.

A picture emerges of a large pool of 'poor performers' that contributes to the UK's overall weak performance in international rankings. The UK therefore faces a two-pronged challenge: to stretch those at the top, while the performance of those that are falling behind needs to be raised. In terms of the number of pupils, the latter is the bigger challenge, with around a fifth of pupils failing to get the basic skills required to succeed in life.

3.1.2.2 *The Socioeconomic Gradient in UK Educational Attainment*

The extent to which the long tail discussed above is driven by socioeconomic disadvantage is not directly discernible. The relationship between socioeconomic background and educational attainment is called the socioeconomic gradient of education. It is a well-established empirical fact that children from disadvantaged backgrounds are over-represented in the group of poor performers, while children from wealthier families are over-represented in the group of high performers.

According to the PISA results from 2009 (the most recently published), 14% of the variation in student performance in the UK is explained by students' socioeconomic background. This is in line with the OECD average but contrasts with Canada and Japan, where the equivalent figure is 9%. If we consider the wider family context (including, for example, whether or not children's parents are immigrants or the language spoken at home), differences in family background characteristics explain 25% of the differences in performance across UK students; this compares with a figure of 22% for the typical OECD country and a figure of 19% in Canada, Finland, Japan and South Korea. These numbers suggest a weaker relationship

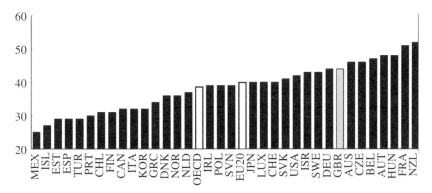

Figure 3.4. The impact of socioeconomic
background on PISA 2009 reading score.

Source: OECD (2012). *Notes.* Differences in PISA test scores associated with increases in
the PISA index of social and cultural status.

between socioeconomic background and educational inequality in other
OECD countries than is found in the UK.

The same message from a different perspective is given by figure 3.4,
which shows the impact of socioeconomic background on PISA scores:
it shows that, of the OECD countries, the impact in the UK is among the
most acute. Moreover, the share of UK students from weak socioeconomic
backgrounds that perform well is low: the average PISA score of the worst-
performing 10% of UK students is below the average for the same group
in other OECD countries (OECD 2012).

The PISA study also reports on the percentage of 'resilient students':
those who come from the lower quartile of the distribution of socioeconomic background but go on to score in the top quartile of PISA test
results. On this measure, the UK trails both the OECD average and its key
competitors, with only 6% of students considered 'resilient' according to
this criterion.

Schuetz *et al.* (2005) relate family background to student test scores
across countries using TIMSS. Although a gradient is present in most
countries, the estimated effect is higher in England than in any other
country for this particular survey. Achievement gaps between children
from rich and poor backgrounds are evident from a very early age and
continue to widen as children grow up. As a result the achievement gap
between rich and poor is considerable at age 16 when it comes to GCSE
results.[4]

---

[4]The fact that these achievement gaps are present even before school suggests that
the educational system should not take sole responsibility.

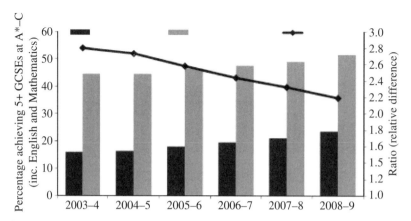

Figure 3.5. Percentage of children achieving five or more GCSEs at grades
A*–C (including English and mathematics) by FSM eligibility.

One way to analyse this pattern is to look at the school attainment
of children eligible for free school meals (FSM).[5] In 2008, while half of
all children from higher-income families (not eligible for FSM) achieved
five good GCSEs (A*–C) inclusive of English and mathematics, less than
a quarter of FSM children achieved that benchmark (figure 3.5). However, figure 3.5 also shows that this gap has narrowed in relative terms
in recent years.[6] Despite the improvement, the current achievement gap
is still large and negatively impacts on later-life income and earnings
inequalities with the potential risk of being passed on to future generations (Chowdry *et al.* 2010).

However, the problem is much wider and goes beyond FSM pupils.
Indeed, there is a clear and consistent link between deprivation and academic achievement wherever you are on the scale (figure 3.6). Those
pupils living in the most-disadvantaged postcodes score on average
320 points at GCSE (approximately the equivalent of eight C grades),
and the results gradually improve as you move towards better (less-
disadvantaged) postcodes. Pupils living in the wealthiest postcodes score
on average 380 points (equivalent to just over eight B grades). It is therefore not possible to identify a particular level of deprivation at which
performance falls. This challenges the assumption that programmes

---

[5]Children are classified as 'eligible' for FSM in administrative data only if they are both
eligible for them and claiming them. Only families with a low income and no adults in full-
time paid work are eligible for FSM. *A priori*, therefore, we would expect FSM 'eligibility'
to identify children in the lowest-income households.

[6]It is worth noting that only part of this narrowing reflects a real improvement in
pupils' performance owing to the 'grade inflation' phenomenon.

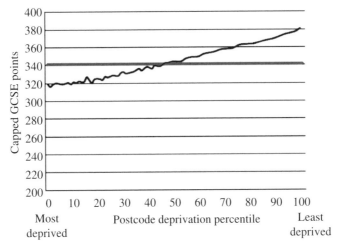

Figure 3.6. Capped GCSE points by postcode deprivation.
Source: Clifton and Cook (2012).

targeted towards pupils who are eligible for free school meals will be sufficient to close the gap, as the problem is much wider than just this group of pupils.[7]

More importantly, in contrast with popular belief, disadvantaged children are not all concentrated in a small number of poorly performing schools (though, of course, poorer areas will generally tend to have larger shares of disadvantaged children than wealthier areas). Disadvantaged children are spread across the entire school system, and they perform poorly compared with their wealthier peers in the vast majority of schools. Figure 3.7 illustrates this problem. The darker line shows the average point score for all pupils in each percentile of schools. The lighter line shows the average point score for only poorer children within those schools (those living in the bottom fifth of households, as measured by the deprivation level of the postcode). While the darker line's slope increases rapidly, the pink one is flatter. In other words, the problem is not just that there are a few schools that have all the disadvantaged children in them performing poorly, it is also that disadvantaged children

---

[7] Another striking feature of the 'long tail' is the higher variability in GCSE results of poorer pupils compared with wealthier pupils. The highest-achieving pupils from disadvantaged postcodes score almost as well as the highest-achieving pupils from wealthier areas (about 40 points less at GCSE). However, low-achieving pupils from disadvantaged neighbourhoods score much worse than low-achieving pupils from wealthier areas (about 120 points less at GCSE).

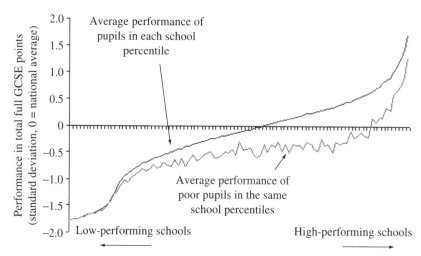

Figure 3.7. Attainment of poor pupils against the
(within-school) average by school deprivation.
Source: Cook (2012).

perform poorly (compared with their wealthier peers) in the vast majority
of schools.

Low income is the attribute of disadvantage that, over the years, has
attracted most attention from academics, politicians and the general public. The simple correlation between low income and poor educational outcomes (the so-called socioeconomic gradient of education) is long established (Rowntree 1901; Glennerster 1995b). Income is often used as a
measure of disadvantage for three main reasons:

(i) the income gradient gives a measure of educational inequality in its
own right;

(ii) some other features of disadvantage discussed below are associated
with income;[8] and

(iii) the relationship between family income and education is one of the
key drivers of intergenerational income mobility across time (see,
for example, Blanden *et al.* 2007).

There are a multitude of possible reasons for the children of low-
income families doing less well at school; some of them are causal (family
income actually influences a child's educational attainment), while others

[8]This could be because those features are a causal driver of income, because they are
caused by income, or it could be because both those features and income are commonly
determined by a third factor.

are non-causal (for example, income simply acts as an indicator of many other aspects of disadvantage, such as parental education level or social class). Different studies suggest that sustained income shocks do impact on children's educational outcomes, and that low household income is likely to be one of the primary drivers behind the developmental deficits of poor children.[9] Adults in low-income families may have characteristics that negatively impact on children's educational achievement, such as poorer innate ability, a lower emphasis on educational achievement in parenting, a reduced ability to translate parenting time into educational development, or lower ambitions (Blanden and Gregg 2004).

3.2 THE IMPORTANCE OF HUMAN CAPITAL

Educational outcomes and human capital formation are among the most important drivers of economic growth. Theoretical models of economic growth have considered different determinants of economic growth and a range of theoretical approaches. The standard neoclassical growth model of Solow (1957) considers the output of the macro economy as a direct function of only its capital and labour (and technological level) in a given period. Augmented neoclassical growth theories, developed by Mankiw *et al.* (1992), also include human capital among the factors of production: a change in the education level induces growth. However, in these models, technology, the key driver of growth rates, is exogenous. A different view comes from the 'endogenous growth' models developed by Lucas (1988), Romer (1990) and Aghion and Howitt (1998), whereby technology is now endogenous to the model. This literature stresses the role of education in increasing the innovation capacity of the economy through developing new ideas and new technologies. Other macro-models on technological diffusion (such as those of Nelson and Phelps (1966), Welch (1970) and Benhabib and Spiegel (1994)) argue that education and training facilitate the adoption and implementation of new technologies, which has a positive effect on growth and development.

Empirical analysis based on growth- and development-accounting models has generally shown that education accounts for a large share of economic growth and development. Growth-accounting models (such as those of Griliches (1970), using US data, Barro and Lee (1993, 2001), Mankiw *et al.* (1992), Barro and Sala-i-Martín (2004), Sala-i-Martín *et al.*

---

[9]For example, Stevens and Schaller (2011) and Gregg *et al.* (2012) analyse fathers' job displacement, Dahl and Lochner (2012) examine the introduction of the Earned Income Tax Credit in the US, and Milligan and Stabille (2011) study the variation in child tax benefits across time and Canadian provinces.

(2004), de la Fuente and Domenech (2006) and Cohen and Soto (2007), using cross-country data) relate educational attainment (in growth or level) to economic growth (measured as GDP or GDP per capita); while development-accounting models seek to explain cross-country differences in income levels and education's role in these differences (see, for example, Lagakos *et al.* (2012) and Gennaioli *et al.* (2011); see also Hall and Jones (1999) and Caselli (2005) for a theoretical foundation).

Human capital has usually been measured in terms of educational attainment/years of education. More recently, thanks to the development of new data sets, authors have been able to consider different measures; for instance, they have been able to make a distinction between the education levels of entrepreneurs/managers and workers (Bloom and Van Reenen 2007, 2010; La Porta and Shleifer 2008; Syverson 2011), or consider the quality of education (or cognitive skills) using PISA or TIMSS results (see Hanushek and Woessmann (2008) for a review of these studies). These new empirical approaches have confirmed the critical role that human capital plays in the growth and development processes of countries, regions and firms.

Hanushek and Woessmann (2007) and Hanushek and Kimko (2000) emphasize the positive effect of the quality of education, rather than its quantity alone, on economic growth. Hanushek and Shultz (2012) state that a one standard deviation difference on test performance (100 points on the PISA assessment) is related to a two percentage point difference in annual GDP per capita growth rates. OECD (2010b) estimated that the UK would gain more than $US6 trillion by increasing its average performance by only 25 PISA points (or by one-quarter of a standard deviation). These are obviously long-run calculations, but they do give some indication of the huge potential prize: if the UK could attain the quality of education in Germany or Australia, this would put us on a path that would more than double our income per person. Following the more ambitious goal of reaching Finland's PISA performance, the UK would record a GDP improvement of more than $US7 trillion, tripling its current level of GDP.

The major criticism of these cross-country analyses is that they show associations between human capital and growth but not necessarily causation, i.e. they do not address issues of endogeneity: estimates of school attainment could reflect reverse causality, since improved growth could lead to more schooling rather than the reverse (Bils and Klenow 2000). Whether or not there is a causal relationship is a very important issue from a policy point of view (OECD 2010a,b). However, this problem is not easily solved by using standard econometric techniques since the potential instruments for education are often correlated with institutional features (Glaeser *et al.* 2004). Nonetheless, Hanushek and Woessmann (2009) and Gennaioli *et al.* (2011) have tried to account for the endogeneity problem using different estimation methods: although none of these approaches addresses all the critical issues, they provide some assurance that the results are not biased by any of the most obvious problematic issues (OECD 2010b).

3.2.1 *Human Capital Inequality and Growth*

In addition to the overall accumulation of human capital, inequality of human capital within a country is an important factor in determining growth. In practical terms, reducing human capital inequality means improving the educational attainment of pupils at the bottom of the distribution, so focusing on the worst-performing students is imperative. The OECD (2010b) have estimated how GDP would improve if OECD countries addressed education inequality and tried to ensure that all students reach a level of minimal proficiency (i.e. a PISA score of 400). Under this scenario of raising the level of achievement of those at the bottom of the distribution, the OECD estimates that the current level of UK GDP would be more than US$6 trillion, or 2.7 times its current level.

Recent literature has focused on human capital inequality and its influence on demographic variables to explain the negative relationship between human capital inequality and growth. De la Croix and Doepke (2003) and Moav (2005) study the link between human capital inequality and increasing fertility (which has a negative effect on growth), while Castelló-Climent and Doménech (2008) focus on how human capital inequality may dampen growth by reducing life expectancy and investment in education.

Some authors analyse the effect of inequality on growth under imperfect credit markets (see, for example, Galor and Zeira 1993; Mookherjee and Ray 2003) or at different levels of a country's development. Galor and Zeira (1993) show that in the presence of credit market imperfections and indivisibilities in investment in human capital, the initial distribution of wealth affects investment in education both in the short term and in the long term. With regards to development studies, Castelló-Climent (2010) shows that a greater degree of human capital inequality was associated with lower per capita income growth rates in most developing countries during the period 1965–2005, where the life expectancy and fertility channels seem to play a prominent role. However, the effect disappears in higher-income economies. Moreover, he finds that the effect is stronger in countries where there is limited access to credit.

3.2.2 *Human Capital Inequality and Social Mobility*

On average, disadvantaged students perform worse than pupils from rich families. Poor educational outcomes for disadvantaged students reduce social mobility later in life, which in turn perpetuates low intergenerational social mobility.[10] Two facts help us understand the size of the problem of educational inequality. Firstly, 24% of disadvantaged students in the UK are 'resilient', in the sense that they come from the most socioeconomically disadvantaged 25% of students in the country but perform much better than expected on the basis of their socioeconomic background (31% is the OECD average) (see OECD 2010a). Secondly, it is also true that the odds of a young person from a family with low levels of parental education attaining higher education is 0.61 in the UK, which is well above the OECD average of 0.44. This suggests that if socioeconomic disadvantages were not allowed to hold back educational attainment, social mobility could be high in the UK.

A series of reports have highlighted the UK's low levels of social mobility, showing how children from poorer backgrounds struggle to gain access to university, enter professional jobs and earn decent wages (see Milburn 2012; Higgins *et al.* 2011; Blanden *et al.* 2005). This, in turn, means that disadvantage can become entrenched across generations. Low levels of social mobility have been rooted in wider changes to the British economy since the 1970s, following the loss of decent jobs at the bottom of the labour market, the professionalization of jobs at the top of the labour market, and an increase in income inequality, which have all combined to make it harder for people to climb the ladder of opportunity (Duncan and Murnane 2011).

A high level of education has become more important for getting a good job over the past thirty years, meaning that those families that are unable to invest in education are left further behind (Lindley and Machin 2012). Education can provide access to many opportunities later in life, and schools can help to create a level playing field for young people as they start out (Clifton and Cook 2012). Research has identified a causal

---

[10]It is important to remember that raising achievement alone is not enough. There also needs to be sufficient demand for the gained skills and qualifications in the labour market, so that young people can put their education to good use. Recent cuts to the funding of post-16 education, a weak youth labour market and the prevalence of low-quality jobs will also have to be tackled for improvements to social mobility to be realized (Lawton and Lanning 2012; Keep *et al.* 2006). Other factors can also be important when it comes to social mobility, such as having access to social networks and inherited wealth. Raising achievement in schools is therefore just one piece of a much bigger jigsaw (Clifton and Cook 2012).

relationship between high levels of education and a number of outcomes in later life, including higher earnings (Dickson 2009), lower teenage pregnancy (Black *et al.* 2008), healthier lifestyles and a lower likelihood of serving a prison sentence (Heckman *et al.* 2006).

There is wide empirical evidence to strongly support the idea that education is one of the major drivers of intergenerational social mobility, particularly income mobility. The UK has recorded a fall in intergenerational mobility between the cohorts born at the end of the 1950s and those born in the 1970s. Blanden and Gregg (2004) argue that it was mainly due to a disproportionate increase in educational opportunities biased towards individuals from better-off backgrounds.

The link between intragenerational income inequality and intergenerational social mobility is rather complex. Recent evidence shows that higher inequality is associated with lower intergenerational mobility (OECD 2012). Firstly, this can be explained by the fact that higher wage dispersion allows for higher returns to education, and this may benefit individuals whose families do not face any constraints when it comes to investing in education. Secondly, if income inequality increases the severity of credit constraints, mobility decreases. Thirdly, large differences in educational outcomes raise income inequality and lower intergenerational social mobility. As discussed above, the children of high-income (and better-educated) parents tend to get better results than their peers (Blanden *et al.* 2007).

3.3 The Drivers of Educational Attainment: A Review of the Literature

In this section we will briefly discuss the factors that the economics of education has identified as driving educational attainment. A complex interplay of factors contributes to attainment gaps between advantaged and disadvantaged children. These factors include the following.

- Broad contextual drivers, such as the socioeconomic background of a child (e.g. family income and parental education), and their knock-on effect on the home learning environment.
- Pupil-level factors: for example, having been in care at some stage, having English as another language (EAL) status, having special educational needs (SEN) status,[11] mobility and ethnicity. These factors have a complex relationship with material disadvantage.

---

[11] SEN is a multifaceted classification that brings together children with innate cognitive/learning difficulties and children who are underperforming for reasons other than

- School-level factors that determine the quality of the child's formal learning environment, such as teaching, peer composition, resources and the general effectiveness of individual schools in overcoming material barriers.

Recent evidence (Kramarz *et al.* 2009) on the relative contributions of pupils, schools and peers shows that the variance of test scores is mostly explained by the pupil effect.[12] The standard deviation of pupil effects is between four and five times larger than the standard deviation of school effects,[13] which is the second largest source of variance in the results. Many other studies suggest that families are much more important than schools and peers in explaining the variance in results (Teddlie and Reynolds 2000; Todd and Wolpin 2003).

We now consider in more detail the literature on the key factors driving educational outcomes. We start with pupil effects, then move on to school and teacher effects, and then to peer effects. Finally, we consider the effects of expenditure.

3.3.1 *Pupil Effects*

The finding that pupil effects account for the majority of the variance in test scores implies that the influence of home environment and socioeconomic background on schooling outcomes is very important.

Even before pupils start school, there is a large gap in cognitive ability between children from high and low socioeconomic backgrounds. Feinstein (2003) finds significant gaps between children from high and low socioeconomic backgrounds in an index of development. Another way to illustrate pre-school gaps is to look at vocabulary skills by gender and

---

their innate ability (e.g. a strong negative impact of family background and/or poor teaching quality and/or unsupportive peer effects). The first subgroup is defined by a characteristic that puts it at a disadvantage. The second subgroup is defined by its (poor) performance level, and may or may not be disadvantaged (depending on whether family background or other factors drive poor performance). In that sense, SEN conflates discretionary inputs (e.g. teaching quality), non-discretionary inputs (e.g. an unsupportive family background), and outputs (e.g. low attainment).

[12]In this context, pupil effects consist of a range of educational experiences that pupils carry with them, reflecting parental background, the quality of the schools previously attended, innate ability, etc. This research measures the relative contributions of pupils, schools and peers without restricting the analysis to observable proxies for peers' characteristics or school quality.

[13]However, any assessment of the relative merits of various policy alternatives (e.g. those targeted at individual effects versus those targeted at school effects) needs to allow for the fact that school quality has an impact on multiple pupils.

Table 3.2. Age 5 differences in vocabulary by gender and ethnicity (Millennium Cohort Study).

Ethnic group	Boys	Girls
White British	55.9	56.5
Black, Caribbean	48.4*	51.0*
Black, Other	44.2*	47.2*
Bangladeshi	40.4*	41.7*
Pakistani	40.6*	40.7*
Indian	49.8*	50.3*
Chinese	41.2*	55.2
Number of children	4,587	4,452

Source: McNally (2012). *Notes.* Based on table 3 of Dustmann *et al.* (2010). The vocabulary test is standardized to have a mean of 50 and a standard deviation of 10. Asterisks denote statistically significant differences relative to white British boys or girls, respectively.

ethnic group at the time of school entry. Table 3.2 shows gaps in the vocabulary skills of 5-year-olds in the Millennium Cohort Study.

This illustrates that human capital acquisition is not something that begins at school and that inequality is evident even at an early stage. Breaking the link between family background and educational attainment (and improving educational attainment generally) seems to require policies directed at families before the start of formal schooling. This might involve close attention to the quality of early childcare and pre-school settings. However, if part of the issue is poverty and worklessness, then the policy solutions may also lie in other areas of social policy such as housing, employment benefit and childcare provision (McNally 2012).

As discussed in section 3.2, low income is the attribute of disadvantage that, over the years, has attracted most attention from academics, politicians and the general public. The simple correlation between low income and poor educational outcomes (the so-called income gradient of education) has long been established (Rowntree 1901; Glennerster 1995a,b). However, the most significant social background characteristic is parental education, which has been shown to account for between a quarter and two-fifths of the deficits of low-income children (Gregg *et al.* 2008).[14] While a range of other family background characteristics (e.g. parents' employment status or family structure) have occasionally been linked to child attainment, the evidence of their effects, conditional on other

---

[14]Chowdry *et al.* (2009) also found that differences in parental education between young people from different socioeconomic backgrounds provide a major explanation for differences in their educational attainment, and some of the evidence presented points towards the relationship being causal.

economic circumstances, is still mixed (see box 3.1 for evidence on the relationship between family income and educational attainment).

Box 3.1. Family income and educational attainment.

Blanden and Gregg (2004) give evidence of a significant impact of family income on educational attainment in the UK. The results suggest that a reduction of one-third in income from the mean decreases the probability of a child getting five GCSEs at grade A*–C by on average 3–4 percentage points, and reduces the probability of getting a degree by a similar magnitude. These results imply that the probability of a young person at the 90th percentile of the income distribution getting a degree is 42%, compared with 21% for students at the 10th percentile.

The results of Gregg and Macmillan (2009) show that a unit change in the log of income predicts a gap of over one-tenth of a standard deviation in both IQ and Key Stage 1 scores. In their analysis, the magnitude of this effect is much larger than the contributions of both adverse family structures and poor parental labour market outcomes, and the effect also has double the importance of being in a disadvantaged local neighbourhood when it comes to IQ. Only low parental education is a more important predictor of low-income children's cognitive deficits.

Chowdry *et al.* (2009) estimate that differences in the availability of material resources for educational purposes play a key role in explaining why teenagers from poor families tend to make less progress between Key Stage 3 and Key Stage 4 than teenagers from rich families. After accounting for differences in material resources, the gap in Key Stage 4 test scores between young people from the richest and poorest fifths of their sample falls by 37% compared with its value after controlling for parental education, and demographic and other family background characteristics.

Gregg *et al.* (2012) have shown how, in England, a child's educational progress suffered if his/her father lost his job in the recession of the 1980s—something that did not happen for children whose parents remained in work. Similar results have been found after spikes in job losses in the US (Ananat *et al.* 2011).

Dahl and Lochner (2012) estimated the effect of income on children's mathematics and reading achievement in the US using data from the Earned Income Tax Credit. Their estimates suggest that a $1,000 increase in annual income raises combined mathematics and reading test scores by 6% of a standard deviation in the short term. Test gains are larger for children from disadvantaged families.

3.3.2 *School and Teacher Effects*

It is widely acknowledged in the theoretical and empirical literature that the key driver of school quality (defined as the value added of the school) is the quality of teaching staff. There are a large number of anecdotes about the positive impact of excellent teaching on pupils' performance. However, trying to quantify this effect is difficult, principally because of the data requirements. Slater *et al.* (2009) use a unique primary data set to estimate the effect of individual teachers on student outcomes, linking over 7,000 pupils to the individual teachers who taught them in each of their compulsory subjects and to the results of the exams they take at age 16. Their results suggest that being taught by a high-quality teacher (75th percentile) rather than a low-quality teacher (25th percentile) adds 0.425 of a GCSE point[15] per subject (25% of the standard deviation of GCSE points).

Rivkin *et al.* (2005) relate the teacher quality measure to the socioeconomic gap in outcomes. They measure the gap in GCSE points between a poor student and a non-poor student (equal to 6.08 GCSE points) and suppose that this gap arises over eight subjects that they both take. If the poor student had good (75th percentile) teachers for all eight subjects and the better-off student had poor (25th percentile) teachers for all eight, this would account for 3.4 GCSE points. This is a powerful effect that is not typically addressed in explaining the socioeconomic educational gap.

Similar studies for the US suggest that having a teacher at the 25th percentile versus the 75th percentile of the quality distribution would imply a difference in learning attainments of roughly 0.2 standard deviations in a single year. This would induce a move in a student at the middle of the achievement distribution to the 59th percentile. The magnitude of such an effect is large relative to the estimated effects (around 0.1–0.3 standard deviations (Hanushek and Rivkin 2010)) of a ten-student reduction in class size.

The academic literature has also sought markers for high-quality teachers, looking in particular at pay, teachers' experience and their academic level.

There is a great deal of literature on the impact of teachers' pay. One strand investigates the effect of teacher salaries on school performance. Although initial evidence on this was mixed,[16] more recent work has

---

[15]An increase from one grade to the next, a B to an A, say, is one point.

[16]For example, Hanushek (1989) highlights that only nine out of sixty teacher salary studies found a positive effect of teacher wages on school performance.

mostly found different results (see box 3.2 for a review of the literature). The evidence suggests that teaching staff respond to pecuniary and market incentives aimed at increasing their effort and 'output' (i.e. learning). However, it is worth making a distinction between a general increase in teachers' wages (due, for example, to a general increase in the national pay scheme) and an improvement in pay linked to geographical disparities in costs of living or teachers' outcomes. Only the latter types of intervention seem to have a positive impact on teachers' performance and pupils' achievement (Propper and Britton 2012).

Box 3.2. Teachers and head teachers' payment incentives.

The volume of empirical and theoretical literature on the functioning of the labour market for teachers (and head teachers) has increased in recent years. Overall, it suggests that teachers and head teachers respond to monetary and market incentives aimed at increasing their effort and 'output' (i.e. learning). Using different methodologies and data, Dolton and Van Der Klaauw (1999), Hanushek (2003), Murnane and Olsen (1989, 1990) and Chevalier *et al.* (2007) show that individuals respond to (relative) wage incentives in their decision to start teaching or leave the occupation. Loeb and Page (2000) find that teachers' wages are a significant determinant of their performance and their decision to stay in the profession: a 10% increase in teachers' wages would reduce quit rates among US teachers by 3–6%. Dolton and Marcenaro-Gutierrez (2011) (using panel data on thirty-nine countries) show how both relative and absolute levels of teachers' salaries strongly impact on pupil performance. Propper and Britton (2012) provide further evidence favouring the argument that teachers' wages are important for school performance in England.

There is also a growing body of work investigating the impact of performance-related pay. Whilst again there is some mixed evidence, the general consensus appears to be that performance-related pay for teachers does improve student attainment in a variety of settings. Examples include Lavy (2009) in Israel, Muralidharan and Sundararaman (2009) in India, Jackson (2010) in Texas, Bettinger (2010) in Ohio, and Atkinson *et al.* (2009) in England. Hanushek and Luque (2003) and Lavy (2002) show that teacher performance-related pay schemes could effectively attract good teachers and improve their motivation with positive outcomes on pupils' attainment. Woessmann (2011) uses cross-country data to show that the introduction of performance-related pay is significantly associated with improved mathematics, science and reading achievement across countries. In particular, countries that adopt this type of teacher compensation record about one-quarter of a standard deviation higher scores. Atkinson *et al.* (2009) evaluate the impact of a performance-related pay scheme for teachers in England, using teacher-level data matched with pupils' test scores and value added. They show that the introduction of a payment scheme based on pupil attainment improved test scores and value added, on average by about half a grade per pupil. They also find heterogeneity across subjects, with mathematics teachers showing no improvement. Green *et al.* (2008) show that private schools in the UK—which are characterized by staff with higher education levels and which attract a lot of teachers from the state system each year—are used to paying a premium for teachers of subjects for which there is a teacher shortage, such as mathematics and science. They use pay flexibility as an effective strategy to attract more and better teachers in these subjects.

Looking at teachers' decisions to stay in the profession, Lazear (2003) argues that a reduction in teacher pay in the US and Sweden has caused adverse selection, inducing the highest-quality teachers to leave the job; the author further suggests that linking compensation to performance would improve teacher quality and school effectiveness. Clotfelter *et al.* (2006) report that a monetary bonus given to qualified teachers in North Carolina greatly reduced their probability of leaving high-poverty schools. This incentive was especially effective for teachers with more years of experience, who are usually associated with better pupil outcomes (Hanushek *et al.* 2005).

With regards to head teachers, Besley and Machin (2008) investigate the link between the pay and performance of school principals. They show that, in line with the evidence on the pay and performance of private sector chief executive officers, school principals' salaries are linked to publicly observable performance measures, and poorly performing principals face a higher chance of being replaced. The results of Branch *et al.* (2013) show that highly effective principals increase the performance of a typical student by between two and seven months of learning in a single school year; ineffective principals lower achievement by the same amount.

In particular, evidence indicates that relative salaries and alternative employment opportunities are important influences on the attractiveness of teaching as a profession (Santiago 2004). As discussed in OECD (2005), teachers' salaries relative to those for other occupations influence

(i) the decision to become a teacher after graduation, as graduates' career choices are associated with relative earnings in teaching and non-teaching occupations, and their likely growth over time;

(ii) the decision to return to teaching after a career interruption, as returning rates are generally higher among those teaching subjects that provide the fewest opportunities for employment elsewhere;

(iii) the decision to remain a teacher, as, in general, the higher that teachers' salaries are, the fewer people leave the profession.

Relative earnings seem to be less important when the decision is whether to enrol in teacher education or another college course (Hanushek and Pace 1995). McKinsey (2007) suggested that while raising salaries in line with other graduate salaries is important, raising them above the graduate market average level would not lead to substantial further increases in the quality or quantity of applicants.

Using data on university graduates in the UK, Dolton (1990) showed that increasing teacher salaries by a small amount (10%) resulted in a large rise in applications (30%). The 'wage elastic' teacher supply could be explained by the comparatively low level of teachers' wages. Wolter and Denzler (2004) ran a similar analysis for Switzerland and showed that since salaries were already relatively high, further increases had little impact on the number or quality of applicants to teaching. While starting salaries in general are high in England,[17] low top wages at higher career levels may discourage more experienced teachers from remaining in the profession and also deter good graduates from starting a teaching career.

There is also a growing body of work investigating the impact of performance-related pay. Whilst again there is mixed evidence, the general consensus appears to be that performance-related pay for teachers does improve student attainment in a variety of settings.[18]

However, a good salary is not necessarily the only, or even the main, motivation for teaching. The status of the teaching profession, the career opportunities it presents and the decisional power given to teachers are all important factors in explaining their performance. For example, Hoxby (2002b) provides evidence that school choice affects the teaching profession by increasing the demand for staff with higher qualifications (especially in mathematics and science) as well as prompting greater effort from teachers and a greater degree of autonomy.

While the literature has long identified an association between the experience of a teacher (i.e. his/her years of teaching experience) and that teacher's performance (i.e. the quality of their teaching), recent studies

---

[17]Working hours in teaching are also fairly long compared with many other OECD countries.

[18]See box 3.2 for a review of the literature.

have consistently found that the impact of experience is concentrated in the first one or two years of teaching and that subsequent years have little impact (Hanushek 2008). A teacher's education also tends not to be correlated with his or her quality.[19]

Given the critical role of teacher quality on pupils' performance, recruiting and maintaining the most efficient teachers should be prioritized. The issue is how to attract and select good teachers. This is not a straightforward process since it is difficult to assess *ex ante* if a candidate would be a good teacher. Qualitative research suggests that top-performing school systems manage to attract better people into the teaching profession, leading to better student outcomes. They do this by introducing highly selective teacher training, developing effective selection processes for identifying the right candidates, and paying good (but not great) starting compensation. Conversely, lower-performing school systems rarely attract the right people into teaching (McKinsey 2007). The success in attracting talented people into teaching is linked to specific country features such as history, culture and the status of the teaching profession. However, there are some policies that can be implemented to attract the best graduates, such as effective mechanisms for selecting teachers, good teacher-training programmes, good starting compensation and increasing professional autonomy in schools. All these policies could contribute to an increase in the status of the teaching profession and the attractiveness of teaching as a career, and teaching could then attract the best graduates (see box 3.3 for an overview of different recruitment processes).

Box 3.3. The recruitment process.

It is difficult to assess *ex ante* if a candidate would be a good teacher, therefore it is essential to have better-designed recruitment mechanisms together with effective teacher training for one or two years. For example, in 2007 Finland introduced a three-round selection process for teaching. The first round consists of a first examination designed to test numeracy, literacy and problem-solving skills. The top-scoring candidates go through to the second round, which tests a wide range of the candidates' aptitudes, such as communication skills, willingness to learn, academic

---

[19]Some have argued, however, that if teachers have higher academic qualifications, this could produce benefits for the education system in other forms. For example, more highly educated teachers may increase the success of school autonomy, by providing better input into the design of the school's curriculum and in developing new teaching methods. Furthermore, the perceived status of the teaching profession is linked to the level of education and training required to become a teacher (Day *et al.* 2006).

ability and motivation for teaching, and gives them access to teacher training. In Finland all teacher-training programmes are 'Master of Education' degrees, with a duration of four years. After graduating from teacher training, the prospective teachers need to pass further tests at the individual schools to which they apply for teaching positions. As advocated by Ostinelli (2009), the Finnish model presents some advantages over the English one. However, its implementation is not straightforward.

It is important to carefully design teacher training and select graduates into those programmes. It can be done either by controlling entry directly, or by limiting the number of places on teacher-training courses, so that supply matches demand. Indeed, failing to control entry into teaching training would lead to an oversupply of candidates, which, in turn, would have a significant negative effect on teacher quality. Indeed, if too many students are involved in these programmes, they would struggle to find jobs as teachers when they graduate. Moreover, training quality could be affected because of the reduced level of resources per candidate, and because of the lower average quality of the people involved in the programme. While Singapore makes teacher training selective to manage supply, England focuses on limiting the funding for teacher training to manage supply, and ensures that all training providers meet certain general standards for the selection of the students on their courses (McKinsey 2007).

A well-performing system must also find a way to recruit more experienced graduates. The teacher-training requirement that experienced graduates must undergo training for a year creates a barrier, since applicants would lose a year's earnings as well as having to bear the costs of their courses. Creating new routes into teaching in which entrants can avoid this financial burden significantly increases the pool of potential applicants into the profession. The UK has massively diversified its recruitment process and has developed many entry points into teaching in an attempt to maximize recruitment. By 2006, there were thirty-two different ways of entering the teaching profession in the UK, though there is some homogeneity across the routes when it comes to expectations about the skills, knowledge and behaviour that teacherss should demonstrate by the time they have completed their training (McKinsey 2007).

3.3.3   Peer Effects

Another driver of educational attainment is believed to be peers' behaviour and characteristics. This has been documented empirically (Coleman 1966) as well as theoretically (Angrist and Lang 2004; Hoxby 2000; Lavy and Schlosser 2011; Gould *et al.* 2009). The main rationale is that group actions or attributes might influence individual decisions and outcomes. However, the estimation of peer effects is empirically challenging. Manski (1993) highlights the pitfalls of endogenous peer selection and the difficulty of distinguishing between average school effects and peer effects.

Recent empirical evidence based on better data and better identification strategies has reached a consensus: to capture peer effects, analyses should not focus on average students but should instead consider pupil distributions. There is little conclusive evidence to suggest that studying with a higher-ability peer group leads to better outcomes for all pupils (see, for example, Atkinson *et al.* (2008), Bradley and Taylor (2008), Dills (2005) and Summers and Wolfe (1977)), while the presence of low-ability peer groups can decrease general outcomes (Lavy *et al.* 2012; Gibbons and Telhaj 2008; Winston and Zimmerman 2004; Zimmerman 2003; Henderson *et al.* 1978; Summers and Wolfe 1977).[20] Lavy *et al.* (2012) show that it is only the very bottom 5% of students that (negatively) affect average outcome and not 'bad' peers in any other part of the ability distribution. They also find evidence that the presence of students in the top 5% of the ability distribution does not impact average outcomes. Henderson *et al.* (1978) show that mixing weak and strong students lowers educational attainment for higher achievers. Similar results are also found by Bradley and Taylor (2008), who use pupils moving between schools to address the problems inherent with estimating peer effects, and find that the effects of a more able peer group are stronger for low-ability students than they are for higher-ability students. On the other hand, Betts and Shkolnik (2000) find little evidence of differential effects of ability grouping for high- or low-ability pupils.

Some academics associate the negative impact of low-ability students on the outcomes of other students to the fact that more-homogeneous groups of students might be taught more effectively (Duflo *et al.* 2010) or by pointing at the classroom disruption and decrease in attention paid by the teachers (Lavy *et al.* 2012). Some studies suggest that these general findings mask some heterogeneity along the gender dimension by showing that girls are significantly affected by interactions with peers (Lavy *et al.* 2012; Stinebrickner and Stinebrickner 2006).

To overcome the difficulties of endogenous peer selection, a number of studies use the random allocation of accommodation within higher

---

[20]For a slightly different message see Carrell *et al.* (2011).

education establishments in the US. Sacerdote (2001) finds that peers have an effect on grade point average. In a similar framework, Zimmerman (2003) and Winston and Zimmerman (2004) find no credible effect at the top of the SAT ability distribution, but do find evidence of a negative impact on students in the middle of the distribution when they are grouped with students in the bottom 15% of the distribution.

Taking a step further, Carrell *et al.* (2011) use a random experiment to determine whether student academic performance can indeed be improved through systematic sorting of students into peer groups. They design peer groups for the United States Air Force Academy and, using an experimental design, sort the incoming college freshman cohorts at the academy into these peer groups. The objective was to improve the grades of the bottom third of incoming students by academic ability. The experiment yielded unexpected results. For the lowest-ability students there is a negative and statistically significant treatment effect; for middle-ability students, who were expected to be unaffected, there is a positive and significant treatment effect of 0.067. High-ability students were unaffected by the treatment.

Finally, Gibbons and Telhaj (2008) offer an alternative interpretation of the peer effect. They suggest that peer effects may impact factors other than school attainment, such as subsequent educational decisions, and may provide other immediate and long-run benefits, such as lifetime friendship networks, that make schools with good peer groups desirable commodities.

3.3.4 *How Significant Is Expenditure?*

Existing research has struggled to show a clear causal relationship between the amount that schools spend and student achievement, suggesting that how money is spent is typically much more important than how much is spent (see Hanushek (2008) for a review of the literature). Analysing the effect of spending on reduced pupil–teacher ratios, most studies find no significant relationship with achievement.

Levacic and Vignoles (2002) find that in the British context, the impact of school resources is small. Holmlund *et al.* (2010) find that after controlling for the range of pupil and school-level characteristics, the estimated effect of an increase of £1,000 in average expenditure per pupil would raise standardized test scores by about 5% of a standard deviation. They find evidence of a consistently positive effect of expenditure across subjects.

The studies looking at resource effects for primary schools (Gibbons *et al.* 2011; Holmlund *et al.* 2010) find that effects are substantially more pronounced for economically disadvantaged students. These findings are encouraging in policy terms because they suggest that despite large imperfections, mechanisms can be designed to ensure that disadvantaged students benefit from increasing school resources (see the discussion about the Pupil Premium in section 3.4.4). This provides some support for the recommendation to increase targeted resources for the disadvantaged.

There is also evidence to suggest that targeted investments, which address problems in specific areas or subjects and are specifically designed for pupils with learning disadvantages, deliver larger benefits. A case in point is the 'Excellence in Cities' programme (Machin *et al.* 2010) and the 'Literacy Hour' policy (Machin and McNally 2004).

3.4 THE UK INSTITUTIONAL FRAMEWORK

Having considered the drivers of success and failure in educational systems, we turn to a critical appraisal of the UK institutional framework, highlighting areas that are working or improving and pointing to problem areas that still need to be addressed.

3.4.1 *Accountability*

An important feature of an education system is the way in which its performance is held to account. A growing body of literature posits that the key to improving education outcomes lies in altering the incentives structure, so that it promotes strong schools with high-quality teachers (Hanushek 2008; Hanushek and Woessmann 2006, 2011). For example, there is empirical evidence suggesting that schools that face external exit exams tend to have better results than schools that face no such exam. The same literature reports a negative link between accountability and autonomy, i.e. in the absence of central accountability frameworks, schools with greater autonomy tend to underperform (Hanushek *et al.* 2013).

The UK accountability system is based on two pillars:

(i) school performance tables (or 'league tables'), which have traditionally focused on schools' average GCSE results; and

(ii) inspection reports from the Office for Standards in Education (Ofsted), the statutory agency responsible for monitoring schools' performance.

Both have significant limitations.

School performance tables are useful tools for parents and government to evaluate school performance and educational outcomes.[21] Allen and Burgess (2011a,b) use seven years of pupil census to show that using the performance tables to select schools does on average lead to better choices than choosing at random. However, test scores and value added as published in the league tables are not accurate measures of school quality (Kramarz *et al.* 2009).

Furthermore, league tables may encourage behavioural distortions. For example, in order to improve average exam results, individual teachers might focus their effort more towards exam preparation ('teaching to the test'); schools may also decide to develop a more selective intake approach or change the mix of subjects offered to students so that examination success is more probable. The consequences of such distortions are grade inflation and an increasing focus on the average student's performance rather than looking at the entire distribution. It also distorts funding allocations within the school.

The second pillar of the accountability system is the role played by Ofsted. Recent empirical evidence suggests that Ofsted's inspections are effective in improving poor school performance (Hussain 2012). Allen and Burgess (2012a,b) show that schools only just failing to reach the minimum standards expected by school inspectors do indeed see an improvement in scores over the following two to three years, over and above those schools that only just make it above the threshold. The effect size is moderate to large at around 10% of a pupil-level standard deviation in test scores. Moreover, this improvement occurs in core compulsory subjects, which suggests that schools are not altering their subject mix.

The results mentioned above, however, indicate little positive impact on lower-ability pupils, with equally large effects for those in the middle and at the top end of the ability distribution. This raises doubts about the effectiveness of the incentives given to schools to improve the performance of disadvantaged children. These doubts are exacerbated by the fact that the performance of disadvantaged children appears to be diluted in the criteria Ofsted applies while judging the overall effectiveness of schools.

3.4.1.1 *Floor Targets and the Academies Act*

One of the government's flagship policies to tackle poor school quality is based on the definition of a 'floor target'. This sets an expectation that

---

[21]The use of benchmarking is more widespread in the UK than in virtually any other OECD country (Gonand *et al.* 2007).

a minimum of 35% of children at every secondary school should get five A*–C passes at GCSE level, including English and mathematics. A primary school will be below the floor if less than 60% of pupils achieve the 'basic' standard of level 4 in both English and mathematics and if fewer pupils than average make the expected level of progress between Key Stage 1 and Key Stage 2. Schools that fail to meet this target (and a few other criteria) are at risk of having their management replaced (the so-called sponsor academy conversion). Where there has been long-term underperformance, little sign of improvement and serious Ofsted concern, the government converts schools into academies, partnering them with a strong sponsor or outstanding school.

Unfortunately, the impact of this program on the socioeconomic gradient is likely to be rather limited, as is illustrated by figure 3.8. The thin black line in the figure gives every 16-year-old who took GCSEs at a state school in 2010 a point score for their exam performance: eight points for an A* down to one point for a G. It standardizes the lot, and divides them up according to the poverty of their neighbourhoods. Children in disadvantaged postcodes are to the left of the graph and the richest are to the right. The thicker grey line strips out the failing schools (according to the floor target mentioned above) and assumes that the children who previously attended those schools are dispersed into the rest of the school system in a way that does not damage the performance of those other schools. The resulting improvement in the gradient is very limited.

This is yet another reminder of the point we highlighted on pages 96–101: the problem is not that there are a few schools that contain all the disadvantaged children and perform poorly. The problem is that disadvantaged children perform poorly (compared with their wealthier peers) in the vast majority of schools.

3.4.1.2 *Targeting Symptoms, Not Causes*

Over the years, most central government policy interventions have not been systematically targeted at economically disadvantaged/FSM children but have instead focused on a number of pupil characteristics that are (imperfectly) associated with economic disadvantage (such as special educational needs status, ethnic minorities and low attainment).[22]

---

[22]Under the previous government, there were only a handful of interventions designed to directly target disadvantaged/FSM children (e.g. apart from additional funding, there was a 2-year-old childcare pilot, an extended services subsidy and the Education Maintenance Allowance).

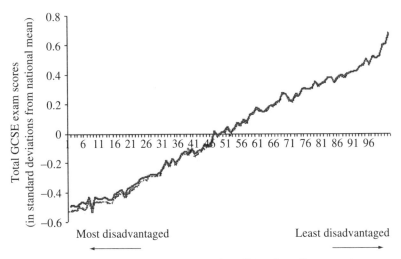

Figure 3.8. GCSE exam scores (pupil-level performance) by neighbourhood deprivation level.

Source: Cook (2012).

Although there are significant overlaps between these groups (see figure 3.9), there are drawbacks to this approach. First, it fails to account for a large number of children who are socioeconomically disadvantaged but not income disadvantaged. Second, some of these groups conflate pupil deprivation with poor teaching performance (low attainment could be driven simply by poor teaching). Third, it provides mixed messages to schools and blurs their priorities: anecdotal evidence suggests that schools/teachers struggle to understand why and how they should target the needs of FSM pupils rather than pupils with more visible types of need (e.g. special educational needs children, or those who have English as another language status).

3.4.1.3 *The Main Measure of Deprivation Is Subject to Substantial Limitations*

FSM status is widely used as the main measure of deprivation. The Pupil Premium is also based on this indicator. FSM is a crude indicator of parental income. Hobbs and Vignoles (2010) examined the relationship between children's FSM 'eligibility' and their net household income (figure 3.10) and found that there is considerable overlap between the range of household incomes of children taking up FSM and those not taking up FSM. In other words, many children taking up FSM are in households with higher incomes than children not taking up FSM. This makes it likely that

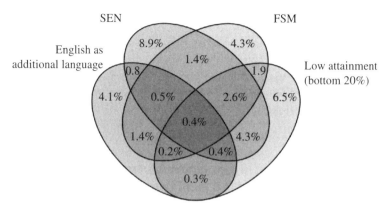

Figure 3.9. GCSE-targeting symptoms: a Venn diagram.
Source: data from the 2009 National Pupil Database.

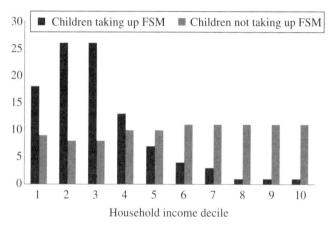

Figure 3.10. Distribution of household income
by children's FSM take-up status.
Source: Hobbs and Vignoles (2010).

many children eligible for and claiming FSM are not in the lowest-income households.

Other well-established limitations of the FSM measure include the following.

- Dropping out of the FSM category could simply mean that children are not claiming FSM although they would be entitled to do so (this is known to be particularly significant in the later stages of secondary education).

- Changes in FSM status may reflect increases in income beyond the thresholds defining the FSM category, but not to the extent of having meaningful impacts on attainment.

- Even if reductions in the proportion that are eligible for FSM from one year to the next reflect significant improvements in household income, we would not expect this to lead to an instant improvement in pupil attainment. The effects of earlier poverty are likely to persist.

- It is well established in the empirical literature that it is being eligible for FSM at any point in a pupil's academic career rather than the number of years a pupil is eligible that is most strongly associated with attainment.

3.4.1.4 *Recent Reforms*

The government has partially addressed the issue of targeting the right groups by redefining the target group for the Pupil Premium. From April 2012 the Pupil Premium was extended to include children who have been eligible for FSM at any point in the last six years.

Since January 2012, the government has also started to publish new league tables that report GCSE results by groups of pupils (*within* schools) defined by their prior attainment at Key Stage 2. Specifically, for each school the tables report the percentage of pupils attaining at least five A*–C grades (including English and mathematics) separately for low-attaining pupils, high-attaining pupils and a middle group. This is a change for the better as the main differences between schools in the performance of different groups will tend to emerge from variation in schools' teaching effectiveness.

However, a particular disadvantage of the new measure is that it uses very broad pupil bands. The groups are defined to cover the entire pupil population: the low-attaining group are students below the expected level (Level 4) in the Key Stage 2 tests; the middle-attaining group are those at the expected level; and the high-attaining group comprises students above the expected level. The disadvantage of this is that the broad groups (about 45% of students fall in the middle group) hide the significant variation in average ability within that group across schools. This implies that differences in league table performance between schools will still reflect differences in intake in addition to effectiveness—even within the group—thus partly undermining the aim of group-specific reports.

3.4.2 *Autonomy*

Schools are only as good as their teachers. Since it is hard to find good *ex ante* predictors of teaching quality, it is likely to be important to give schools the tools and incentives to hire and reward high-performing teachers and to remove low-performing ones. The case for giving schools more freedom is based on the notion that this will allow them to take advantage of local knowledge to operate more efficiently and become more innovative.

Accordingly, several countries have enabled a certain proportion of state-funded schools to operate with greater autonomy than the norm within the state system. The structure and rules differ between (and some-times within) countries but they also have much in common: for example, 'charter schools' in the US, 'free schools' in Sweden and 'academies' in England (see box 3.4 for more detail on academies). In an international context, English schools are high up in the autonomy rankings, second only to the Netherlands according to OECD (2012).

Box 3.4. The structure and freedoms of academies.

What are academies? Academies are independent schools that are pub-licly funded. They benefit from greater freedoms to innovate and raise standards. These include (a) freedom from local authority control; (b) the ability to set their own pay and conditions for staff; (c) freedoms around the delivery of the curriculum; and (d) the ability to change the lengths of terms and school days. Head teachers are given the freedom to innovate with the curriculum, pay staff more, extend school hours and develop a personal approach to every pupil. Academy schools enjoying direct fund-ing and full independence from central and local bureaucracy. The prin-ciples of governance are the same in academies as in maintained schools, but the governing body has greater autonomy. Academies are required to have at least two parent governors.

Funding. Academies cannot charge fees and receive the same level of funding per pupil from the local authority as a maintained school, plus additions to cover the services that are no longer provided for them by the local authority. However, academies have greater freedom over how they use their budgets. Funding comes directly from the Education Funding Agency rather than from local authorities.

Staffing. When a school converts from a local authority maintained school to a new academy, staff from the predecessor school must be transferred to the new academy school under the 1981 Transfer of Undertakings (Protection of Employment), or TUPE, regulations, in which case their existing terms and conditions of employment are upheld. Once open, the academy trust may consult with staff and their union representatives on changes to these terms and conditions, e.g. to enable the academy to operate over different term times or change the length of the school day. Thus, the governing body is able to authorize changes to the terms and conditions of employment and approve personnel practices regarding staff development and discipline.

Admission. Academies are also required to give priority to children 'who are wholly or mainly drawn from the area' in which the school is located. This means that the majority of pupils admitted must live close to the school. All schools, whether maintained or academy, are required to comply with the 'Greenwich Judgement', which requires schools to avoid treating pupils living outside the local authority area less favourably than it does those living within the same local authority. Put more simply, the local authority boundary cannot be used to define the admission catchment area.

Academies will need to take part in their local coordinated admissions process, and so parents apply for places for their child in the same way as they do for any other local school. Maintained schools that have previously selected some or all of their pupils by ability are able to continue this practice when they become academies, but schools becoming academies cannot decide to become selective schools if they were not previously selective. Independent selective schools joining the academies sector are not legally able to continue to select by ability. However, any school with a relevant specialism can select 10% of its intake by aptitude in sport, modern foreign languages, visual arts or performing arts.

Expansion. A little-known reform in 2011 allowed academy and voluntary aided schools to expand in size without the permission of the local authority.

The empirical evidence (both for the UK and for other countries) provides support for the hypothesis that increasing school autonomy can lead to improvements in pupil performance and might also have positive effects on neighbourhood schools (see box 3.5 for a review of the literature). In the UK, recent studies that have investigated the conversion of disadvantaged schools into academies have noted an improvement in pupils' performance compared with pupils in similar schools.

Box 3.5. School autonomy and educational outcomes.

Machin and Wilson (2009) provide some early research into academies, comparing the GCSE performance of schools that turn into academies with a comparison group of similar schools. There was an improvement in the GCSE performance of schools that became academies, but it was no different from the improvement for schools in the comparison group. Wilson (2011) finds that intake into academies over the period 1997–2007 has consisted of a lower proportion of pupils from relatively disadvantaged backgrounds (measured by those on FSM).

Machin and Vernoit (2011) evaluate the schools that became academies up to 2008/9. Their main findings were as follows. Firstly, schools that became academies started to attract higher-ability students. Secondly, there was an overall improvement in performance in GCSE exams. These results were strongest for schools that had been academies for longer and for those that experienced the largest increase in their autonomy. Thirdly, schools in the neighbourhood of academies started to perform better as well. This might be because of increased competition or the sharing of school facilities and expertise with the local community.

Gibbons and Silva (2008) investigate the effects of the emergence of the private sector in education on the performance of public sector schools and find no evidence that a higher concentration of privately managed schools improves the performance of neighbouring public sector schools in England. However, the authors find that certain types of state schools (voluntary aided schools) that have autonomous governance and admission procedures react positively to greater competition with local schools: their students' value-added attainment scores improve by about 1.6 points for each additional competitor.

The evidence for other countries is in line with that for the UK. Böhlmark and Lindahl (2008) look at both the long-term and the short-term effects of academies in Sweden. They find evidence of only small positive effects in the short term, and these effects do not persist. Other studies adopting non-experimental methods tend to produce more mixed results.

In the US, there are charter schools that are similar in mandate and autonomy to academies in the UK. In the US, some charter schools use lotteries to allocate places when the school is oversubscribed. Abdulkadiroglu *et al.* (2011) exploit this randomization to estimate the impact of charter school attendance on student achievement in Boston. They find that charter school attendance leads to significant increases in pupils' English language and mathematics scores compared with students not attending charter schools. Interestingly, they find that the highest achievement gains are for students who performed poorly before they attended the charter school.

Similarly, using data from New York, Hoxby and Murarka (2009) found that pupils who won the lottery to attend charter schools experienced significant improvements in both mathematics and reading scores between the third grade and the eighth grade compared with pupils who lost the lottery and remained in traditional public schools.

Angrist *et al.* (2010) evaluate the impact of a specific charter school that is targeted at low-income students that qualify for free school meals. They find significant increases in the mathematics and reading scores for students who attend this academy: increases of 0.35 standard deviations and 0.12 standard deviations, respectively, were found for each year that pupils spent enrolled at the academy, compared with pupils not attending the academy. Most importantly, they find that pupils with limited English proficiency, special educational needs or lower baseline scores achieve the highest gains in both scores.

The spillover effects of charter schools in the US has been studied by Bettinger (2005), who looks at the spillover impact of charter schools in Michigan, Hoxby (2002a), who evaluates the effect of charter schools in Michigan as well as in Arizona, and Booker *et al.* (2007), who look at the impact of charter schools in Texas. All three studies find improvements in the traditional public schools that can be attributed to the introduction of charter schools.

The important discussion for policy, though, is not so much whether autonomy is a good idea in general but in what spheres and contexts schools should be made more autonomous. Hanushek *et al.* (2013) provide a good discussion on where autonomy may and may not be desirable. In their view, some decisions—such as hiring and budget allocations— require significant local knowledge and are more appropriately made at the school level. In contrast, where standardization is important (e.g. in setting course offerings and requirements), decisions should be made at a higher level.[23] Furthermore, the impact of autonomy may vary with other elements of the schools system, e.g. whether there is a strong system of accountability in place.

---

[23]In a cross-country analysis, Woessmann (2003) found that school autonomy in setting educational standards and the size of the school budget was negatively related to pupil performance. The opposite was true of school autonomy in personnel management and process decisions, e.g. hiring teachers and setting salaries.

In the UK, community schools (which still represent a large portion of the schools system) enjoy limited autonomy[24] compared with other types of school such as academies and voluntary aided schools. Localizing hiring and making pay conditions more flexible would put these schools on a more similar footing to independent schools, academies, Free Schools and faith schools. It could also help overcome the problem of regional disparities in real salaries associated with the national pay scale (see box 3.6 for a discussion of teacher pay in the UK).

Box 3.6. Teacher pay and autonomy in the UK.

Although better remuneration and work conditions could improve the quality of the pool of teachers, teacher wages in the UK are set by local education authorities based on guidelines issued by the central government Department for Education. Despite the existence of four pay bands ('Inner London', 'Outer London', 'The fringe' and 'The rest of England'), teacher wages have exhibited very little regional variation relative to private sector wages since the early 1970s. For example, the average teacher wage differential between the northeast of England and inner London is approximately 9%, while the equivalent private sector wage differential is larger than 30%.

Since its formation in the 1990s, the School Teachers' Review Body, an advisory board that comments on teaching conditions and pay, has frequently argued that the Department for Education should be doing more to encourage locally flexible wages. Although an increasing amount of discretion over wages has been granted to local education authorities, they have almost entirely failed to utilize the option. This is likely to be due, in part, to the fact that local authorities face relatively strong national teaching unions (Zabalza *et al.* 1979).

Following the recommendations from the School Teachers' Review Body—which advocates more freedom for school leaders in deciding pay—in January 2013 the education secretary, Michael Gove, announced that performance-related pay for teachers will begin in September 2013. He argues that this method will reward good staff and help schools in disadvantaged areas recruit and keep the best teachers.

Propper and Britton (2012) find that pay regulation reduces school performance. They also find that the response is non-convex across

---

[24]The 1988 Education Reform Act gave community schools the option to become 'grant-maintained' community schools, where they were free from local authority control. The Act also gave community schools greater local management rights whereby schools could control their budgets.

heterogeneous labour markets, so that the losses from keeping wages too low in high-cost areas outweigh the gains from overpaying in low-cost areas. The average effect is relatively small. A 10% increase in the local labour market wage would result in an average increase of 2% in the scores attained in the high-stakes exams taken by pupils at the end of compulsory schooling in England. But the number of pupils who would benefit from any gain in teacher performance, the fact that the associated gain in education would have returns over a long time period and the non-convexity in the response to wage regulation mean that the long-term gains from the removal of regulation could be very large. A potential drawback of a regional payment system is that it could reduce wages in a school that is performing badly (e.g. in Newcastle) and raise them in the best-performing schools (such as London schools). In particular, it could become tougher to attract good teachers to the urban north, where schools are weakest, if wages were regionalized according to labour market conditions. Many areas already face problems recruiting good teachers with the pay scales as they are.

In practice, this movement towards greater school autonomy is taking place through a piecemeal *academization* of the schools system. In the Academies Act of 2010, the coalition government specified that any primary, secondary or special school that has been rated outstanding by Ofsted should be allowed to become an academy on a fast-track route.

From November 2010, all other primary and secondary schools that wished to benefit from Academy freedoms will be able to apply to convert, provided they work in partnership with a high-performing school that will help support improvement or with another sponsor, such as a large charity or a small federation of schools. Over time, the government has removed many of the requirements from the Academy funding agreement. There are no longer any prescriptions on curriculum or qualifications, there is no target setting and no production of rigid plans.

The share of academies in the school system is rapidly increasing. Figure 3.11 shows the number of new converters each month. Twenty-nine schools converted in the first month of the programme, September 2010. Conversions remained below fifty per month for each of the next two terms. More than 150 converted at the start of the summer and autumn terms in 2011, and a peak number of 300 converted during August 2011. Moreover, as shown in table 3.3, the phenomenon of academy chains is emerging, since some sponsors control more than one school. For example, the Academies Enterprise Trust (AET) is the largest sponsor,

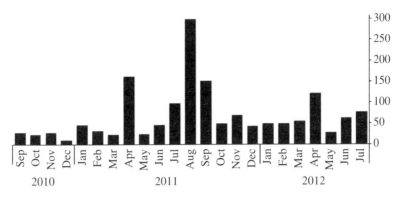

Figure 3.11. Schools converting to academies, by month.
Source: House of Common Library (SNSG/6233, July 2012).

administering more than sixty schools. This raises the challenging issue—both for academics and policymakers—of identifying the optimal structure of the academies system. Looking at the US charter schools system could provide useful hints. For example, KIPP, one of the major US charter school networks, has adapted the franchise model to manage its expansion. Each KIPP school pays 1% of its annual revenues to the KIPP foundation; teachers and school leaders are carefully selected and trained; KIPP schools are subject to annual inspections on financial, academic, real estate and legal issues, and schools who fail to maintain the system's quality lose the KIPP brand and the foundation's support. However, unlike a typical business franchisor, KIPP grants its new schools considerable freedom in deciding how they will earn and keep the brand. However, the majority of charter management organizations opt for greater control over each school and adopt a corporate-style growth approach that ensures that each new site replicates the organization's standards for building design, staffing and programmes (Bennett 2008).

The government has also introduced Free Schools, whereby parents, teachers or non-profit organizations can set up a school that enjoys the same independence as an academy (Braconier 2012).

Another initiative in the direction of academization has been the creation of Free Schools, which are being set up in response to real parental demand within a local area for a greater variety of schools. The first such schools opened in September 2011. Free Schools are non-profit-making, independent, state-funded schools. The model is flexible: Free Schools may be primary or secondary schools, they may be located in traditional school buildings or in appropriate community spaces, and they may be set up by a wide range of proposers.

Table 3.3. Academy chains in the UK.

Sponsor	Prim. open	Prim. upcoming	Sec. open	Sec. upcoming	Total (including schools not shown)
Academies Enterprise Trust	18	15	20	12	66
E-ACT	7	3	18	1	30
United Learning Trust	—	—	17	—	21
Ormiston Trust	1	—	18	—	19
School Partnership Trust	4	6	5	3	19
Kemnal Academies Trust	9	5	2	—	16
ARK Schools	3	1	7	1	15
Harris Federation	2	1	11	1	15
Greenwood Dale Foundation Trust	4	1	5	—	11
Academies Transformation Trust	1	4	—	5	10

Source: Department of Education data and Guardian Datablog.

Like academies, Free Schools are funded on a comparable basis to other state-funded schools. The groups running these schools cannot make a profit and are subject to the same Ofsted inspections as state schools. Free Schools cannot be academically selective and must take part in their local coordinated admissions process.

However, Free Schools have additional freedoms compared with academies, a key example being that teachers in Free Schools do not necessarily need to have qualified teacher status.

3.4.3 *School Choice and Competition*

Increasing parental choice is often a frontrunner when it comes to policies designed to promote competition and improve school outcomes (see, for example, OECD 2012). The rationale is that, as schools compete to attract students, parental demands will create strong incentives for schools to improve performance.

In the UK, parents' ability to choose schools is limited. While parents have been able to apply to any state school since the 1980s, schools are allowed to discriminate in the case of oversubscription according to an enforced code of practice. The most important oversubscription criterion is usually proximity to the school. This means that some people have greater empowerment to exercise choice than others, and this tends to work against lower-income families and those with difficulties in accessing and understanding the school performance information provided through league tables and Ofsted reports.

There is evidence from England and from other countries that many parents act on available information when they are purchasing a home (for England, see Rosenthal (2003), Gibbons and Machin (2003), Gibbons *et al.* (2013) and Burgess *et al.* (2009)). Higher-income parents move to locations with better schools, and this is reflected in a high correlation between house prices and the quality of the school in the neighbourhood. The consequence is that parents from lower-income households are not able to exercise meaningful choice because they cannot afford to live very close to a popular school. West and Pennell (2000) also show that higher socioeconomic households have better information about and understanding of school performance. Thus, 'school choice', as desirable as it is, is not an effective instrument for addressing attainment gaps by household background (McNally 2012).

As discussed in section 3.4.2, there are some types of school that are more autonomous from the local authority and their admission criteria are not linked to residence criteria. These include faith-based schools, academies and independent schools. The ability to make effective choices is thus highly influenced by whether families can afford independent schools, whether they have access to faith-based schooling, whether they have children with specific aptitudes, and whether they are able to move close to attractive local authority maintained schools (Braconier 2012).

International evidence on choice and competition is voluminous but its findings are still mixed. Evidence on competition and choice focusing specifically on the UK is very limited (see Allen and Vignoles (2009) for a good review of the existing literature), and what little there is focuses mainly on secondary education. Gibbons *et al.* (2008) was the first (pupil-level) analysis that investigated the effects of choice and competition on academic achievement in primary schools in England. The study reports little evidence of a causal link between achievement and either choice or competition. Encouragingly, they find some positive effects of competition for children in primary schools that are in the tail of the performance distribution.

3.4.4 *Funding System*

Central government provides additional funding per disadvantaged student to local authorities (equivalent to roughly £4,000 per year in 2010). Local authorities use their own individual funding formulas to transfer funds to schools. In 2010, on average, local authorities passed through roughly £3,000 per disadvantaged student to schools, with the difference spread across all schools within the local authority. A complex funding system makes it difficult for local authorities to understand the share of deprivation funding in their total grants. The partial pass-through may also reflect local authorities disagreeing with central government priorities. This may be one reason why local authorities sometimes do not express support for extensive deprivation funding.

At the school level, if funding for deprivation is lower than the perceived costs, the school may engage in 'cream skimming': trying to dissuade disadvantaged children from admission while recruiting more-able students. The lag in receiving deprivation funding also incentivizes schools not to retain disadvantaged students (Sibieta *et al.* 2008).

The current government introduced a Pupil Premium to help mitigate these incentive biases and make funding directly tied to the disadvantaged (Jarrett and Bolton 2012). In 2011/12 schools received a premium amounting to £488 per child, on top of base funding, for pupils entitled to FSM and for pupils in care who had been continuously looked after for six months. The premium amount increased to £600 per pupil for 2012/13.

The Pupil Premium increases central government's notional funding for deprivation. But at this stage it is still unclear whether the level of funding proposed is sufficient, whether schools will use the funds to tackle the performance of disadvantaged pupils, whether local authorities will divert their grants away from deprivation funding, and whether schools will continue to 'cream skim'.

Recent research by the Sutton Trust also casts doubt on the impact of the premium. Less than 2% in a survey of primary and secondary school teachers said it would be used to improve feedback between teachers and pupils and less than 1% said they will introduce peer-to-peer tutoring schemes (the National Foundation for Educational Research Omnibus Survey, February 2012). The Sutton Trust argues that these two schemes, if implemented well, could indeed boost recipients' performance by the equivalent of an extra eight or nine months in a school year.

Similar results were obtained in a recent Ofsted survey[25] that aimed to identify how schools were using the Pupil Premium to raise achievement and improve outcomes for its recipients. The qualitative survey found that in the more disadvantaged areas, only one in ten school leaders thought it had significantly changed the way they worked. Schools often failed to disentangle the Pupil Premium from their main budget, and said

---

[25]The survey was based on the views of 262 school leaders gathered from additional survey questions during routine inspections and telephone interviews.

that they were not using the funding to put in place new teaching initiatives. Pupil Premium funding was most commonly used to pay for teaching assistants. In summary, there seems to be a significant risk that the Pupil Premium will not benefit the students who need it most, and that it will be used to fund existing programmes with no real impact in terms of additionality.

Ways of alleviating this problem include making schools directly accountable for the achievement of Pupil Premium recipients. One particular policy option is to publish school-level information on the attainment of pupils eligible for the Pupil Premium. This transparency and accountability may incentivize schools to use the funding to improve the attainment of the target group. The coalition government has recently taken steps in this direction, by requiring schools to publish how they spend the Pupil Premium on their websites and by asking Ofsted to survey how the money is spent. They have also started to document the performance of students eligible for the Pupil Premium in the performance tables of schools. Although these initiatives are arguably going in the right direction, it is doubtful they will be strong enough to counteract the bias in incentives created by the complexity and opacity of the way in which schools are funded in the UK.

3.4.5 *Teacher Recruitment and Training*

In the UK, the prestige of the teaching profession (or the lack thereof) is reflected in the fact that overall, 3.7% of graduates enter teaching; the average for Russell Group universities was 2.7%, and for Cambridge, Bristol, Imperial College, UCL and LSE it was less than 2%, with Oxford only just over 2%.

Teachers are not civil servants in the UK: they are employed directly by individual schools. In order to teach in local authority maintained schools, teachers must hold qualified teacher status. There are a number of different routes available for gaining this status. Initial teacher training is a complex system, involving both undergraduate and postgraduate programmes in university-led, school-centred and employment-based provision. The question is, how should this be set up to produce the most effective teachers who will have the greatest impact on pupil progress?

Traditionally, teachers were trained either on undergraduate (Bachelor of Education or BA Primary Education with Qualified Teacher Status) or postgraduate (Postgraduate Certificate in Education) courses run by higher education institutions. In 1994, School-Centred Initial Teacher Training was introduced; this is a full-time postgraduate course based in a school or a group of schools. Employment-based routes into teaching were first introduced in 1990. These are designed for qualified mature people for whom it was necessary to earn a living while in training. They included the Graduate Teacher Programme, the Registered Teacher Programme and the Overseas Trained Teacher Programme.

Initial teacher training, as a route into the teaching profession, plays two roles for the profession: training and selection, with the emphasis typically placed on the former. Allen and Burgess (2012b) argue that selection seems to be the most important and that it should apply at the point where evidence on ability is strongest. According to these authors, the final decision on who can become a teacher should be made at a stage when there is sufficient evidence on the candidate's teaching effectiveness, i.e. after completing their training. Given that variations in teacher effects on pupil progress are very substantial, and that the future effectiveness of a potential teacher is hard to judge from their own academic record, a broader group (with a relatively low academic entry requirement) should be allowed to try out teaching. But, towards the end of the training programme, a much stricter probation policy should be enforced.

The coalition government has proposed significant changes to the teacher training landscape, where selection is tight at the beginning but negligible thereafter. The current policy direction[26] of tightening academic entry requirements for teaching is not helpful: it will restrict the quantity of recruits and have no impact at all on average teaching effectiveness. The key decision on final certification should be made after a significant probation period (three years, say), and ideally the probation should involve classes of varying ability and year group (Allen and Burgess 2012a).

One of the successful recruitment routes has been the Teach First Programme. Teach First is a charitable organization that introduced a training programme in London in 2003 for graduates who were willing to commit to teaching for two years in challenging London secondary schools. According to an early-stage evaluation by Hutchings *et al.* (2006), after the first two years of its operation it had been successful in recruiting star graduates.[27]

---

[26] See 'Great teachers: attracting, training and retaining the best' at www.publications .parliament.uk/pa/cm201012/cmselect/cmeduc/1515/1515.pdf.

[27] The Institute for Policy Studies in Education was commissioned by the Teacher Training Agency in 2003 to conduct an evaluation of innovative practice on the Teach First Programme, with the aim of ensuring that initial teacher training as a whole is able to benefit from innovative practice developed within the programme. The evaluation was conducted between September 2003 and September 2005: the first two years of the Teach First Programme, at which time it operated only in London.

The key attractions for potential participants were that one could keep one's career options open while gaining a qualification, making a social contribution and soaking up the prestige that surrounded the programme: participants were encouraged to view themselves as a privileged group. They underwent both teacher training (in the first year) and a programme of leadership training. Qualified teacher status is normally gained at the end of the first year. Teaching in challenging London schools gave a sense of mission to the graduates.

Once teachers have been carefully recruited and trained, mechanisms for teachers, schools leaders and local authorities to share best practice should be more strongly encouraged. The London Challenge and the more general City Challenge programmes have shown how successful this could be. The City Challenge was launched in April 2008, building on the success of the London Challenge (2003–8). Its aim was to improve the educational outcomes of young people and 'to crack the associated cycle of disadvantage and underachievement in the Black Country, Greater Manchester and London' (DfES 2007). In particular, its goals were to reduce the number of underperforming schools, especially in English and mathematics; increase the number of good and outstanding schools; and improve the educational outcomes of disadvantaged children.

City Challenge took a different approach to other government interventions. First of all, it was built on the belief that educational problems should be addressed at local level, with local authorities and schools working together. Secondly, it focused on all aspects of education (leadership, accountability through better data collection, pupil attainment, school-to-school collaboration) and involved all the interested parties (local authorities, school leaders, teachers, parents and pupils). Thirdly, it was characterized by a great degree of flexibility, allowing the modification of activities on the basis of changing school needs. Finally, there was not one single approach: the support package was bespoke for each school and was agreed by school leaders, local authorities, civil servants and a local team of advisors.

Based on the findings of a mixed-methods evaluation, City Challenge areas achieved the majority of their initial targets. Indeed, London schools in each quintile of 2008 attainment improved significantly compared with areas not included in the City Challenge programme (with the exception of the highest quintile of secondary schools). In Greater Manchester and the Black Country the picture was less clear, since only schools in the lowest quintiles of attainment improved significantly more than those outside City Challenge areas. The attainment of FSM pupils increased by more than the national figure in all areas (with the exception of primary pupils in Greater Manchester), and the attainment gap of FSM pupils narrowed for London primary and secondary pupils and for Greater Manchester primary pupils. Also, the proportion of 'good' and 'outstanding' schools increased in all three areas, despite the introduction of a more challenging Ofsted inspection framework (Hutchings *et al.* 2012). In addition, thanks to the high level of involvement of schools and their staff in the decision and implementation process, London Challenge also had a positive impact on inspiring teachers that were already in the system and attracting new ones into the profession.

Additional evidence on the importance of teacher satisfaction in attracting better teachers is provided by Green *et al.* (2008). They show an increasing outflow of teachers from state schools to private schools: the net annual flow of teachers from public to private has quadrupled over the last fifteen years, rising from 400 in 1993 to 1,600 in 2008. Moreover, private schools employ a higher proportion of teachers with a postgraduate degree than state schools do, and the gap has grown over time. In the period since 2000, 60% of male teachers in the private sector had a higher degree compared with 45% in the state sector. Given that the wage gap between these two groups of schools is negligible (at least in subjects that are not classed as 'shortage subjects'), what really matters in explaining this teacher flow are the better working conditions and, in particular, the higher level of satisfaction in private schools.

3.4.6 *Individual Policies Have Not Been Properly Evaluated*

Evaluating educational reforms and identifying efficient policies is often difficult. Firstly, evaluations of long-term labour market and social outcomes cannot be performed immediately after the programmes have been initiated. Secondly, education systems are very context specific: different countries perform well under different institutional settings. This means that policy evaluations have to be interpreted in a context-specific institutional framework.

In the UK there has been a lack of rigorous and independent evaluation of the policies that have been implemented over the years. Even where evaluations exist, they are not always considered in the policy-making process. The abolition of the Education Maintenance Allowance (EMA) is a case in point. The EMA was launched nationally in the UK in 2004. It provided low-income 16–19-year-olds with payments of up to £30 per week if they stayed on at school or college. This policy was independently and rigorously evaluated, yet that evaluation seems to have been ignored when the policy was scrapped in 2010. The Department for Education cited research by the National Foundation for Educational Research that showed that 90% of students who received EMA would continue with their education even without the payment. However, this was a gross misrepresentation of the evaluation evidence and research. Extensive quantitative and econometric evaluations of the EMA by the Institute for Fiscal Studies in 2005 showed that the scheme significantly improved both staying-on rates and qualifications for students from poorer backgrounds. The government had chosen to ignore this rigorous and independent evidence and had instead argued that the abolition of EMA was justified by high levels of 'deadweight'.

There are, nevertheless, notable exceptions. The more recent and rather encouraging exception concerns the Education Endowment Foundation, established in 2010 to look at what interventions work to overcome educational disadvantage. The Education Endowment Foundation aims to build a rigorous evidence base of what works to raise the attainment of the lowest-performing, and most-disadvantaged, children. It has very generous resourcing (the Department for Education has given a grant of £125 million over ten years to the winner of a tender process). The creation an independent organization[28] such as this is a positive step towards rigorous policy evaluation, and a similar approach should be encouraged more widely to inform the debate around education policymaking.

There are many advantages to using this kind of platform, i.e. an independent, well-resourced organization with a very clear remit to focus on the evidence around what works: (i) a dedicated and focused team without the distractions of the normal business of government; (ii) insulation from the demands of other government departments, to rule options out before they have a chance to be considered; (iii) insulation from 'political' vetoes; (iv) research continuity and strong institutional memory; and (v) the ability to bring in multidisciplinary expertise.

3.5   POLICY RECOMMENDATIONS

3.5.1   *Core Recommendations on Education*

Our proposals go with the grain of the academies movement. But the system needs to deal more squarely with the UK's failure to develop the

---

[28]The Education Endowment Foundation has no one from the Department for Education on its board, which also contains no politicians; it is an independent organization supported by charities.

talents of disadvantaged pupils. We therefore propose some direct steps, particularly financial and non-financial incentives, to address this fundamental problem.

The 'academization' of the school system should deepen into a 'flexible ecology', building on aspects of the higher education system (see below). There are four integral parts: greater school autonomy, strengthened central accountability (transparent information and inspection), wider parental choice and more flexibility for successful schools and their sponsors to expand.

To improve school governance, leadership and management, it must become easier for outstanding sponsored academies to grow. Ideally, this operates at the school level by making physical expansion easier. But there may be spatial limitations, which is why expansion through the growth of networks of sponsored academies is also an important way to spread better practices. By the same token, it should be made easier for underperforming schools to shrink and, if they do not improve, to be taken over or, in extreme cases, closed down.

Changes to help to develop the talent of disadvantaged pupils include the following.

- Information on school performance needs to be changed so that it also reflects the performance of disadvantaged children within the school. Such changes should apply to league tables and targets and they should be more closely reflected in Ofsted's inspection regime. Improving the performance of disadvantaged children should be given a central role when Ofsted awards an 'outstanding' grade to a school.

- 'Floor targets' must be redesigned to become effective in addressing poor school performance and should be aligned with the guidelines defined in the framework for schools inspection. This should involve moving away from undifferentiated average performance targets (such as the current target, which requires 40% of pupils to obtain five A*–C passes at GCSE level). These are 'blind' targets that distort schools' incentives to target resources and support towards those children who can more readily be expected to reach the predefined threshold.

- Contextual value added (school exam results adjusted for intake quality) should be published by schools for Pupil Premium children and for the medium-performing Key Stage 2 group.

The expansion of new sponsored academies should be focused on under-performing schools serving disadvantaged children. The original pro-gramme was shown to be very successful in doing this (Machin and Vernoit 2011), but the post-2010 academies are less focused on this group of schools.

Teacher quality needs to be improved through better conditions for both entry and exit. Teacher recruitment and training could be improved through implementation of the following measures.

- Teach First (which is renowned for its outstanding track record in recruiting high-quality graduates) should expand until it becomes one of the main routes into school teaching.

- Mainstream teacher recruitment should become more concentrated in the best universities and schools, following a national recruitment process.

- The probation period for teachers should be extended in length: by doubling it from two to four years, for example.

- There should be a relaxation of policies that insist on grades, qualifications and backgrounds in order to encourage a wider range of applicants to reflect the fact that teacher effectiveness is not highly correlated with crude background indicators.

- Mechanisms for teachers and schools to share best practice should be more strongly encouraged. The London Challenge programme has shown how successful this could be.

Our proposed measures would, we believe, work together to increase the skills that are needed to make the UK economy a more competitive and dynamic place to do business and directly tackle the long-standing problem of poor intermediate and low-level skills. Together they would ensure that fewer of our children leave school ill equipped to work in the competitive international environment that we now face. These proposals would also reduce disadvantage without compromising the achievements of other children.

3.5.2 *Further Recommendations for Schools*

To provide additional support for disadvantaged pupils, the criteria for receiving the Pupil Premium should be expanded to reflect a wider measure of disadvantage than simply free school meals. This need has now been acknowledged by making eligibility for the Pupil Premium dependent on whether a family has been eligible for free school meals at any time in the last six years. But available databases could expand the definitions of eligibility further.

The Pupil Premium is planned to increase from £600 to £900 in 2014/15. We recommend that part of the premium should be given in cash to the pupils and their families to provide an individual incentive. This should be conditional on improvements in performance after age 14, such as attendance and grade improvement beyond pre-agreed baseline expectations. This kind of 'conditional cash transfer' programme has proved to be effective in a wide variety of programmes (in welfare reform, for example, re-employment vouchers are usually more effective if the bonus is kept by the job seeker rather than the firm that hires them). The precursor to this approach was the EMA, which evaluations show was effective in encouraging children from disadvantaged backgrounds to remain in school. We recommend that the bursary scheme that replaced EMA should be wrapped back into this.

More resources should be made available for programmes that provide better information to low-income children and parents on the economic returns to different subjects.

In the spirit of encouraging better teaching, a more flexible system of rewards should be introduced for pay and promotion. This would include ending automatic increments, basing pay on performance and local market conditions, and extra rewards for teachers of core subjects in tough schools. We need swifter action on improved professional development and movement out of the classroom for underperforming teachers. Some of these changes are starting to happen and we would expect this process to accelerate under the flexible education system that we are recommending, which should give head teachers the incentives and capabilities to make these reforms.

UK education policy has traditionally lacked rigorous, independent evaluations. Positive steps have been taken in this direction with the creation of the Education Endowment Foundation, but much more could be done. For example, we recommend piloting the release of teacher-level information on performance (in a similar vein to the NHS data on surgeons that is available).

References

Abdulkadiroglu, A., J. D. Angrist, S. M. Dynarski, T. J. Kane and P. Pathak. 2011. Accountability and flexibility in public schools: evidence from Boston's charters and pilots. *Quarterly Journal of Economics* **126**(2), 699–748.

Aghion, P., and P. Howitt. 1998. *Endogenous Growth Theory.* Cambridge, MA: MIT Press.

Allen, R., and S. Burgess. 2011a. Can school league tables help parents choose schools? *Fiscal Studies* **32**(2), 245–261.

Allen, R., and S. Burgess. 2011b. Evaluating the provision of school performance information for school choice. Working Paper 11-10, Department of Quantitative Social Science.

Allen, R., and S. Burgess. 2012a. How should we treat under-performing schools? A regression discontinuity analysis of school inspections in England. Working Paper 12/87, Centre for Market and Public Organisation; Working Paper 12/02, Department of Quantitative Social Science.

Allen, R., and S. Burgess. 2012b. Reforming teacher training. CMPO Viewpoint.

Allen, R., and A. Vignoles. 2009. Can school competition improve standards? The case of faith schools in England. Working Paper 09-04, Department of Quantitative Social Science.

Ananat, E. O., A. Gassman-Pines, D. V. Francis and C. M. Gibson-Davis. 2011. Children left behind: the effects of statewide job loss on student achievement. Working Paper 17104, National Bureau of Economic Research.

Angrist, J. D., and K. Lang. 2004. Does school integration generate peer effects? Evidence from Boston's Metco Program. *American Economic Review* **94**(5), 1613–1634.

Angrist, J. D., S. M. Dynarski, T. J. Kane, P. A. Pathak and C. Walters. 2010. Inputs and impacts in charter schools: KIPP Lynn. *American Economic Review Papers and Proceedings* **100**(2), 239–243.

Atkinson, A., S. Burgess, P. Gregg, C. Propper and S. Proud. 2008. The impact of classroom peer groups on pupil GCSE results. Working Paper 08/187, Centre for Market and Public Organisation.

Atkinson, A., S. Burgess, B. Croxon, P. Gregg, C. Propper, H. Slater and D. Wilson. 2009. Evaluating the impact of performance-related pay for teachers in England. *Labour Economics* **16**(3), 251–261.

Barro, R. J., and J.-W. Lee, 1993. International comparisons of educational attainment. *Journal of Monetary Economics* **32**(3), 363–394.

Barro, R. J., and J.-W. Lee. 2001. International data on educational attainment: updates and implications. *Oxford Economic Papers* **53**(3), 541–563.

Barro, R. J., and X. Sala-i-Martín. 2004. *Economic Growth*, 2nd edn. Cambridge, MA: MIT Press.

Becker, G. 1974. A theory of social interaction. *Journal of Political Economy* **82**, 1063–1093.

Benhabib, J., and M. M. Spiegel. 1994. The role of human capital in economic development evidence from aggregate cross-country data. *Journal of Monetary Economics* **34**(2), 143–173.

Bennett, J. 2008. Brand-name charters: the franchise model applied to schools. *Education Next* (Summer), pp. 28–34.

Besley, T., and S. Machin. 2008. Are public sector CEOs different? Leadership wages and performance in schools. LSE Mimeo.

Bettinger, E. P. 2005. The effect of charter schools on charter students and public schools. *Economics of Education Review* 24(2), 133–147.

Bettinger, E. P. 2010. Paying to learn: the effect of financial incentives on elementary school test scores. Working Paper 16333, National Bureau of Economic Research.

Betts, J. R., and J. L. Shkolnik. 2000. The effects of ability grouping on student achievement and resource allocation in secondary schools. *Economics of Education Review* 19(1), 1–15.

Bils, M., and P. J. Klenow. 2000. Does schooling cause growth? *American Economic Review* 90(5), 1160–1183.

Black, S. E., P. J. Devereux and K. G. Salvanes. 2008. Staying in the classroom and out of the maternity ward? The effect of compulsory schooling laws on teenage births. *Economic Journal* 118, 1025–1054.

Blanden, J., and P. Gregg. 2004. Family income and educational attainment: a review of approaches and evidence for Britain. *Oxford Review of Economic Policy* 20(2), 245–263.

Blanden, J., and S. Machin. 2004. Educational inequality and the expansion of UK higher education. *Scottish Journal of Political Economy* (Special Issue on the Economics of Education) 54, 230–249.

Blanden, J., P. Gregg and S. Machin. 2005. Educational inequality and intergenerational mobility. In *What's the Good of Education? The Economics of Education in the UK* (ed. S. Machin and A. Vignoles). Princeton University Press.

Blanden, J., P. Gregg and L. Macmillan. 2007. Accounting for intergenerational income persistence: non-cognitive skills, ability and education. *Economic Journal* 117(519), C43–C60.

Bloom, N., and J. Van Reenen. 2007. Measuring and explaining management practices across firms and countries. *Quarterly Journal of Economics* 122(4), 1351–1408.

Bloom, N., and J. Van Reenen. 2010. Why do management practices differ across firms and countries? *Journal of Economic Perspectives* 24(1), 203–224.

Böhlmark, A., and M. Lindahl. 2008. Does school privatization improve educational achievement? Evidence from Sweden's voucher reform. Discussion Paper 3691, Institute for the Study of Labor (IZA).

Bolton, P. 2012. Education spending in the UK. Standard Note SN/SG/1078, House of Commons Library.

Booker, K., S. Gilpatric, T. Gronberg and D. Jansen. 2007. The impact of charter school student attendance on student performance. *Journal of Public Economics* 91, 849–876.

Braconier, H. 2012. Reforming education in England. Working Paper 939, OECD Economics Department.

Bradley, S., and J. Taylor. 2008. Do peers matter? Estimation of peer effects from pupil mobility between schools. Department of Economics, Lancaster University.

Branch, G. F., S. G. Rivkin and E. A. Hanushek. 2013. School leaders matter: measuring the impact of effective principals. *Education Next* 13(1), 62–69.

Brighouse, T. 2007. The London challenge: a personal view. In *Education in a Global City: Essays from London* (ed. T. Brighouse and L. Fullick). Bedford Way Papers. London: IOE Press.

Burgess, S., E. Greaves, A. Vignoles and D. Wilson. 2009. What parents want: school preferences and school choice. Working Paper 09-01, Department of Quantitative Social Science.

Carrell, S. E., B. Sacerdote and J. E. West. 2011. From natural variation to optimal policy? The Lucas critique meets peer effects. Working Paper 16865, National Bureau of Economic Research.

Caselli, F. 2005. Accounting for cross-country income differences. In *Handbook of Economic Growth* (ed. P. Aghion and S. Durlauf), volume 1, chapter 9, pp. 679–741. Elsevier.

Castelló-Climent, A. 2010. Channels through which human capital inequality influences economic growth. *Journal of Human Capital* 4(4), 394–450.

Castelló-Climent, A., and R. Doménech. 2008. Human capital inequality, life expectancy and economic growth. *Economic Journal* 118(528), 653–677.

Chevalier, A., P. Dolton and S. McIntosh. 2007. Recruiting and retaining teachers in the UK: an analysis of graduate occupation choice from the 1960s to the 1990s. *Economica* 74, 69–96.

Chowdry, H., C. Crawford and A. Goodman. 2009. Drivers and barriers to educational success: evidence from the Longitudinal Study of Young People in England. Research Report RR102, DCSF.

Chowdry, H., E. Greaves and L. Sibieta. 2010. The Pupil Premium: assessing the options. Institute for Fiscal Studies.

Clifton, J., and W. Cook. 2012. A long division: closing the attainment gap in England's secondary schools. Report (September), Institute for Public Policy Research.

Clotfelter, C. T., E. J. Glennie, H. F. Ladd and J. L. Vigdor. 2006. Teacher bonuses and teacher retention in low-performing schools: evidence from the North Carolina $1,800 Teacher Bonus Program. *Public Finance Review* 36(1), 63–87.

Cohen, D., and M. Soto. 2007. Growth and human capital: good data, good results. *Journal of Economic Growth* 12(1), 51–76.

Coleman, J. S. 1966. Equality of educational opportunity. US Department of Health, Education, and Welfare, Office of Education.

Cook, C. 2012. FT data: blogs. http://blogs.ft.com/ftdata/author/christopher cook/.

Dahl, G. B., and L. Lochner. 2012. The impact of family income on child achievement: evidence from the Earned Income Tax Credit. *American Economic Review* 102(5), 1927–1956.

Day, C., G. Stobart, P. Sammons, A. Kington, Q. Gu, R. Smees and T. Mujaba. 2006. Variations in teachers' work, lives and effectiveness! Final report for the VITAE Project. London: Department for Education and Skills.

de la Croix, D., and M. Doepke. 2009. To segregate or to integrate: education politics and democracy. *Review of Economic Studies* 76(2), 597–628.

de la Fuente, A., and R. Domenech. 2006. Human capital in growth regressions: how much difference does data quality make? *Journal of the European Economics Association* **4**(1), 1–36.

Demirgüç-Kunt, A., and R. Levine. 2009. Finance and inequality: theory and evidence. *Annual Review of Financial Economics* **1**(1), 287–318.

DfES. 2007. City challenge for world class education. Department for Education and Skills.

Dickson, M. 2009. The causal effect of education on wages revisited. Report 09/220, Centre for Market and Public Organisation.

Dills, A. K. 2005. Does cream-skimming curdle the milk? A study of peer effects. *Economics of Education Review* **24**(1), 19–28.

Dobbie, W., and R. G. Fryer. 2009. Are high quality schools enough to close the achievement gap? Evidence from a social experiment in Harlem. Working Paper 15473, National Bureau of Economic Research.

Dolton, P. 1990. The economics of UK teacher supply: the graduate's decision. *Economic Journal* (Conference Papers) **100**, 91–104.

Dolton, P., and O. Marcenaro-Gutierrez. 2011. If you pay peanuts do you get monkeys? A cross country analysis of teacher pay and pupil performance. *Economic Policy* **26**(65), 5–55.

Dolton, P., and W. van der Klaauw. 1999. The turnover of teachers: a competing risks explanation. *Review of Economics and Statistics* **81**(3), 543–550.

Duflo, E., P. Dupas and M. Kremer. 2010. Peer effects, teacher incentives, and the impact of tracking: evidence from a randomized evaluation in Kenya. Massachusetts Institute of Technology Mimeo.

Duncan, G. J., and R. J. Murnane. 2011. Introduction: the American dream, then and now. In *Whither Opportunity: Rising Inequality, Schools, and Children's Life Chances* (ed. G. J. Duncan and R. Murnane). New York: Russell Sage Foundation.

Dustmann, C., S. Machin and U. Schönberg. 2010. Ethnicity and educational achievement in compulsory schooling. *Economic Journal* **120**(546), F272–F297.

Feinstein, L. 2003. Inequality in the early cognitive development of British children in the 1970s cohort. *Economica* **70**, 73–97.

Galor, O., and J. Zeira. 1993. Income distribution and macroeconomics. *Review of Economic Studies* **60**(1), 35–52.

Gennaioli, N., R. La Porta, F. Lopez-de-Silanes and A. Shleifer. 2011. Human capital and regional development. Working Paper 17158, National Bureau of Economic Research.

Gibbons, S., and S. Machin. 2003. Valuing English primary schools. *Journal of Urban Economics* **53**(2), 197–219.

Gibbons, S., and O. Silva. 2008. Urban density and pupil attainment. *Journal of Urban Economics* **63**(2), 631–650.

Gibbons, S., and S. Telhaj. 2006. Peer effects and pupil attainment: evidence from secondary school transition. Discussion Paper 0063, Centre for the Economics of Education.

Gibbons, S., and S. Telhaj. 2008. Peers and achievement in England's secondary schools. Discussion Paper SERCDP0001, Spatial Economics Research Centre.

Gibbons, S., S. Machin and O. Silva. 2008. Choice, competition, and pupil achievement. *Journal of the European Economic Association* **6**(4), 912–947.

Gibbons, S., H. G. Overman and P. Pelkonen. 2010. Wage disparities in Britain: people or place? Discussion Paper 0060, Spatial Economics Research Centre.

Gibbons, S., S. McNally and M. Viarengo. 2011. Does additional spending help urban schools? An evaluation using boundary discontinuities. Discussion Paper 90, Spatial Economics Research Centre.

Gibbons, S., S. Machin and O. Silva. 2013. Valuing school quality using boundary discontinuity. *Journal of Urban Economics* **75**, 15–28.

Glaeser, E. L., R. La Porta, F. Lopez-de-Silane and A. Shleifer. 2004. Do institutions cause growth? *Journal of Economic Growth* **9**(3), 271–303.

Glennerster, H. 1995a. *British Social Policy Since 1945.* Oxford: Blackwell.

Glennerster, H. 1995b. Opportunity, costs, education: finance needs change if we are to build a high skill Britain. *New Economy* **2**(2), 110–114.

Gonand, F., I. Joumard and R. Price. 2007. Public spending efficiency in primary and secondary education: institutional indicators. Working Paper 543, OECD Economics Department.

Gordon, B. D., and L. Lochner. 2012. The impact of family income on child achievement: evidence from the Earned Income Tax Credit. *American Economic Review* **102**(5), 1927–1956.

Gould, E. D., V. Lavy and M. D. Paserman. 2009. Does immigration affect the long-term educational outcomes of natives? Quasi-experimental evidence. *Economic Journal* **119**, 1243–1269.

Green, F., S. Machin and R. Murphy. 2008. Competition for private and state school teachers. *Journal of Education and Work* **21**(5), 383–404.

Gregg, P., and L. Macmillan. 2010. Family income and education in the next generation: exploring income gradients in education for current cohorts of youth. *Longitudinal and Life Course Studies* **1**(3), 259–280.

Gregg, P., C. Propper and E. Washbrook. 2008. Understanding the relationship between parental income and multiple child outcomes: a decomposition analysis. Working Paper 08/193, Centre for Market and Public Organisation.

Gregg, P., L. Macmillan and B. Nasim. 2012. The impact of fathers' job loss during the 1980s recession on their child's educational attainment and labour market outcomes. Working Paper 12/288, Centre for Market and Public Organisation.

Griliches, Z. 1970. Notes on the role of education in production functions and growth accounting. In *Education, Income, and Human Capital*, pp. 71–128. Cambridge, MA: National Bureau of Economic Research.

Hall, R., and C. Jones. 1999. Why do some countries produce so much more output per worker than others? *Quarterly Journal of Economics* **114**(1), 83–116.

Hanushek, E. A. 1989. The impact of differential expenditures on school performance. *Educational Researcher* **18**(4), 45–51.

Hanushek, E. A. 2003. The failure of input-based schooling policies. *Economic Journal* **113**(485), F64–F98.

Hanushek, E. A. 2008. Education production functions. In *The New Palgrave Dictionary of Economics* (ed. S. Durlauf and L. Blume). Basingstoke: Palgrave Macmillan.

Hanushek, E. A., and D. D. Kimko. 2000. Schooling, labour force quality, and the growth of nations. *American Economic Review* **90**(5), 1184–1208.

Hanushek, E. A., and J. A. Luque. 2003. Efficiency and equity in schools around the world. *Economics of Education Review* **22**(5), 481–502.

Hanushek, E. A., and R. Pace. 1995. Who chooses to teach and why? *Economics of Education Review* **14**(2), 101–117.

Hanushek, E. A., and S. J. Rivkin. 2010. Generalizations about using value-added measure of teacher quality. *American Economic Review* **100**(10), 267–271.

Hanushek, E. A., and G. P. Shultz. 2012. Education is the key to a healthy economy. *Wall Street Journal*, 30 April.

Hanushek, E. A., and L. Woessmann. 2006. Does educational tracking affect performance and inequality? Differences-in-differences evidence across countries. *Economic Journal* **116**(510), C63–C76.

Hanushek, E. A., and L. Woessmann. 2007. The role of education quality for economic growth. Working Paper 4122 (February), World Bank Policy Research.

Hanushek, E. A., and L. Woessmann. 2008. The role of cognitive skills in economic development. *Journal of Economic Literature* **46**(3), 607–668.

Hanushek, E. A., and L. Woessmann. 2009. Do better schools lead to more growth? Cognitive skills, economic outcomes, and causation. Working Paper 14633, National Bureau of Economic Research.

Hanushek, E. A., and L. Woessmann. 2011. Overview of the symposium on performance pay for teachers. *Economics of Education Review* **30**(3), 391–393.

Hanushek, E. A., J. F. Kain, D. M. O'Brien and S. G. Rivkin. 2005. The market for teacher quality. Working Paper 11154, National Bureau of Economic Research.

Hanushek, E. A., S. Link and L. Woessmann. 2013. Does school autonomy make sense everywhere? Panel estimates from PISA. *Journal of Development Economics* **104**, 212–232.

Heckman, J., J. Stixrud and S. Urzua. 2006. The effects of non-cognitive abilities on labour market outcomes and social behaviour. *Journal of Labor Economics* **24**(3), 411–482.

Henderson, V., P. Mieszkowski and Y. Sauvageau. 1978. Peer group effects and educational production functions. *Journal of Public Economics* **10**(1), 97–106.

Higgins, S., D. Kokotsaki and R. Coe. 2011. Toolkit of strategies to improve learning: summary for schools, spending the Pupil Premium. Research Report (May), Sutton Trust.

Hobbs, G., and A. Vignoles. 2010. Is children's free school meal 'eligibility' a good proxy for family income? *British Educational Research Journal* **36**(4), 673–690.

Holmlund, H., S. McNally and M. Viarengo. 2010. Does money matter for schools? *Economics of Education Review* **29**(6), 1154–1164.

Hoxby, C. M. 2000. Peer effects in the classroom: learning from gender and race variation. Working Paper 7867, National Bureau of Economic Research.

Hoxby, C. M. 2002a. School choice and school productivity (or could school choice be a tide that lifts all boats?). Working Paper 8873, National Bureau of Economic Research.

Hoxby, C. M. 2002b. Would school choice change the teaching profession? *Journal of Human Resources* **37**(4), 846–891.

Hoxby, C. M., and S. Murarka. 2009. Charter schools in New York City: who enrols and how they affect their students' achievement. Working Paper 14852, National Bureau of Economic Research.

Hussain, I. 2012. Subjective performance evaluation in the public sector: evidence from school inspections. Discussion Paper 135, Centre for Economics of Education.

Hutchings, M., U. Maylor, H. Mendick, I. Menter and S. Smart. 2006. An evaluation of innovative approaches to teacher training on the Teach First programme: final report to the Training and Development Agency for Schools. Institute for Policy Studies in Education.

Hutchings, M., C. Greenwood, S. Hollingworth, A. Mansaray, A. Rose, S. Minty and K. Glass. 2012. Evaluation of the City Challenge programme. Research Report DFE-RR215 (June), Department for Education.

Jackson, C. 2010. The effects of an incentive-based high-school intervention on college outcomes. Working Paper 15722, National Bureau of Economic Research.

Jarrett, T., and P. Bolton. 2012. School funding, including the Pupil Premium. Commons Library Standard Note.

Jerrim, J. 2013. The reliability of trends over time in international education test scores: is the performance of England's secondary school pupils really in relative decline? *Journal of Social Policy* **42**(2), 257–279.

Keep, E., K. Mayhew and J. Payne. 2006. From skills revolution to productivity miracle—not as easy as it looks? *Oxford Review of Economic Policy* **22**(4), 539–559.

Kounali, D., T. Robinson, H. Goldstein and H. Lauder. 2008. The probity of free school meals as a proxy measure for disadvantage. Available at www.bristol.ac.uk/cmm/publications/fsm.pdf.

Kramarz, F., S. Machin and A. Ouazad. 2009. What makes a test score? The respective contributions of pupils, schools and peers in achievement in English primary education. Discussion Paper 0102, Centre for the Economics of Education.

Lagakos, D., B. Mollz, T. Porzio and N. Qian. 2012. *Experience Matters: Human Capital and Development Accounting.* Princeton University Press.

La Porta, R., and A. Shleifer. 2008. The unofficial economy and economic development. *Brookings Papers on Economic Activity* **2008**, 275–352.

Lawton, K., and T. Lanning. 2012. No train, no gain: beyond free-market and state-led skills policy. Report (April), Institute for Public Policy Research.

Lavy, V. 2002. Evaluating the effect of teacher group performance incentives on students achievements. *Journal of Political Economy* **110**(6), 1286-1317.

Lavy, V. 2009. Performance pay and teachers' effort, productivity, and grading ethics. *American Economic Review* **99**(5), 1979-2011.

Lavy, V., and A. Schlosser. 2011. Mechanisms and impacts of gender peer effects at school. *American Economic Journal: Applied Economics* **3**(2), 1-33.

Lavy, V., M. D. Paserman and A. Schlosser. 2012. Inside the black box of ability peer effects: evidence from variation in the proportion of low achievers in the classroom. *Economic Journal* **122**(559), 208-237.

Lazear, E. 2003. Output-based pay: incentives, retention or sorting? Discussion Paper 761, Institute for the Study of Labor.

Levacic, R., and A. Vignoles. 2002. Researching the links between school resources and student outcomes in the UK: a review of issues and evidence. *Education Economics* **10**(3), 313-331.

Lindley, J., and S. Machin. 2012. The quest for more and more education: implications for social mobility. *Fiscal Studies* **33**(2), 265-286.

Loeb, S., and M. Page. 2000. Examining the link between teacher wages and student outcomes: the importance of alternative labor market opportunities and non-pecuniary variation. *Review of Economics and Statistics* **82**(3), 393-408.

Lucas Jr, R. E. 1988. On the mechanics of economic development. *Journal of Monetary Economics* **22**(1), 3-42.

Machin, S., and S. McNally. 2004. The evaluation of English education policies. Discussion Paper 131, Centre for the Economics of Education.

Machin, S., and R. Murphy. 2010. The social composition and future earnings of postgraduates. Interim Report of a research project commissioned by the Sutton Trust.

Machin, S., and J. Vernoit. 2011. Changing school autonomy: academy schools and their introduction to England's education. Discussion Paper 0123, Centre for the Economics of Education.

Machin, S., and J. Wilson. 2009. Public and private schooling initiatives in England. In *School Choice International: Exploring Public-Private Partnerships* (ed. R. Chakrabarti and P. Peterson). Cambridge, MA: MIT Press.

Machin, S., S. McNally and C. Meghir. 2010. Resources and standards in urban schools. *Journal of Human Capital* **4**(4), 365-393.

Mankiw, N. G., D. Romer and D. N. Weil. 1992. A contribution to the empirics of economic growth. *Quarterly Journal of Economics* **107**(2), 407-437.

Manski, C. 1993. Identification of endogenous social effects: the reflection problem. *Review of Economic Studies* **60**, 531-542.

McKinsey. 2007. How the world's best-performing school systems come out on top. Report (September), McKinsey.

McNally, S. 2010. Evaluating education policies: the evidence from economic research. CEP Election Analysis Series.

McNally, S. 2012. Education and skills. Submission to the LSE Growth Commission.

Milburn, A. 2012. University challenge: how higher education can advance social mobility. A progress report by the Independent Reviewer on Social Mobility and Child Poverty.

Milligan, K., and M. Stabile. 2011. Do child tax benefits affect the well-being of children? Evidence from Canadian child benefit expansions. *American Economic Journal* **3**(3), 175–205.

Moav, O. 2005. Cheap children and the persistence of poverty. *Economic Journal* **115**(500), 88–110.

Moffitt, R. 2001. Policy interventions, low-level equilibria, and social interactions. In *Social Dynamics* (ed. S. Durlauf and P. Young). Cambridge, MA: MIT Press.

Mookherjee, D., and D. Ray. 2003. Persistent inequality. *Review of Economic Studies* **70**(2), 369–393.

Muralidharan, K., and V. Sundararaman. 2009. Teacher performance pay: experimental evidence from India. Working Paper 15323, National Bureau of Economic Research.

Murnane, R., and R. J. Olsen. 1989. Will there be enough teachers? *American Economic Review* **79**(2), 242–246.

Murnane, R., and R. J. Olsen. 1990. The effects of salaries and opportunity costs on length of stay in teaching: evidence from North Carolina. *Journal of Human Resources* **25**(1), 106–124.

Nelson, R. R., and E. Phelps. 1966. Investment in humans, technology diffusion and economic growth. *American Economic Review* **56**(2), 69–75.

OECD. 2005. *Attracting, Developing and Retaining Effective Teachers—Final Report: Teachers Matter.* Paris: OECD Publishing.

OECD. 2010a. *Viewing the United Kingdom School System Through the Prism of PISA.* Paris: OECD Publishing.

OECD. 2010b. *The High Cost of Low Educational Performance.* Paris: OECD Publishing.

OECD. 2012. *Education at a Glance 2012.* Paris: OECD Publishing.

Ostinelli, G. 2009. Teacher education in Italy, Germany, England, Sweden and Finland. *European Journal of Education* (Special Issue: The Training of Adult Education Professionals in Europe) **44**(2), 291–308.

Propper, C., and J. Britton. 2012. Does wage regulation harm kids? Evidence from English schools. Working Paper 12/293, Centre for Market and Public Organisation.

Rivkin, S. G., E. A. Hanushek and J. F. Kain. 2005. Teachers, schools, and academic achievement. *Econometrica* **73**(2), 417–458.

Romer, P. 1990. Endogenous technological change. *Journal of Political Economy* **99**(5), S71–S102.

Rosenthal, L. 2003. The value of secondary school quality. *Oxford Bulletin of Economics and Statistics* **65**(3), 329–355.

Ross, A., and M. Hutchings. 2003. United Kingdom country background report: attracting, developing and retaining effective teachers. OECD.

Rowntree, B. S. 1901. *Poverty: A Study of Town Life.* London: Macmillan.

Sacerdote, B. 2001. Peer effects with random assignment: results for Dartmouth roommates. *Quarterly Journal of Economics* **116**(2), 681–704.

Sala-i-Martín, X., G. Doppelhofer and R. I. Miller. 2004. Determinants of long-term growth: a Bayesian averaging of classical estimates (BACE) approach. *American Economic Review* **94**(4), 813–835.

Santiago, P. 2004. The labour market for teachers. In *International Handbook on the Economics of Education* (ed. G. Johnes and J. Johnes), pp. 522–578. Cheltenham: Edward Elgar.

Schuetz, G., H. Ursprung and L. Woessmann. 2005. Education policy and equality of opportunity. Working Paper 1518, CESifo.

Shultz, G. P., and E. A. Hanushek. 2012. Education is the key to a healthy economy: if we fail to reform K-12 schools, we will have slow growth and more income inequality. *Wall Street Journal*, 1 May.

Sibieta, L., H. Chowdry and A. Muriel 2008. Level playing field? The implications of school funding. Reading, UK: CfBT Educational Trust.

Slater, H., N. Davies and S. Burgess. 2009. Do teachers matter? Measuring the variation in teacher effectiveness in England. Working Paper 09/212, Centre for Market and Public Organisation.

Solow, R. M. 1957. Technical change and the aggregate production function. *Review of Economics and Statistics* **39**(3), 312–320.

Stevens, A. H., and J. Schaller. 2011. Short-run effects of parental job loss on children's academic achievement. *Economics of Education Review* **30**(2), 289–299.

Stinebrickner, R., and T. R. Stinebrickner. 2006. What can be learned about peer effects using college roommates? Evidence from new survey data and students from disadvantaged backgrounds. *Journal of Public Economics* **90**, 1435–1454.

Summers, A. A., and B. L. Wolfe. 1977. Do schools make a difference? *American Economic Review* **67**(4), 639–652.

Syverson, C. 2011. What determines productivity? *Journal of Economic Literature* **49**(2), 326–365.

Teddlie, C., and Reynolds, D. 2000. *The International Handbook of School Effectiveness Research*. London: Falmer Press.

Todd, P. E., and K. I. Wolpin. 2003. On the specification and estimation of the production function for cognitive achievement. *Economic Journal* **113**, F3–F33.

Walcher, P. 2013. Teachers' pay rises to be based on performance, Michael Gove confirms. *The Guardian*, 15 January.

Welch, F. 1970. Education in production. *Journal of Political Economy* **78**(1), 35–59.

West, A., and H. Pennell. 2000. Publishing school examination results in England: incentives and consequences. *Educational Studies* **26**(4), 423–436.

Wilson, J. 2011. Are England's academies more inclusive or more 'exclusive'? The impact of institutional change on the pupil profile of schools. Discussion Paper 125, Centre for the Economics of Education.

Winston, G. C., and D. J. Zimmerman. 2004. Peer effects in higher education. In *College Choices: The Economics of Where to Go, When to Go, and How to Pay for It* (ed. C. M. Hoxby), pp. 395–421. NBER Conference Report Series. University of Chicago Press.

Woessmann, L. 2003. European education production functions: what makes a difference for student achievement in Europe? European Economy: Economic Paper 190, Directorate of General Economic and Monetary Affairs, European Commission.

Woessmann, L. 2011. Cross-country evidence on teacher performance pay. *Economics of Education Review* **30**(3), 404–418.

Wolter, S. C., and S. Denzler. 2004. Wage elasticity of the teacher supply in Switzerland. *Brussels Economic Review* **47**, 387–408.

Zabalza, A., P. Turnbull and G. Williams. 1979. *The Economics of Teacher Supply.* Cambridge University Press.

Zimmerman, D. J. 2003. Peer effects in academic outcomes: evidence from a natural experiment. *Review of Economics and Statistics* **85**(1), 9–23.

Infrastructure and Growth

By Novella Bottini, Miguel Coelho and Jennifer Kao

4.1 THE ECONOMICS OF INFRASTRUCTURE

Energy, water, transport, digital communications, and waste disposal networks and facilities are essential ingredients for the success of a competitive modern economy.

Research has shown that well-designed infrastructure investments have long-term economic benefits; they can raise economic growth, productivity and land values while providing significant positive spillovers. However, growing evidence suggests that the UK performs poorly by international standards. For example, the World Economic Forum ranked the UK twenty-fourth for 'quality of overall infrastructure' in its 2012 report on global competitiveness.

What sets investment in infrastructure apart from other types of investment is its high-risk, long-term, capital-intensive nature, reflected in the creation of long-lived assets with high sunk costs. The resulting gulf between marginal and average costs creates a time-inconsistency problem as investors always face the problem that they will be 'held up'. This requires suitable government intervention.

In turn, government intervention exposes infrastructure investment to an additional layer of risks and decision-making biases—these are the root cause of underinvestment in UK infrastructure.

In this chapter we examine all aspects of infrastructure and growth in the UK and make policy recommendations designed to strengthen

We are grateful to a large number of people for kindly submitting written or oral evidence to the Secretariat. We are particularly grateful to Kate Barker, Alex Bowen, Ricky Burdett, Paul Cheshire, Stephen Fries, Stephen Glaister, Ralf Martin, David Newbery, James Rydge, Mattia Romani, Bridget Rosewell, Dimitri Zenghelis, the OECD and officials at the Department for Business, Innovation & Skills. We are also thankful to Anna Valero for providing useful comments on previous versions of this paper, and to Jo Cantlay and Linda Cleavely for logistical support. The views expressed here do not necessarily reflect the views of the individuals or institutions mentioned above.

the governance, strategic planning and financing of major infrastructure investment through the creation of a new institutional architecture.

4.2 INFRASTRUCTURE AND GROWTH

Infrastructure is a heterogeneous term,[1] including physical structures of various types used by many industries as inputs to the production of goods and services (Chan *et al.* 2009). This description encompasses 'social infrastructure' (such as schools and hospitals) and 'economic infrastructure' (such as network utilities). The latter includes energy, water, transport and digital communications. They are the essential ingredients for the success of a modern economy, and they are the focus of this chapter (Stewart 2010).

Conceptually, infrastructure may affect aggregate output in two main ways:

(i) directly, through its sector contribution to GDP and as an additional input in the production process of other sectors;[2] and

(ii) indirectly, raising total factor productivity by reducing transaction and other costs and therefore allowing a more efficient use of conventional productive inputs.

Infrastructure can be considered as a complementary factor for economic growth.

How big is the contribution of infrastructure to aggregate economic performance? The answer is critical for many policy decisions: to gauge the growth effects of fiscal interventions in the form of public investment changes, for example, or to assess if public infrastructure investments can be self-financing.

The empirical literature is far from unanimous (see, for example, Gramlich 1994) but a majority of studies report a significant positive effect of infrastructure investment on output, productivity and long-term growth rates. Infrastructure investment is complementary to other investment in the sense that insufficient infrastructure investment constrains other investment, while excessive infrastructure investment has

---

[1] Infrastructure has been understood to include many different things, and a universally accepted definition has remained elusive. One well-known attempt reads (Gramlich 1994): 'The definition that makes the most sense from an economics standpoint consists of large capital intensive natural monopolies such as highways, other transport facilities, water and sewer lines, and communications.'

[2] For example, the total direct contribution of the energy sector to the UK economy in 2011 (measured by contribution to GDP) was £20.6 billion, an increase of 16% from 2007 (Energy UK 2012).

no added value. To the extent that suboptimal infrastructure investment constrains other investment, it constrains growth (Newbery 2012).

Empirical estimates of the magnitude of infrastructure's contribution display considerable variation across studies.[3] Overall, however, the most recent literature tends to find smaller (and more plausible) effects than those reported in the earlier studies (Aschauer 1989; Calderón *et al.* 2011), probably as a result—at least in part—of improved methodological approaches[4] that also allow better estimates of the causal relationship. This empirical correlation is the subject of considerable heterogeneity depending on the countries and time periods under study, possibly indicating asset-quality issues, complementarities with other production factors, non-linearity due to the network character of infrastructure,[5] and larger policy and institutional factors that still need to be better understood.[6]

4.3 THE CHANGING ROLE OF INFRASTRUCTURE

It is necessary to realign the nation's infrastructure with the changing world economy. The UK's infrastructure must be secure, flexible and well interconnected in order to support the UK's long-term economic growth.

Infrastructure security and stability concerns the quantity of spare capacity (or the security of supply). Instead of acting on the efficiency frontier, infrastructure projects must operate with spare capacity to contribute to economic growth through ensuring reliable service provision

---

[3] See Romp and Haan (2007) for a review of the relevant empirical literature.

[4] The empirical literature on the contribution of infrastructure to aggregate output is subject to major caveats. In particular, it ignores the non-stationarity of aggregate output and infrastructure capital, potential simultaneity between infrastructure and income level, and potential heterogeneity across countries (Calderón *et al.* 2011; Esfahani and Ramírez 2003).

[5] This problem mainly arises using a Cobb–Douglas production function, since under this functional form the elasticity of substitution among factors is constrained to be 1. The key argument with infrastructure is complementarity. Given that the assumptions underlying a Cobb–Douglas production function do not account for complementarity, infrastructure's impact on growth could be underestimated.

[6] Egert *et al.* (2009a,b) sought to identify the wider economic benefits of transport infrastructure investments using a panel growth regressions framework for 1960–2005. The results suggested massive variation across the OECD, in both the signs and the magnitudes of the benefits, and the authors conclude that the impacts are country specific and depend *inter alia* on the pre-existing level of provision. In the case of the UK, both road and rail infrastructure investments were found to have significant indirect productivity impacts. This finding is consistent with recent evidence of quite strong agglomeration effects on productivity in the UK (Graham 2007; Crafts 2009).

in energy and transport. For instance, it was the spare capacity generated by Victorian (and later) transport investment that provided for the structural shifts in London jobs over the past forty years, from manufacturing (mainly in outer London) to services (which are much more centrally located). Crossrail is another example: it has been estimated that without it 35,000 people would be crowded out of access to central London jobs by 2035 (Rosewell 2012). (This represents a loss of additional output to the UK economy of £80 billion, simply on the basis of the higher productivity that is generated across all activities in a dense location (Rosewell 2012).)

Spare capacity is a necessary condition for a properly functioning energy system. In the absence of storage, to ensure there is a level of spare capacity the system needs to have excess supply. However, no rational profit-seeking company will deliberately create conditions of excess supply, since it would produce a marginal cost lower than the average cost (Helm 2012). Given this market failure, the government needs to create the right incentives to ensure security of energy supply, since the social and economic costs of a blackout or a train crash (due to insufficient supply) are much higher than the losses of the company involved.

Greater flexibility in infrastructure systems is necessary to respond to changing economic needs. For instance, within the energy sector the UK needs to ensure energy security and at the same time meet its decarbonizing target in the coming decades. Allowing energy to be supplied by different sources makes it easier to achieve both these aims. But this requires a different, and more flexible, energy system than the one that is currently in place. One possible solution is the development of a 'supergrid', i.e. an international network of electricity cables, that integrates offshore renewables generation into the transmission system, as well as allowing electricity to be traded across borders. The opportunity to connect houses, and hence the final consumer, to the grid (through the smart grid) would further increment the flexibility and efficiency of energy supply.[7] London's Oyster card is another example of flexible technology that has the potential to introduce flexible pricing policies to public sector networks (e.g. using the same underground ticket on urban rail (Eddington Review 2006)).

Finally, *interconnection and complementarities* across different infrastructure sectors are key elements for increasing service efficiency,

---

[7]For a review on smart grids see IEA (2011), Deutsche Bank Research (2011), Greenpeace (2011), Patsy (2012b), House of Commons (2011), Macilwain (2010) and Nature (2010).

supporting the adoption of innovative technologies and supporting growth. Good connections between cities and airports, via rail, roads and underground, decrease travel times and cost and increase the appeal of airports to both airline companies and passengers. Other examples include broadband and information and communications technology, which play a critical role in the development, installation and operation of the smart grid across the UK: smart grids manage the supply and demand of power through the national distribution network more effectively by introducing high-tech communication to the system. Interconnection also has an effect on the implementation costs and the feasibility of a given project. Moreover, in a crowded and busy network decisions have knock-on effects: for example, Crossrail will offer new opportunities to explore the economies of agglomeration that central London has to offer (Rosewell 2012).

4.4 UK INFRASTRUCTURE PERFORMANCE

Over the years, the UK has developed mature and extensive infrastructure networks that are among the largest and most widely used in Europe. While there has been a strong history of investment, levels have fluctuated significantly over time. The move of the water, energy and communications sectors to regulated private ownership during the 1980s provided a basis for renewal of major parts of these networks.[8] At the same time, and partially as a result of the withdrawal of state funding from these areas, public capital spending has been falling since the late 1960s onwards: net public investment has never regained its 1968 level, either in absolute terms or as a share of GDP.[9]

Growing evidence suggests that the UK performs poorly by international standards. The World Economic Forum ranked the UK twenty-fourth for 'quality of overall infrastructure' in its 2012 report on global competitiveness. The Doing Business project ranks access to UK electricity supply fifty-fourth in the world and Ofgem (the energy sector regulator) warns of the risks of power shortages by 2015. The Eddington Review predicted that increased congestion could potentially cost the UK £22 billion per year by 2025 if the transport network fails to keep up with demand (Eddington Review 2006).

---

[8]For example, £85 billion has been invested in water infrastructure alone since privatization (Water UK 2010).

[9]As a share of GDP, net public investment fell from a level of 5.6% in 1975/76 to 3% in 2008.

This chapter focuses mainly on energy and transport, where the problems are well understood and where potential growth implications are likely to be more severe.

Other areas that deserve attention are broadband and housing: the former given its critical role in the UK economic system and its future competitiveness, and the latter because of the currently low investment level and increasing housing demand.

Energy

Energy Risk

The UK, like other OECD countries, faces significant challenges in its aim to achieve a sensible balance of security, stability and affordability when it comes to energy supply, while at the same time complying with relatively stringent carbon targets.

Energy security is determined by the margin of spare generating capacity in excess of maximum electricity demand. This should be maintained at around 20%. However, within the next ten years, over a fifth of the UK's electricity generating capacity (built in the 1960s and 1970s) will be going offline, pushing the 'capacity margin' below 10% by 2015 (Redpoint–DECC 2010; Ofgem 2012). This problem is becoming more pressing than it was in previous decades.[10]

Energy stability refers to the ability to provide a constant supply of energy. This could become compromised by a shortage in spare capacity. While nuclear power and gas would ensure stable energy supply, renewable energy generators (such as wind farms) are characterized by intermittent supply and require additional flexible reserves to prevent blackouts.

The decarbonization objective is based on EU and UK carbon targets. At the inception of the Kyoto Protocol, the EU-15 committed to reducing emissions by an average of 8% over the 2008–12 period, compared with base-year emissions. Under the EU's burden-sharing agreement the UK

---

[10]The 1980–82 recession changed the composition of the economy and this period was followed by a process of relative deindustrialization. The capacity built in the 1970s for electricity was greatly in excess of demand in the 1980s and 1990s. During the 1990s there was the first 'dash for gas', partly linked to the privatization process and regulator pressure in the name of 'competition' and partly for environmental reasons, since the UK had begun to implement new climate change policies directly targeted at energy efficiency and emission reductions. Finally, the Great Recession (since 2007) meant that GDP was at a much lower level in 2012 than was expected to be the case in 2005, and this has also lowered energy demand.

committed to a 12.5% reduction in emissions. More recently, the UK has introduced a system of carbon budgets that set legally binding emissions limits over five-year periods for the periods 2008-12, 2013-17, 2018-22 and 2023-27. The average level of emissions in the fourth budgeted period (2023-27) will have to be 50% lower than the 1990 level. These new climate change policies have contributed to the decline in energy-related CO_2 emissions per head during the 2000s, after the 'dash for gas' and the effect of privatization started to dissipate.[11] Indeed, the UK registered the largest energy emissions decrease of any country between 1990 and 2005, when the average decrease was 0.7% per year per head, well above the OECD, EU-15 and world averages. These reductions were strongly linked to the privatization of the electricity industry in the early 1990s. Indeed, privatization was accompanied by reduced gas prices and improvements in electricity generation technology, both of which favour greater use of the cleaner energy sources, especially gas (the so-called dash for gas), which replaced coal and oil (Bowen and Rydge 2011).

The EU has also adopted a target of deriving 20% of final energy demand from renewables by 2020 and has agreed on individual country targets to achieve this. The UK's target is 15%. Although this target is not accompanied by any EU-wide policy instrument, over the past decade the UK has promoted different policies that support renewable energy, has aimed to reduce the carbon intensity of energy and has diversified supply (Bowen and Rydge 2011). In sharp contrast with the performance on emission reductions, the contribution of renewables to energy supply and electricity generation in the UK is lower—in both absolute and relative terms—than in other OECD countries. Indeed, most of the UK's electricity is produced by burning fossil fuels, predominantly natural gas (47% in 2010) and coal (28%). Only 16% of UK electricity comes from nuclear reactors, and renewable energy (mainly wind, wave, marine, hydro, biomass and solar) made up 7% of the total electricity generated in 2010 (Energy UK 2012). Stronger measures are therefore required to accelerate the transition from fossil-fuel-based electricity generation towards cleaner energy supplies to sustain the downward trend in emissions and meet the EU renewable target (Bowen and Rydge 2011).

All these challenges imply higher costs for end users, which raises concerns about affordability for households and cost efficiency for firms. Germany's biggest companies have recently warned that Europe's ability

---

[11]The economic downturn brought an extra stimulus to the emissions decline during this period (Bowen and Rydge 2011). However, the reduction in emissions has been slower than it was in the previous decade.

to compete against the US as a manufacturing centre is being damaged by rising energy costs as North America benefits from cheap natural shale gas.

Moreover, supply-side policies alone will not achieve the targets. In order to decrease energy demand, both consumers and businesses have to be empowered with facts so that they can make the right decisions about their energy consumption and become greener (Helm 2010b; CBI 2012b).

The Current Institutional Architecture

The economics profession is divided on the specifics of an optimal energy policy framework. This divide manifests itself in current debate around energy market reform, with some commentators advocating the need for a radical departure from current government policy to increase simplification of the policy instruments and their targets, increase competition and increase competitive bidding (see, for example, Helm 2012), while others claim that moderate changes to the current system could enable the UK to achieve its energy objectives (see, for example, Newbery 2012).

However, there seems to be broad consensus—among academics and business alike—that current policy arrangements have failed to deliver a stable, credible, long-term policy/regulatory environment that is capable of attracting private investment on the scale required to meet the challenges described above. In particular, the reliance of the economic viability of most low-carbon technologies on government policy presents a unique challenge to investors, who often see policy as uncertain and susceptible to change, either through ad hoc tinkering or through major changes in political objectives (CBI 2012b).[12]

Since the late 1980s the Department of Energy and Climate Change has proposed and developed a complex set of measures to reduce emissions. Most domestic UK energy policies, such as quantity-based instruments

---

[12]For example, the slippage of the review into support for renewable energy generation under the existing Renewables Obligation mechanism and the uncertainty over the level of subsidy for wind projects cause uncertainty about the long-term energy market framework. This creates major challenges in term of planning and financing projects, with negative outcomes on private investment. Of equal concern are the sudden and unexpected policy changes that have recently been implemented, including the increase in the North Sea oil and gas tax, the removal of revenue recycling from the Carbon Reduction Commitment and the cut to the solar photovoltaic feed-in tariff. These have been damaging to business confidence, with implications not just for immediate investment decisions but for longer-term trust in government policy (CBI 2012b).

(e.g. the Renewables Obligation[13]) and price-based instruments (e.g. the Climate Change Levy[14]), have been designed to be 'market friendly'. Several schemes have been hybrids or have taken the form of regulations mandating specific actions (such as labelling requirements for energy efficiency). Owing to this multitude of energy measures, many policies have risked overlapping with others (Bowen and Rydge 2011). The Electricity Market Reform programme is geared towards simplifying the energy market, providing a clearer framework for investment. But the fact that it came after many years of indecision means that it will take time to build confidence. The four pillars of the Energy Market Reform programme are as follows (Patsy 2012a).

A Feed-in Tariff with Contracts for Difference (FIT CfD) to provide long-term price-supporting contracts to different types of energy generation. It is a static payment on top of that obtained from selling electricity in the wholesale market.

A capacity mechanism to encourage flexible reserve/cushion plants or demand-reduction measures to ensure the 'appropriate' level of energy supply and spare capacity.

A carbon price floor to 'underpin' carbon price support, providing a minimum guaranteed level. This would provide a more stable and certain target than the EU emissions trading scheme.

An emissions performance standard to limit how much carbon coal power stations can emit, so that no new coal is built without demonstrating carbon capture and storage (CCS) technology or being 'CCS-ready' (that is, not necessarily fitted).

A number of bodies play advisory, implementation and accountability roles. The Department for Energy and Climate Change is responsible for

---

[13]The Renewables Obligation was introduced in 2002 and requires electricity end suppliers to purchase a certain fraction of their annual electricity supply from producers using specific renewable technologies. In return, they receive tradable Renewables Obligation Certificates. The supplier can also 'buy out' the obligation by paying a set price per megawatt hour. The buy-out revenue is recycled to participating suppliers in proportion to their Renewables Obligation Certificates.

[14]The Climate Change Levy was introduced on 1 April 2001, effectively replacing the Fossil Fuel Levy. It is a downstream tax on non-domestic energy use by industry and the public sector, and it is designed to incentivize energy efficiency and reductions in emissions, with part of the revenue being used to reduce National Insurance contributions. Energy-intensive firms can receive up to an 80% discount if they join a Climate Change Agreement, which requires meeting energy-efficiency or carbon-saving targets. Renewable electricity suppliers are exempt from the Climate Change Levy. Receipts from the levy amounted to £0.7 billion in 2009.

defining energy policy goals and for designing policy frameworks for achieving them.

The Department for Energy and Climate Change also has some specific functions in the energy sector, including

- granting consent for power stations;
- defining the extent of the regulated industry by deciding on licence exemptions;
- appointing members of the Gas and Electricity Markets Authority, which sets Ofgem's strategy;
- using vetoing power on any proposal by the regulator to modify licences;
- setting wider social and environmental policy relating to energy, and dealing with the growing international energy issues (specifically liberalization of the EU energy market, and imports of oil and gas); and
- looking after areas such as energy efficiency and fuel poverty.

The Energy and Climate Change Committee is appointed by the House of Commons to examine the expenditure, administration and policy of the Department for Energy and Climate Change and its associated public bodies.

In 2008, the Climate Change Act set up the Committee on Climate Change: an independent and authoritative body advising the UK government and devolved administrations on carbon budgets[15] and climate change issues in the UK. It monitors progress towards meeting carbon budgets and recommends actions for keeping budgets on track, and it conducts independent analysis into climate change science, economics and policy, as requested by the national authorities, in collaboration with a wide range of organizations and individuals (Committee on Climate Change 2010, 2012).

Ofgem, the independent energy regulator established by the Utilities Act 2000, is responsible for regulation of the energy markets in England, Scotland and Wales. Gas and electricity companies generally need a license to operate, and Ofgem deals with this duty by issuing, modifying, enforcing and revoking licenses. Its additional key functions include setting price controls in the natural monopoly licensed sectors, and investigating and penalizing those that violate license conditions. Ofgem's

---

[15]The budgets define the maximum level of CO_2 and other greenhouse gases that the UK can emit in each five-year budget period, beginning with 2008–12.

independence ensures that energy regulation is free from political interference, and helps avoid uncertainty in energy markets, which is one of the main constraints when it comes to infrastructure investment. Ofgem's main objective is to protect energy consumers' interests wherever appropriate through effective competition or by other means (Patsy 2012a).

Other bodies that impact on the development and delivery of energy policy include

- the Carbon Trust, which stimulates and supports energy efficiency in business and supports low-carbon technological deployment,
- the Energy Saving Trust, which is government funded and aims to stimulate energy efficiency and renewable energy take-up in the housing sector, and
- the Environment Agency, which applies the Integrated Pollution Prevention and Control regulations to major energy users and implements the EU Emissions Trading Scheme.

Government intervention is not confined to the principles and objectives of energy policy. Instead, it covers a plethora of detailed policy initiatives delivered through Ofgem, the Carbon Trust, the Energy Saving Trust, the Environment Trust and the planning system (see, for example, the National Policy Statements for Energy[16]).

Transport

Transport Risk

Underinvestment, a poor maintenance record and growing demand for road and air travel, coupled with inappropriate resource diversion and inefficiencies within the rail sector, define the current transport challenges. Growing demand on existing connections and dense concentrations at certain times of the day are putting the system under serious strain. The most heavily used and economically significant parts of the transportation network (urban areas, inter-urban corridors and key international gateways) are showing signs of increasing congestion, unreliability and overcrowding.

At the same time, environmental costs demand a different policy direction for a transportation sector that needs to contribute to reductions in the UK's overall greenhouse gas emissions.

---

[16]There are six of these and they cover the following issues: overarching energy, renewable energy, fossil fuels, oil and gas supply and storage, electricity networks, and nuclear power. They are produced by the Department for Energy and Climate Change and receive designation by the Secretary of State for Energy and Climate Change.

The most important type of transport infrastructure is the road network (Crafts 2009; Department for Transport 2008). The UK road network is the country's dominant means of transport, accounting for 73% of passenger travel and 65% of freight moved (Eddington Review 2006).

There is severe congestion on urban roads: 89% of transportation delay is estimated to be on urban roads (Eddington Review 2006). Department for Transport forecasts suggest that congestion across the English road network as a whole will increase from 2003 levels by 27% by 2025 and by 54% by 2035 (Department for Transport 2012b). Congestion in the UK is among the worst in Europe and reflects inadequate investment over previous decades (OECD 2005). Furthermore, as with the aviation sector, there will be a need to reduce carbon intensity. In addition, improvement and maintenance costs are increasing. Road charging has been proposed as a long-term solution to the problem of road investment, maintenance and finance (see the discussion of road pricing that starts on page 186 as well as that in appendix 4A).

Current challenges for UK rail include unreliability (train punctuality is worse in the UK than it is in the rest of Europe), the need to reduce carbon intensity (HM Treasury 2011; Eddington Review 2006), and increasing passenger overcrowding of commuter and intercity routes in the southeast and in the London Underground at peak times. There is also widespread recognition that the rail industry has major problems in terms of low efficiency and high costs.[17]

The challenges facing the aviation sector include reliability issues and constrained airport capacity, particularly hub runway capacity. UK international gateways are subject to some of the highest levels of delay in the EU: 28% of Heathrow flights and 24% of Gatwick flights are delayed by over 15 minutes (Eddington Review 2006). The two busiest UK airports are Heathrow and Gatwick. Heathrow operates at near full capacity in terms of runway utilization and terminal passenger volumes. Gatwick operates

---

[17] The McNulty 'Value for Money' report (2011) on railway costs gave evidence that suggested there was an efficiency gap. The high costs are largely related to the relatively low level of train utilization in the UK. Rail costs would need to be reduced by around 40% in the UK to match comparable costs in France, the Netherlands, Sweden and Switzerland. Passenger fares per passenger-kilometre are, on average, around 30% higher in the UK and, although it is difficult to compare government funding streams in different countries, it is likely that the UK taxpayer is also paying at least 30% more to subsidize the railways than taxpayers elsewhere. One reason for this is the excessive fragmentation between Network Rail, train operators and their suppliers and contractors. The effects of fragmentation are exacerbated by misaligned planning and budgeting cycles between the various players and by having, in effect, two separate regulators: the Office of Rail Regulation and the Department for Transport.

at near full runway utilization but does have some spare terminal capacity. Despite recent efforts to alleviate constrained terminal capacity (such as the £2.3 billion investment in building Terminal 2, which is set to open in 2014), additional runway capacity is still required in many UK airports.

Current Institutional Architecture

Rail. In a recent report sponsored by the Department for Transport and the Office of Rail Regulation, Sir Roy McNulty concluded that inefficiency in the rail industry was largely due to structural fragmentation, the manner of operation and the culture among major players, and inefficient incentives, legal and contractual frameworks (McNulty 2011).

After privatization in 1993, British Rail was divided into two components: the national rail infrastructure (comprised of track, signalling, bridges, tunnels, stations and depots) and the train operating companies that run on that network.

The former is owned by Network Rail, which is regulated by the Office of Rail Regulation and operates under price-cap regulation. While the train operating companies (both passenger and freight) run the trains, the actual train is often leased from a rolling stock company. The network operator owns the railway stations, most of which are leased to the train operating company that is the main user of that station. However, Network Rail is mainly responsible for operating the main passenger terminals.

The Department for Transport is in charge of passenger and train related matters. In particular, the Secretary of State for Transport is responsible for determining the rail budget, setting rail strategy, and letting the passenger rail franchises.

Contrary to expectations at the time of privatization, the level of government support for the rail industry has increased: it now contributes around 40% of total industry revenues. The remaining 60% of revenues currently come from fare box revenues, a share of which Network Rail receives in the form of the track access charges paid by train operators (Smith *et al.* 2011). As a consequence of the level of subsidy, the government plays an important role in relation to investment plans.

Under the new funding structure, every five years the government publishes two documents prior to the start of a periodic review of Network Rail outputs and funding: a 'high level output specification' of the outputs it wishes to see delivered in the forthcoming control period and a 'statement of funds available' (Smith 2009).

Roads. The Department for Transport retains overall responsibility for strategy, policy and funding of the UK road network. The Highways Agency is the executive agency of the Department for Transport and it is responsible for the maintenance, operation and enhancement of the strategic road network on behalf of the Secretary of State. Maintenance and investment in the remainder of the network is the responsibility of local authorities (county councils and unitary authorities).

There is currently a lack of long-term strategic thinking about the road network by the sector's governing bodies (Glaister 2010). Whilst the government has established a systematic process of five-year plans for railways with an associated funding commitment (and private water companies are obligated to plan twenty-five years in advance), there is nothing comparable for roads. Glaister (2010) argues that this means that government may effectively have committed long-term funding to rail projects with relatively low benefit-to-cost ratios over a period when budgetary pressures could lead to cuts in the roads programme, crowding out investments that could potentially offer higher returns.

Aviation. In 1986, the Airports Act dissolved the British Airports Authority and redistributed the organization's property, rights and liabilities to a new company, BAA. The company (since renamed Heathrow Airport Holdings Limited) is currently owned by FGP TopCo Limited, an international consortium of companies, pension funds and sovereign wealth funds, led by the Spanish construction firm Ferrovial (Butcher 2012).

The UK's independent aviation sector regulator, the Civil Aviation Authority, is responsible for the price regulation of Heathrow, Gatwick and Stansted airports and the consumer regulation of all UK airports. The Competition Commission is the competition regulator, but it is also involved in price control determinations for the three London airports.

Other Areas

Housing

The undersupply of housing, especially in high-growth areas of the country, has pushed up house prices (Barker 2004). The UK has been incapable of building enough houses to keep up with growing demand. Many of the long-term issues of strategic planning and delivery that this chapter highlights apply equally to housing investment, even though most of that investment is undertaken by private business (see the discussion about housing on page 186).

Broadband

In comparison with other countries, the UK ranks very highly in terms of broadband penetration (subscribers per hundred inhabitants) and price per megabit. However, the UK does poorly in other areas, such as regional differences in broadband access, broadband technology (owing to the low penetration of fibre-optic[18] and wired broadband subscriptions) and low broadband speed.

In particular, the OECD has ranked the UK eighth in its latest (Q4 2011) fixed wired broadband rankings, with 33.3 subscribers per hundred inhabitants, which compares well with the OECD average of 25.6. Bottom was Turkey with a score of just 10.4 (OECD 2012a).

In technology terms, 55.8% of fixed broadband connections in the OECD came from DSL (e.g. ADSL) services, 30% from cable (e.g. Virgin Media) and 13.7% from fibre-optic connections. The UK remains dominated by DSL connections, has a low but increasing number of cable connections (that allow the diffusion of superfast broadband) and has practically no fibre-optic capacity (OECD 2012a). Looking at wireless broadband diffusion among OECD countries, UK is middle ranking, with just over fifty subscriptions per hundred inhabitants. South Korea, Sweden and Finland lead the OECD classification with (on average) more than ninety subscriptions per hundred inhabitants (OECD 2012b).

In September 2011 the average advertised broadband download speed (i.e. not the real-world performance) within OECD countries was 41 Mbps, while that in the UK was 34.4 Mbps.

The UK is improving quickly in terms of the penetration of superfast broadband and in terms of download speeds. Ofcom (2012) found that only 10% of UK connections had fixed broadband speeds under 2 Mbps in 2012—a significant improvement in comparison to the 14% recorded in 2011. Superfast broadband is now available to 65% of UK premises from commercial providers; a consistent increase has been seen from the comparable figure of 46% in 2010 (Ofcom 2012).

Finally, data on internet utilization in the UK economy show very high penetration into household and businesses activities. Compared with other OECD economies, UK households tend to spend more time online ordering or purchasing goods and services (the UK is ranked first among OECD countries in this area, with more than 60% of individuals involved in these activities against the OECD average of 32%), playing and downloading games, music and films, engaging in social networking,

---

[18]Although cable connections are increasing.

communicating, searching for jobs, or using banking services. However, internet utilization for learning and for obtaining information from the websites of public authorities is well below the OECD average. The UK ranked among the top OECD countries in terms of its businesses' broadband connections, their selling/purchasing activities over the internet, what share of their total revenues came from e-commerce, whether they had a website, the share of their employees using an internet-connected computer and completed forms returned to public authorities. Finally, looking at the economy in general, the value added generated by internet-related activities represents a larger share of GDP than in almost any other country (OECD 2012b).

4.5 CAUSES OF UNDERINVESTMENT: RISK AND BIAS

Infrastructure suffers from a series of market failures that impede the optimal level of investment from being reached.[19] What usually sets investment in infrastructure apart from other types of investment is its long-term, capital-intensive nature: it typically generates long-lived assets with high sunk costs. This creates a gulf between (short-term) marginal and (long-term) average costs, which, in turn, creates a time-inconsistency problem. This is particularly severe in the UK as the majority of UK infrastructure is owned and operated by the private sector rather than the public sector, whereas the reverse applies in most other countries. Indeed, private investors will be prepared to put their money into projects only if potential customers agree, through a long-term contract, to buy the output at average cost and refrain from behaving opportunistically if a better offer subsequently comes along. Problems of credible commitment lie at the heart of the appropriate regulatory design of infrastructure policy (Jamison *et al.* 2005).

The need for these long-term contracts is made more pressing by the possibility of technological change leading to obsolescence, which increases fear among potential private investors that an adequate return will not be made on investments.[20] This can be achieved only if investors have a monopoly or if governments, through regulators, guarantee that future costumers will pay a price that reflects average costs.

---

[19]See, for example, Romani *et al.* (2011) for a description of classical market failures in infrastructure investment.

[20]In almost all major network systems this is a real threat. In electricity, smart grids and meters threaten existing assets. In communications, copper wires face threats from new transmission mechanisms, including wireless ones. Both nuclear and wind technologies may have to compete with new cheaper rivals over the next decade or two.

167

Government intervention is also often required to allow for both positive and negative externalities associated with infrastructure projects, e.g. environmental considerations are an increasingly important factor in infrastructure investment decisions.

Historically, attempts to overcome market failures in infrastructure investment have led to state ownership and/or regulatory intervention. This, in turn, has exposed infrastructure investment to important (policy) risks and (decision-making) biases. Problems of underinvestment in infrastructure are strongly related to these risks and biases, resulting in policy uncertainty, complexity and the lack of a holistic strategy, all of which damage investment prospects, primarily in the energy and transport sectors (CBI 2012a).

Political Risk

In attempting to correct various forms of market failure, governments may regulate private service providers (through concessions, public–private partnerships or fully privately owned companies) or provide the service themselves (as a public monopoly). In the first case (which covers the majority of UK infrastructure), governments make choices about types of infrastructure they are prepared to support through long-term contracts, they facilitate planning and licensing and they seek to create a regulatory environment that offers credible commitments to prospective investors (Helm 2010a).

Private infrastructure investment therefore relies on a political rubber stamp: the state is the ultimate guarantor of the regulatory contracts that allow investors to make a return on their assets. The state also controls the planning system, which means that prospective investors have to engage in the political process right from the outset.

The influence of state intervention on the infrastructure investment climate brings with it, in turn, risks that may lead to underinvestment and/or increases in the costs of capital. The customers of regulated utilities are also voters, who potentially have an incentive to lobby politicians to renege on sunk costs (Helm 2010a). Moreover, when public subsidies are involved, infrastructure investments might be exposed to short-sighted political behaviour and short-term political expediency.[21]

---

[21] For example, land transport infrastructure (road and rail) has an economic life of over thirty years. The 10–20-year capital planning and budgeting cycle is incompatible with 7-year business cycles, 3–5-year political cycles and 2–3-year budgetary cycles (OECD 2007a).

It is not enough for governments to set out policy statements: there need to be institutional mechanisms in place that are capable of delivering sustainable policy commitments. The Nordic countries have achieved this through political systems that revolve around a culture that prioritizes consensus. Other countries, such as the UK, where the political system is much more adversarial in nature, lack the institutional arrangements necessary to achieve the same goal: cross-party consensuses that support stable tax, regulatory and planning investment environments.

Sectoral bodies reveal the potential for advisory bodies to provide independent, expert advice on infrastructure issues within a clearly defined framework. Infrastructure Australia, for example, advises the Australian government, investors and infrastructure owners on a wide range of issues, such as

- the country's current and future infrastructure needs, with a focus on the modernization of the nation's economic infrastructure;

- the mechanisms for financing infrastructure investments and unlocking infrastructure bottlenecks; and

- policy, pricing and regulation issues and their impacts on investment and the operation of national infrastructure networks.

Moreover, it conducts audits to determine the adequacy, capacity and condition of nationally significant infrastructure, taking growth forecasts into account. Infrastructure Australia also reviews and provides advice on proposals to facilitate the harmonization of policies (and laws) relating to the development of (and investment in) infrastructure, and it identifies any impediments to investment in nationally significant infrastructure and tries to devise strategies to remove those impediments. Infrastructure Australia reports regularly to the Council of Australian Governments through the Federal Minister for Infrastructure and Transport (see www.infrastructureaustralia.gov.au/about). The composition of Infrastructure Australia reflects the close relationship between central government, local government and businesses, since all of its eleven members are appointed by the Ministry of Infrastructure and Transport from a pool of experts who have acquired the necessary knowledge or experience in the private sector or in local government (Australian Government 2008; Auditor General 2011).

Examples of sectoral bodies that provide independent advice within the UK include

- the National Institute for Health and Clinical Excellence, which has helped to create a better-informed and less-polarized debate around choices concerning health treatments within the NHS;[22]

- the Migration Advisory Committee, which manages the points-based system for immigration;

- the Low Pay Commission, which advises on the minimum wage;

- the National Pay Review Bodies for public sector workers; and

- the Climate Change Committee.

Although some government attempts to mitigate these problems have been undertaken—such as the introduction of National Policy Statements subject to parliamentary votes, the creation of the Infrastructure Planning Unit (already amended by the Localism Act 2011) and the creation of Infrastructure UK[23]—effective institutional arrangements seem to be absent in the UK. Some parts of the transport sector, for example, are known for involving a large number of players with a variety of different powers, responsibilities and agendas. This has led to a number of problems:

- decisions driven by decision makers who have the largest influence (rather than those with the best solution);

- efficient options not being developed or considered; and

- the need to manage the needs of interlinked administrative units, which leads to extra costs and, at times, gridlock during the decision-making process (Eddington Review 2006).[24]

---

[22]The government remains in charge of overall spending rules but no longer directly manages difficult, detailed decisions where clinical expertise is of primary importance.

[23]Infrastructure UK was introduced in 2010 with the role of providing advice on the UK's long-term infrastructure priorities and facilitating private sector investment over the longer term. It is a unit within the Treasury's Enterprise and Growth Directorate and its chief executive is supported by a non-executive chair, Paul Skinner, who chairs Infrastructure UK's advisory council, which is made up of a group of permanent secretaries from the key infrastructure departments as well as senior representatives from the private sector.

[24]For example, the use of Special Parliamentary Procedures (a further process that some orders of various types must undergo in parliament by virtue of provisions in the Planning Act) has been criticized for creating an open-ended time frame at the end of the planning process, so that businesses effectively have no guarantee of when determination will take place (CBI 2012c).

Analytical Risk

Politics and economics interact in complex ways, exerting powerful influences over each other. For infrastructure investments, these interactions represent an additional source of risk—one more possible threat to the clarity and stability of the investment environment.

The last century witnessed a number of changes in political perspectives that have played influential roles in steering the evolution of public economics.[25] For example, a 'pro-market' era of government retreat and deregulation (from the 1970s onwards) replaced an era during which government took an active role in the economy through increasing taxation and public expenditure (after the Second World War). While there were sound economic arguments for the privatization and regulation of the coal, oil, automotive and steel industries, the benefits of rail privatization and regulation were less well defined, and it required much greater care than that the UK experience relied on.

In that period, and partially as a reflection of the experience during it, public economics was marked by an ideological approach based on the presumption that 'markets know best' on both the micro and macro fronts. This approach, rather than one that allows the possibility of improvements through reform,[26] has had too much influence in determining financial deregulation in rich countries, the infrastructure and pension policies of developing countries, and the process of transition in Eastern Europe and the former Soviet Union.

Just as politics influences economic policy, economists also influence political decisions. Changes in economic orthodoxy can have a profound impact on the direction of policy. For example, measuring the net impact of green growth policies requires allowing for distortions originating in market and government failures. Standard models based on 'first-best' assumptions can usefully assess the benchmark costs of these policies but they are unable to investigate the full benefits, such as changes to incentives to innovate (see, for example, Aghion *et al.* 2012). Shifting to cost–benefit analyses that take these externalities into account generates investment opportunities.

---

[25] See Stern (2010, pp. 255–257) for a thorough description of the historical link between policy and economics.

[26] A canonical statement of this is in the work of James Meade. As Stern (2010) notes, the Meadean tradition frames policy design within the context of imperfect frames policy design within the context of imperfect economies.

Policy Bias

The Evaluation Process: Cost–Benefit Analysis

From project conception to delivery, first-rate evaluation is necessary along the infrastructure pipeline to make sensible decisions in the best interest of current and future generations (Henckel and McKibbin 2010). Independent, rigorous evaluation of policy alternatives is an important component of well-informed political debate that is capable of gathering broad, cross-party consensus and underpinning stable, long-term policy orientation.

In practice, evaluation of policy alternatives in government suffers from a number of important weaknesses. Although the existing evidence is limited, it suggests that project appraisal is often exposed to strategic overestimation of benefits and underestimation of costs (see, for example, Ergas and Robson 2009; Flyvbjerg 2009). Most recently, the National Audit Office (2011) has concluded that departments were unable to demonstrate either that government interventions provided value for money or that they provided poor value for money due to the absence of option appraisals. The following main weaknesses were identified.

- Inadequate development of options against which to judge the preferred course of action.
- Lack of monetization of burdens and benefits. Over 40% of those involved in the appraisal process who were surveyed did not agree that sufficient time and effort went into monetizing impacts.
- Unstructured qualitative analysis. While qualitative arguments were influential in a large proportion of cases, few followed guidance on ways to structure that analysis, or applied a qualitative structure consistently to all options considered.

In the same vein, in a recent review of 189 Impact Assessments, the Regulatory Policy Committee (2011) judged 44% of appraisals not fit for purpose.

In interviews given to the National Audit Office:

> [Chief economists] have acknowledged that departments often consider a narrow range of options and noted that promising options are often dismissed too early or discarded options not revisited when a change in scope would again make them viable. They explained that a lack of option development is common in circumstances where ministerial decisions have limited the number of practical solutions.
>
> National Audit Office (2011, p. 14)

The limitations of project evaluation are not confined to the idiosyncrasies of government, but rather extend to the instruments that analysts have at their disposal to conduct such evaluation. Cost–benefit analysis is the centrepiece of the economist's appraisal toolkit. It is often seen as a tried and tested methodology: it has a relatively well-established body of theory underpinning it, as well as a long list of practical applications. Less well known and debated, however, are its limitations. Dynamic gains, costs and risks, for example, are not usually part of project evaluation. Analysis of important—but theoretically and empirically difficult—social, environmental and economic impacts is often omitted (Romani *et al*. 2011).

A number of experiments that warrant further exploration are underway in OECD countries. These include the use of qualitative multi-criteria analyses to complement standard cost–benefit analysis, and models that compare *ex ante* (i.e. during the decision-making phase) and *ex post* (i.e. after a project's completion) evaluations in order to determine whether the investment's targets have been met (this is a common practice at the World Bank and, more recently, at the European Commission) (Pellegrin and Sirtori 2012).

Limitations of the Planning System and Compensation Mechanisms

Prior to 2008, the British planning process for applications to build nationally significant infrastructure was slow and complex. The consent procedure for major infrastructure projects required a public inquiry. Despite attempts to improve procedures, public inquiries remained notoriously long-winded for controversial cases. For example, Heathrow's Terminal 5 experienced the longest public inquiry in UK planning history and it ultimately took over fifteen years for the terminal to be completed. This stands in marked contrast to France's Charles de Gaulle airport, which constructed four runways and five terminals in twenty years (Corry *et al*. 2012).

Following a public inquiry, the inspector would make a recommendation to the Secretary of State. The Secretary of State genuinely had the last word, and could reject the recommendation provided that (s)he gave reasons. There was no provision for a parliamentary vote—the statements just had to be tabled. That meant that a subsequent government could simply reverse a policy by inserting the word 'not' for a specific project, leading to stranded sunk costs.

In an effort to address this problem, the Planning Act 2008 created a two-tier planning system, thus bringing England and Wales in line with their European neighbours: smaller infrastructure projects and housing construction remained under the jurisdiction of local authorities and the National Planning Policy Framework, while national infrastructure projects were removed from the control of the Town and Country Planning system and placed within a streamlined national scheme, first under the Infrastructure Planning Commission and subsequently administered by the Planning Inspectorate (an executive agency of the Department of Communities and Local Government and the Welsh government).[27]

The Planning Act 2008 introduced new National Policy Statements (NPSs) and provided for a new Infrastructure Planning Commission (IPC) to provide 'development consent' for Nationally Significant Infrastructure Projects (NSIPs).[28]

The Secretary of State would no longer have the final word. Instead, the government would publish an NPS covering that type of infrastructure. The IPC would take its decision largely on the basis of that NPS, using its time to consider points specific to the particular application. NPSs would be published in draft, for consultation and parliamentary scrutiny by a report from a Select Committee, and the amount of policy continuity might increase because the ability of policies to be changed with each new parliament would be limited.[29]

However, political pressures could still bleed through into the planning process and affect the way in which decisions on NSIP applications are made. The NPSs were created within the current parliamentary framework and were subject to a series of other legislative processes and government initiatives (in the form of other white papers and bills). Consequently, the remit of a particular NPS would be subject to the specificity of the government. This, in turn, would influence how the IPC assessed NSIP applications.

---

[27]As described in the section on policy risk, some experts fear that the change imposed by the Planning Act 2008 increases the possibility of politicized or vote-motive lobbying because of the reintroduction of a ministerial decision-making role.

[28]The NPSs give explanations for each proposed policy contained in the statement, and they include an explanation of how the policy relates to the mitigation of, and adaptation to, climate change. The sixteen specified types of NSIPs are electricity-generating projects, overhead electric lines, underground gas storage, liquefied natural gas facilities, gas reception facilities, gas pipelines, other pipelines, highways, airports, harbours, railways, rail freight interchanges, dams/reservoirs, water transfer facilities, waste water treatment plants and hazardous waste facilities. The Planning Regime applies to NSIPs, which require a type of consent known as 'development consent.'

[29]Given their infancy, the exact impact of the NPS in reducing policy risk is still unknown. Rosewell (2012) argues that the nuclear NPS is the only NPS that is being actively used. One argument against their widespread use is their lack of clarity.

Under the Localism Act 2011, the coalition government scrapped a significant part of the 2008 act. The IPC functions were transferred to a new National Infrastructure Directorate within the Planning Inspectorate,[30] part of the Department of Communities and Local Government. While the Planning Inspectorate does not comment on government policy, it continues to make recommendations within the framework provided by the NPSs. It retained the idea of the NPS in order to facilitate the development consent procedure for major infrastructure, and introduced the requirement of a vote in favour by parliament before they are designated as NPSs by the Secretary of State (whose power to interfere with the process was unfortunately reinstated).

While the new system is still in its infancy, it does on paper seem to balance national and local needs better. The Planning Inspectorate has a specified time frame to work with: three months from the application being made to establish the process, six months to consider evidence, and three more months to make a recommendation. The government then has three months to make a decision.

Despite the reforms and suggested time frame, several factors contribute to the continued inefficiency of the planning process.

First, the British planning system continues to rest on a process of 'development control', where the supply of land for each legally defined use is controlled by the planning system. As a result, uses are themselves legally defined. Thus specific planning permission from the planning authority is required to convert land that is designated for agricultural use to housing use. This has led to an inefficient planning system characterized by discrete, stochastic decisions subject to appeal.

Second, there is concern that despite the intention of streamlining infrastructure applications, a Special Parliamentary Procedure that has been retained in the Planning Act for certain types of land[31] could act in competition to the new Planning Inspectorate and more than double the decision time of affected projects, increasing uncertainty and damaging investor confidence (CBI 2012c). In its 2012 budget, the government announced that it would remove duplication by adjusting the scope of the Special Parliamentary Procedure.

---

[30]In England, the Planning Inspectorate examines applications for the energy, transport, waste, waste water and water sectors. In Wales, it examines applications for energy and harbour development, subject to detailed provisions in the act; remaining matters are under the remit of Welsh ministers.

[31]The Special Parliamentary Procedure applies to open space land that was not being replaced, National Trust land, and land belonging to local authorities or statutory undertakers (i.e. utilities) where that body had objected to their land being taken.

And finally, many infrastructure projects that fall below the threshold of an NSIP but are clearly part of the national infrastructure, such as rail depots and wind farms, remain under control of local authorities. In a further attempt to streamline and simplify the planning process, the Department of Communities and Local Government introduced the National Planning Policy Framework in 2012 for smaller infrastructure projects and housing construction.[32] Despite these reforms, English planning authorities following National Planning Policy Framework guidelines are quasi-political bodies operating at a district level, and they are still therefore vulnerable to pressure from local interests.

The Traditional Approach to Compensation: Communal Compensation

There is a fundamental misalignment between the geographically concentrated costs of a major infrastructure development and the benefits that accrue to a larger outside population from that project. This leads to further delays within the planning process.

The Thames Tideway project is a perfect example of infrastructure planning that has experienced delays due to a lack of recognition of the asymmetric benefits and costs of development. Though the Greater London Authority has supported the development on a London-wide basis, many of the borough councils along the proposed route have fought against the project due to local perception of the disruption caused during a five-year construction phase.

There are various strategies that could be used to handle the problems of 'potential losers', such as citizens who will lose access to a desirable local environment and encounter lower property values due to the development of a nearby airport or rail line (Aldrich 2007). A classic non-coercive approach to the problem is a mechanism whereby potential losers can be paid compensation in order to avert or reduce objection, whether those losers are individual citizens who face having an incinerator in their backyard or whether they are corporations that have to spend more on reducing emissions (Frey *et al.* 1996; O'Hare 2010). For more detail on the theory of compensation, see appendix 4B.

In the UK, the traditional method of compensation for those affected by development has been one of communal compensation to larger communities. This has been in the form of Planning Obligations under Section 106 of the Town and Country Planning Act 1990. Section 106

---

[32]The guidance in the National Planning Policy Framework runs to just over 50 pages and replaces over 1,300 pages of guidance and policy contained in forty-four separate documents.

agreements were designed with the intention of ensuring that developers would contribute to the costs of developing local infrastructure, open spaces or affordable housing. Section 106 agreements have been criticized for being highly dependent on the skills of the negotiators involved and for causing lengthy delays due to the time taken to finalize agreements. Only 6% of all planning permissions generated a contribution to local infrastructure. Since 2010, planning policy has marginalized Section 106 agreements in favour of other measures.

The Planning Act 2008 introduced the Community Infrastructure Levy (CIL) as a charge by a local authority on developers and is intended to compensate local authorities for the additional costs that are attached to new development, and to incentivize councils to approve new developments. The money can be used to support development by funding infrastructure in the local interest. The CIL is only charged on buildings to which the public generally have access. As of August 2012, there were forty-eight CIL-charging authorities that had published CIL charging plans, with six of those authorities already charging the levy and a further three authorities due to commence charging by the end of the year.

The CIL, like Section 106 agreements, provides funds for community services and thus does not fully address the asymmetric distribution of benefits and costs associated with development. It does not directly compensate local residents for the loss of asset value or amenity.[33] The CIL focuses on compensating the local authority for the wider infrastructure costs but overlooks costs to the existing local population, who are the individuals who perceive themselves as having the most to lose from development and those likely to create political and legal obstacles to it. Moreover, as only developments that are regularly accessed by the public are liable to pay the CIL, infrastructure such as wind turbines and sewage works are not liable to pay the levy and to therefore offer some community benefit.

In the current UK system, monetary compensation directed at individuals is widely viewed as inadequate. The Land Compensation Act 1973 focuses mainly on assessed market value for compulsory purchase (where compensation is paid at the open value of the property) and exclusively on physical damage and major disturbance from public works (such

---

[33]This point was reiterated in a report by Policy Exchange that further highlighted that a major problem with the CIL is that it misaligns incentives for developers, planners and the local population: 'Despite the size of these [community level] incentives, they did not spur enough building: the benefits were spread too thinly across the local authority as a whole, rather than concentrated on those who had been affected by development' (Morton 2011).

as road building or airport construction), thus excluding house building and loss of value as a result of loss of access to open space or views. This feeds into a highly bureaucratic process in which compensation takes a long time to be settled and paid.

International Examples of Successful Compensation

A variety of schemes to determine and to pay monetary compensation have been put forward, including structured negotiations with a designated body that represents community-level interests, an auction of the facility to the site willing to accept the smallest compensation payment, further investment in infrastructure, medical facilities or in-kind nature restoration, and lump-sum tax refunds.

There is support for the view that monetary compensation can be effective: in a review on compensation schemes for noxious facilities, economic incentives are found to be helpful for the cases of low- or moderate-risk sites such as waste landfill sites and prisons (Kunreuther and Easterling 1996). O'Hare (1977) has stated that the failure in practice to convince locals to accept controversial infrastructure developments is a strategic problem resulting from 'failure to pay compensation to neighbours who suffer costs'.

On the other hand, several authors find that, rather than monetary compensation, good relations with communities, the involvement of community members and persuasion skills are the most important factors at play. Based on survey data in Switzerland, Frey et al. (1996) find that residents consider health and safety as inherent rights that should never be traded and that compensation schemes based solely on price incentives are rarely successful. Therefore, people do not increase their propensity to accept hazardous facilities even if economic incentives are offered. Moreover, pure financial compensation has a disappointing track record, at least in the context of facilities that threaten health or injury risk.

The implication of this is that success in the face of opposition cannot be achieved by any single administrative device. A combination of monetary and non-monetary incentives will usually be needed to elicit support (Carnes et al. 1983).

Compensation schemes from France and the Netherlands indicate that effective use of compensation techniques can shift attitudes and give residents and communities a stronger incentive to support development.

The French planning system is widely regarded as more successful than the UK system for driving development. There are generous compensation schemes in France designed to provide incentives for residents affected by development. For example, in order to avoid delays and political conflict when Charles de Gaulle airport was built, the French Prime Minister authorized payments of four times the estimated market value for affected local residents who voluntarily sold their land. While compensation is primarily provided at community level through levies on developers, the major difference between the UK and French planning systems is the closeness of the *commune* to local residents. French communes number 36,000, while England has just 326 local authority planning bodies. In France, communes are intimate enough to allow a series of developer-funded compensation schemes to make a difference to public attitudes, while in England local authorities are too large and the fruits of any developer payments too removed to generate the same effect.

Holland has the highest levels of population density in Europe and has been highlighted by the International Academic Association of Planning, Law and Property as having one of the most pro-development planning systems in the world. Cash compensation is available to individual residents who are affected by planning decisions. Such compensation is determined by independent experts at the time that planning is approved. Compensation is paid by the local authority, but in practice there are voluntary agreements with developers who reimburse the municipalities for these costs. With major infrastructure projects it is the central government that is responsible for paying out the compensation.

Ongoing Efforts to Improve Compensation

There have recently been a number of positive initiatives in the UK that have moved compensation schemes closer to the best practice described in the previous section.

For example, across the construction sector it is normal practice for voluntary compensation mechanisms to be established by developers. Property Market Bond schemes have been advanced by BAA: local residents who will potentially be impacted are issued with bonds to the value of pre-development property prices. These will be redeemed by the developer in exchange for property if the property fails to sell on the open market.

Moreover, to accompany the development of the High Speed 2 rail route between London, the Midlands and the north of England, the Department for Transport has stated that compensation will be 'significantly beyond statutory requirements'. As of October 2012, the compensation package is valued at £1.3 billion (more details can be found in box 4.1).

Box 4.1. High Speed 2 compensation. (*Source*: Department for Transport (2012a).)

The Property and Compensation Consultation for HS2 between London and the West Midlands has put forward a series of proposals.

- A system of advanced and voluntary purchase to provide greater ease and certainty for those in and immediately outside the safeguarded area.

- A sale and rent-back scheme to allow homeowners whose property will need to be demolished to sell their homes but continue to live in them up until the accompanying land is required.

- A hardship scheme to help those outside the safeguarded area and the voluntary purchase zone who need to move during the development of HS2 but are unable to sell their home.

- A series of schemes aimed at maintaining confidence in properties above tunnels.

- A framework for working with local stakeholders to design a strategy to replace any social rented housing that is lost during the process.

Public Accounting

Public sector net debt (PSND) is one of the key public sector finance statistics used by the Treasury to manage and monitor fiscal policy and by the Office for Budget Responsibility to forecast and evaluate the path of public finances.[34] It is based on information reported in the UK National Accounts, produced by the ONS following an accrual accounting procedure.

PSND measures how much the UK public sector owes at a given point in time. When the government borrows money—or increases its financial liabilities through other channels—it raises the country's debt level. Net debt, for the purposes of UK fiscal policy, is defined as total gross financial liabilities less liquid financial assets. Liquid assets include cash and short-term assets that can be converted into cash at short notice and without significant loss. They mainly comprise foreign exchange reserves and bank deposits. Since the National Accounts measure only

---

[34] Another measure used by the current government for its fiscal policy is the Surplus on Current Budget, i.e. a measure of the amount by which current receipts are greater than current expenditure after allowing for depreciation.

financial liabilities and liquid assets, tangible and intangible assets are not included. Net additions of fixed assets are treated as capital spending in the National Accounts and they contribute to Public Sector Net Borrowing, which is the difference between total accrued expenditure (both current and capital) and total accrued revenue (or receipts).

PSND does not distinguish between economic stimuli that increase consumption and debt liabilities and those that increase productive investment and add (or prevent the depreciation of) assets to balance the liabilities issued. As a result, if a government created assets that improved growth and generated higher value than debt, it would improve the public sector balance sheet but would not reduce PSND. This emphasis on debt—without adequately accounting for assets—imposes constraints on rational decision making (Newbery 2012). The failure to use proper public accounting methods makes public investment (e.g. in road maintenance) look artificially expensive and hampers good decision making. It is like judging a firm solely on its profit and loss account while ignoring its balance sheet.

Positive steps in the direction of adequately accounting for the value of assets have been taken through the development of Whole of Government Accounts (WGA): a consolidated set of financial statements for the UK public sector.[35] WGA is based on EU-adopted International Financial Reporting Standards, the system of accounts used internationally by the private sector and adapted for the public sector context.[36] The closest equivalent to PSND in the WGA is the so-called Net Balance Sheet Position. The latter is a broader measure of the public sector's balance sheet, including a wider range of both assets (fixed assets and all financial assets) and liabilities (Daffin and Hobbs 2011; Office for Budget Responsibility 2012).

---

[35]The WGA covers the financial statements of central government departments, local authorities, devolved administrations, the health service, academies and public corporations. However, not all government bodies take part in the WGA. In particular Network Rail, further education colleges, some academies, some local authority school buildings and the banks (such as RBS) that are fully owned by the Treasury are not included. The Bank of England and the Bank of England Asset Purchase Facility Fund were included in the 2010–11 WGA but were excluded from the 2009–10 one. All private finance initiative projects, which are required under accounting standards to be recognized in the account, are included in the WGA (see the National Audit Office FAQs at www.nao.org.uk/highlights/whole-of-government-accounts/ and Morse (2011)). In terms of its content, the WGA does not include everything that accounting standards require, and this has been a concern voiced by the Comptroller and the Auditor General.

[36]See Morse (2011) for an international comparison of WGA-equivalent accounts.

Figure 4.1. A new institutional architecture for infrastructure.

To date, the WGAs have not been used as the basis of fiscal policy targets.

4.6 CORE POLICY RECOMMENDATIONS

Core Recommendations on Infrastructure

The persistent failure of infrastructure policy in the UK requires us to look for a new approach. Our main proposal is for a new architecture to govern infrastructure strategy, delivery and financing that would facilitate long-term planning and reduce policy instability in those critical areas.

Our proposal has three core institutions (see figure 4.1).

- An Infrastructure Strategy Board (ISB) to provide strategic vision in all areas: its key function being to provide independent expert advice on infrastructure issues. It would lay the foundation for a well-informed, cross-party consensus to underpin stable long-term policy. The ISB would support evidence gathering from experts and operate thorough, transparent and wide-ranging public consultations, engaging interested parties and members of the public in the debate over the costs and benefits of policy options. The ISB would obtain its authority from, and be accountable to, parliament. Its mandate would be laid down by statute. As a standing body, it would produce regular reports on infrastructure needs and long-term priorities and challenges. The ISB would be governed by a high-profile,

independent management board, which would be directly accountable to and appointed by parliament.

- An Infrastructure Planning Commission (IPC), which would be
charged with delivering on the ISB's strategic priorities. This body
existed in the recent past. It has now been replaced by the Infrastructure Planning Unit under the auspices of the Department for
Communities and Local Government. This change reintroduced
ministerial approval for projects and we believe that independence
from ministerial decision making should be restored. The IPC is
designed to give predictability and effectiveness to (mostly private)
investment that drives implementation of strategy. It must not be
misunderstood as a 'central planner'.

- An Infrastructure Bank (IB) to facilitate the provision of stable, long-
term, predictable, mostly private sector finance for infrastructure.
There are good theoretical reasons for the creation of such a bank:
it can help to overcome key market failures in capital markets in
a direct and constructive way. In particular, it can help to reduce
policy risk and, through partnerships, to structure finance in a way
that mitigates and shares risk efficiently. This will require a whole
range of financial instruments including equity and structured guarantees. There are good practical examples that show the advantages of a bank with this sort of mandate, such as Brazil's BNDES,
Germany's Kreditanstalt für Wiederaufbau (KfW) and the European
Bank for Reconstruction and Development (and, to some extent,
the European Investment Bank). The IB would develop banking and
sector-specific skills in new and important areas. It would use its
special ability to make investments that could then provide powerful examples with catalytic effects on private investment through
its partnerships. It could have a very strong multiplicative impact
so that its investments have effects much larger than the amount
of capital it puts in. The IB would be governed by an independent
board with a clearly defined mandate and access to capital markets.
See chapter 5 for further details.

We need to institute generous compensation schemes to extend the benefits of infrastructure projects to those who might otherwise stand to
lose, either due to disruption caused by the construction phase or by
the long-term impact on land and/or property values. The principle is
to share the broad value that the implementation of the national strategy will bring. Such compensation schemes should be enshrined in law
and built into the thinking of the ISB and the operations of the IPC. At

present, the UK does not provide adequate compensation for individuals who bear the costs of development. This contrasts with other countries, where mandatory compensation due to noise, travel or other disruptions, for example, is commonplace. The UK's problem arises partly because the level of compensation is low and partly because existing compensation schemes are primarily communal. Both communal and individual schemes are necessary.

Our proposed infrastructure institutions would facilitate long-term planning and reduce policy instability in the planning, delivery and financing of an infrastructure strategy for the UK. The new institutional architecture would allow government to choose its priorities and decide on strategy. But, crucially, it would ensure that political decisions are taken in the right place, that they do not expand to aspects of strategy and/or implementation where they add little value and can be a costly source of instability (e.g. planning), and that they represent credible commitments for current and prospective investors. In addition, the new framework would support a political debate informed by rigorous, independent assessment of policy alternatives, fostering the formation of cross-party consensus where possible, making political procrastination harder and thus generally improving the quality of policymaking.

The projects considered by the Infrastructure Strategy Board, delivered by the Infrastructure Planning Commission and financed by the Infrastructure Bank would be those of highest national priority, such as ones in roads, aviation and energy. But the programme of work could also be responsive to large-scale regional project infrastructure proposals from outside parliament. For example, local enterprise partnerships (collaborations of businesses, local authorities and other groups in an economically meaningful unit) may put together a bid for building a cluster of science parks, which would involve spending on transport, buildings, energy and telecoms.

Allowing such sub-national bids would ensure a more bottom-up approach to major regional projects that involve strategic thinking. This would help to use more local initiative and decentralized information than would be available at a national level. The abolition of Regional Development Agencies and regional offices has left a strategic planning vacuum between the national level and the very micro-level (districts). Indeed, the institutions that support regional economic development in England are a classic example of policy instability, being the subject of numerous reforms, often with radical policy swings following national elections.

Box 4.2. An example of how our infrastructure proposals would help the impasse over the shortfall in runway capacity in the southeast.

The ISB would be a permanent, dedicated source of independent and analytically robust advice that would help to align political views. If it already existed, it would have avoided the need to set up the Davies Commission to investigate the problem again from scratch. The expansion of Heathrow has already been discussed by numerous other inquiries (e.g. the 1968 Roskill Commission). Rigorous information about the costs and benefits of different policy options would have been available from a team of experts long immersed in the strengths and weaknesses of the existing evidence.

The IPC would operate under the rules defined by NPSs like those currently used. It would ensure that planning is not used to reopen political debates every step of the way while implementing policy. The IPC would deal with the ensuing planning practicalities: namely, reviewing and deciding on specific applications for development consent. It would also decide about compensating those who stood to lose from the expansion of an existing airport or the building of a new one, following a set of clear rules enshrined in law. This would help to mitigate political bickering and deliver transparent and predictable planning decisions.

Other Ways of Supporting Infrastructure Investment

Public Sector Accounts

Public investment should not be hamstrung by accounting methods that impede a focus on economic returns. Therefore, for fiscal targets to be useful as a strategic management tool, they should incorporate the value of public sector assets rather than concentrating solely on public sector debt. Otherwise there is no distinction between extra borrowing to finance consumption and borrowing to finance investment in new assets or to repair existing assets. The failure to use proper public accounting methods makes public investment (e.g. in road maintenance) look artificially expensive and hampers good decision making. It is like judging a firm solely on its profit and loss account while ignoring its balance sheet. The UK is leading efforts to improve public sector accounts (for example, through the publication of Whole of Government Accounts). It is time for government to use these new accounts as the basis for policymaking.

Road Pricing

Road pricing is an idea whose time has come. There are no major technological impediments to a system that would manage congestion, be fairer and improve incentives for road building and maintenance. To the extent that there are political impediments with moving to comprehensive road pricing, these can be overcome in the longer term. A new regulator should administer the system following a regulatory asset base model: an approach that has proved to be successful in other areas of infrastructure. By creating dedicated revenue streams, this would help to provide a long-term solution to the problem of road investment, maintenance and financing. Road pricing could be made attractive to the electorate by accompanying its introduction with a cut in fuel duty, as a large component of the tax is currently rationalized by the need to limit congestion. In some circumstances, national roads (operated by the Highways Agency) could be auctioned off and shadow tolls introduced in this section of the road network.

Housing

The ISB and IPC should also take responsibility for long-term strategy and delivery of housing throughout the UK where this is naturally complementary with infrastructure goals. Schemes to increase the amount of land available for development need to overcome local resistance. Institutionalizing a flexible system of compensation for those who stand to lose from new developments is important: for example, via funding local amenities, reductions in council tax payments or straightforward cash payments. Appropriately generous compensation schemes should, in particular, help to diminish local opposition to development.

Broadband

With regards to telecoms, broadband plays an increasingly important role in connectivity. But the UK's broadband infrastructure is not outstanding compared with that in other countries. The UK typically ranks in the middle of the table in terms of raw broadband performance and deployment (including broadband speed and network coverage). But compared with other advanced economies, we tend to spend more time online, buy more online and the value added generated by internet-related activities represents a larger share of GDP than in almost any other country (OECD 2012b). To continue taking advantage of the extraordinary opportunities that the internet offers, we must continue to be prepared to respond flexibly and promptly to a rapidly changing technological environment. Again, the institutional architecture we propose could help with problems here as they arise.

Appendix 4A: Road Pricing

There is evidence to suggest that the gradual introduction of a road regulator to administer a regulatory asset base model in the road sector would provide a long-term solution to the problem of road investment, maintenance and financing (see, for example, Glaister 2010).

Several academics have argued that the regulatory model that works well for profitable privatized networks—which has led to significant improvements in efficiency, investment levels and quality—would work well for the public, but potentially profitable, road network. This regulatory regime sets price limits based on periodic reviews of investment requirements, efficiency and outputs (Glaister 2010; Helm *et al.* 2009). Consequently, companies—who must operate under a licence, which defines a range of supply and conduct requirements—are forced to guarantee their ability to properly finance their functions.

In a series of recommendations for generating long-term funding, Glaister (2010) suggests creating a regulated private utility with shadow tolls or with direct road user charges. Unlike in France and Italy, among other countries, direct charges in the UK are limited to the M6 Toll Road north of Birmingham and a handful of bridges. Some English roads, such as the M40, are currently provided and maintained under a system of shadow tolls, where a private contractor receives payment from government based on the extent of utilization. This goes unseen by road users and does not therefore influence their behaviour.

Crafts (2009) argues that road pricing is potentially a more efficient solution to combating road congestion than a large road-building programme, and tolling portions of the existing road network could deliver increases in productivity for the transport-using sector. The Eddington Review (2006) notes that resources need to be directed towards improving the performance of the existing network since the UK is already well connected. Benefits of increasing the usage of road-pricing schemes include spreading demand, minimizing congestion and overcrowding, improving reliability and delivering benefits to the wider economy. A road-pricing scheme that varies costs according to location and time of the day would help to reflect the full societal costs of transportation and could generate benefits of up to £28 billion by 2025 (based on modelling work within the review). The Eddington Review (2006) cites the area-based congestion charging scheme in central London as an example of a success: since its introduction in 2003, Transport for London estimates that traffic levels within the charging zone have decreased by 15%, congestion levels have fallen by 26% and average traffic speed within the zone has increased by an estimated 2 km per hour.

APPENDIX 4B: THEORY OF COMPENSATION

The traditional economic view posits that opposition by local residents rests on a misalignment between geographically concentrated costs and benefits that are distributed to a larger outside population. Several price-based compensation schemes have been developed to deal with appropriately redistributing the aggregate net benefits to ensure that the host communities receive positive net benefits.

In reality, however, compensation schemes based purely on price incentives have seen mixed results. Many authors argue that the traditional economic theory of compensation is incomplete in important aspects because it neglects the influence of moral principles. In the sphere of politics, where planning battles are typically fought, such moral considerations dampen the effects of price incentives (Frey *et al.* 1996).

Designing Schemes to Share the Benefits

Roughly speaking, there are two strands of empirical research in this area (Coursey and Kim 1997).

The first strand of research emphasizes the importance of psychological and communicational factors rather than of compensation for the loss caused by a policy that creates losers and winners. An extreme in this strand is 'crowding-out theory', which argues that offering financial incentives for hosting a hazardous site reduces citizens' willingness to permit the construction of a noxious facility.

The second strand concerns how to apply and design compensation schemes (Kunreuther *et al.* 1987; Sullivan 1992; Richardson and Kunreuther 1993; Kleindorfer and Sertel 1994). For example, the 2006 United Nations Environment Programme Compensation Policy Issue examined compensation schemes for dams, classifying them into four main categories: (i) monetary compensation for lost assets and loss of access to resources; (ii) livelihood restoration and enhancement; (iii) community development (which includes local infrastructure and financing development); and (iv) nearby nature development.

A variety of schemes for spreading the benefits of development have been proposed (O'Hare *et al.* 1983; Kunreuther and Kleindorfer 1986; Deshpande and Elmendorf 2008), including

- structured negotiations with a designated community body,
- an auction of the facility to an area willing to accept the smallest compensation payment,
- further investment in infrastructure,
- lump-sum tax refunds and
- conditional guarantees, such as property value insurance.

Compensation in the form of property value insurance may be offered to individuals affected by the construction of a transportation link, such as a highway or rail line: a homeowner displaced by noise can avoid any financial losses that occur should his home suffer a loss in property value.

O'Hare (2010) writes that a sincere and credible attempt to compensate affected individuals when they accommodate a socially beneficial project is a necessary beginning, though not the end, of local opposition conflict resolution.

Effectiveness

Existing empirical evidence is conflicted as to whether or not compensation has been effective in reducing the level of opposition to infrastructure projects (White and Ratick 1989; Frey *et al.* 1996; Jenkins *et al.* 2004; Gallagher *et al.* 2008):

Several authors find that good relations with communities, the involvement of community members and persuasion skills are the most important factors when it comes to resolving planning conflict (Kasperson *et al.* 1992; Petts 1992). Based on survey data from Switzerland, Frey *et al.* (1996) find that residents consider health and safety as rights that should never be traded and that compensatory procedures purely based on price incentives are rarely successful. Therefore, people do not increase their propensity to accept hazardous facilities in their communities even if economic incentives are offered. Portney (1991) reports that US states that rely on compensation-based development have experienced no greater success than those using other methods. Moreover, pure financial compensation has a disappointing track record, at least in the context of facilities that threaten health or injury risk (O'Hare 2010).

There is, however, support for the view that monetary compensation can be effective: in a review of compensation schemes for noxious facilities, Coursey and Kim (1997) found that economic incentives were helpful in the case of low- or moderate-risk sites, such as waste landfill sites, incinerators and prisons.

This implies that success in the face of opposition cannot be achieved by any single device, especially cash payments (Frey and Oberholzer-Gee 1996; Frey *et al.* 1996; Gibson 2005; Hermansson 2007; Schively 2007). A compensation mechanism must be viewed as just one component in the overall strategy for dealing with opposition to development (Kunreuther *et al.* 1987). One needs to view citizens and stakeholders as optimizing something more complicated than wealth, or even wealth plus some money equivalent of expected health (O'Hare 2010). Rather, incentive packages consisting of monetary and non-monetary incentives may be just as important in eliciting support as single monetary incentives, if not more so (Carnes *et al.* 1983).

REFERENCES

Aghion, P., A. Dechezlepetre, D. Hemous, R. Martin and J. Van Reenen. 2012. Carbon taxes, path dependency and directed technical change: evidence from the auto industry. Discussion Paper 1178, Centre for Economic Performance. Available at http://cep.lse.ac.uk/pubs/download/dp1178.pdf.

Aldrich, D. P. 2007. Handling the 'biggest losers': compensation in entrepreneurial politics. Occasional Working Paper, Program on US–Japan Relations.

Aschauer, D. 1989. Is public expenditure productive? *Journal of Monetary Economics* **23**, 177–200.

Auditor General. 2011. Performance audit: conduct by Infrastructure Australia of the First National Infrastructure Audit and Development of the Infrastructure Priority List Infrastructure Australia. Audit Report 2, 2010–11.

Australian Government. 2008. Infrastructure Australia Act 2008. An Act to Establish Infrastructure Australia and the Infrastructure Coordinator, and For Related Purposes.

Barker, K. 2004. *Barker Review of Housing Supply*. HM Treasury (March).

Bowen, A., and J. Rydge. 2011. Climate change policy in the United Kingdom. Working Paper 886, OECD Economics Department.

Butcher, L. 2012. Aviation: London Heathrow Airport. Standard Note SN1136, House of Commons Library (July).

Calderón, C., E. Moral-Benito and L. Servén. 2011. Is infrastructure capital productive? A dynamic heterogeneous approach. Policy Research Working Paper 5682, World Bank.

Carnes, S. A., E. D. Copenhaver, J. H. Sorenson, E. J. Soderstrom, J. H. Reed, D. J. Bjornstad and E. Peele. 1983. Incentives and nuclear waste siting: prospects and constraints. *Energy Systems and Policy* **7**(4), 324–351.

CBI. 2012a. Budget 2012 analysis. Report, Confederation of British Industry (March).

CBI. 2012b. The colours of growth: maximising the potential of green business. Report, Confederation of British Industry (July).

CBI. 2012c. Minor measures, major results. Report, Confederation of British Industry (March).

Chan, C., D. Forwood, H. Roper and C. Sayers. 2009. Public infrastructure financing: an international perspective. Staff Working Paper, Productivity Commission.

Committee on Climate Change. 2010. Committee on Climate Change annual report and accounts 2009–2010.

Committee on Climate Change. 2012. Committee on Climate Change corporate plan 2012-15.

Corry, M., G. Mather and D. Smith. 2012. Compensating for development: how to unlock Britain's town and country planning system. Report, The Infrastructure Forum (August).

Coursey, D., and S. Kim. 1997. *An Examination of Compensation Mechanisms to Solve the NIMBY Problem*. University of Chicago Press.

Crafts, N. 2009. Transport infrastructure in investment: implications for growth and productivity. *Oxford Review of Economic Policy* **25**(3), 327–343.

Daffin, C., and D. Hobbs. 2011. Comparison of public sector finance measures from the national accounts and whole of government accounts. Report, National Audit Office.

Deloitte. 2012. Policy essentials: cost–benefit analysis. Report, Business Council of Australia.

Department for Transport. 2008. Annual report 2008 (May).

Department for Transport. 2012a. Property and compensation consultation (London to the West Midlands).

Department for Transport. 2012b. Road transport forecasts 2011 (January).

Deshpande, M., and D. W. Elmendorf. 2008. An economic strategy for investing in America's infrastructure. Hamilton Project Strategy Paper, The Brookings Institution.

Deutsche Bank Research. 2011. Smart grids: energy rethink requires intelligent electricity networks (July).

Eddington Review. 2006. *The Eddington Transport Study. The Case for Action: Sir Rod Eddington's Advice to Government*. Department for Transport.

Egert, B., T. Kozluk and D. Sutherland. 2009a. Infrastructure and growth: empirical evidence. Working Paper 685, OECD Economics Department (March).

Egert, B., T. Kozluk and D. Sutherland. 2009b. Infrastructure investment: links to growth and the role of public policies. Working Paper 686, OECD Economics Department (March).

Energy UK. 2012. Powering the UK: investing for the future of the energy sector and the UK. Joint publication with Ernst and Young.

Ergas, H., and A. Robson. 2009. Evaluating major infrastructure projects: how robust are our processes? Productivity Commission Round Table.

Esfahani, H. S., and M. T. Ramírez. 2003. Institutions, infrastructure, and economic growth. *Journal of Development Economics* **70**, 443–477.

Flyvbjerg, B. 2009. Optimism and misrepresentation in early project development. In *Making Essential Choices with Scant Information* (ed. T. M. Williams *et al.*). London: Palgrave.

Frey, B. S., and F. Oberholzer-Gee. 1996. Fair siting procedures: an empirical analysis of their importance and characteristics. *Journal of Policy Analysis and Management* **15**(3), 353–376.

Frey, B. S., F. Oberholzer-Gee and R. Eichenberger. 1996. The Old Lady visits your backyard: a tale of morals and markets. *Journal of Political Economy* **104**(6), 1297–1313.

Gallagher, L., S. Ferreira and F. Convery. 2008. Host community attitudes towards solid waste landfills infrastructure: comprehension before compensation. *Journal of Environmental Planning and Management* **51**(2), 233–257.

Gibson, T. A. 2005. NIMBY and the civic good. *City and Community* **4**(4), 381–401.

Glaister, S. 2010. Governing and paying for England's roads. Report, RAC Foundation (July).

Graham, D. 2007. Agglomeration, productivity, and transport investment. *Journal of Transport Economics and Policy* **41**, 1–27.

Gramlich, E. 1994. Infrastructure investment: a review essay. *Journal of Economic Literature* **32**(3), 1176–1196.

Greenpeace. 2011. Battle of the grids: how Europe can go 100 per cent renewable and phase out dirty energy. Report.

Helm, D. 2009. Infrastructure investment, the cost of capital, and regulation: an assessment. *Oxford Review of Economic Policy* **25**(3), 307–326.

Helm, D. 2010a. Infrastructure and infrastructure finance: the role of the government and the private sector in the current world. *EIB Papers* **15**(2), 8–27.

Helm, D. 2010b. Market reform: rationale, options and implementation. Policy Paper (October). Available at www.dieterhelm.co.uk/node/931.

Helm, D. 2012. EMR and the energy bill: a critique. Available at www.dieterhelm .co.uk/node/1330.

Helm, D., J. Wardlaw and B. Caldecott. 2009. Delivering a 21st century infrastructure for Britain. Report, Policy Exchange (September).

Henckel, T., and McKibbin, W. 2010. The economics of infrastructure in a globalized world: issues, lessons and future challenges. Working Paper 2010-39, Australian National University, Centre for Applied Macroeconomic Analysis.

Hermansson, H. 2007. The ethics of NIMBY conflicts. *Ethical Theory and Moral Practice* **10**(1), 23–34.

HM Treasury. 2011. National Infrastructure Plan 2011 (November).

House of Commons. 2011. *A European Supergrid: Seventh Report of Sessions 2010–12*, volume I. Energy and Climate Change Committee.

House of Commons. 2012. Quick guide to the railways.

IEA. 2011. Technology roadmap: smart grids. Report, International Energy Agency.

IEA. 2012. Energy policies of IEA countries: the United Kingdom. International Energy Agency 2012 Review.

Jamison, M. A., H. Lynne and S. Berg. 2005. Measuring and mitigating regulatory risk in private infrastructure investment. *Electricity Journal* **18**(6), 36–45.

Jenkins, R. R., K. B. Maguire and C. L. Morgan. 2004. Host community compensation and municipal solid waste landfills. *Land Economics* **80**(4), 513–528.

Kasperson, R. E., D. Golding and S. Truler. 1992. Siting hazardous waste facilities and communicating risks. *Journal of Social Issues* **48**(4), 161–172.

Kleindorfer, P. R., and M. R. Sertel. 1994. Auctioning the provision of an indivisible public good. *Journal of Economic Theory* **64**(1), 20–34.

Kunreuther, H., and Easterling, D. 1996. The role of compensation in siting hazardous facilities. **15**(4), 601–622.

Kunreuther, H., and P. R. Kleindorfer. 1986. A sealed-bid auction mechanism for siting noxious facilities. *American Economic Review* **76**, 295–299.

Kunreuther, H., P. R. Kleindorfer, P. Knez and R. Yarsick. 1987. A compensation mechanism for siting noxious facilities: theory and experimental design. *Journal of Environmental Economics and Management* **14**, 371–383.

Macilwain, C. 2010. Supergrid. *Nature* **468**, 644–625.

McNulty, R. 2011. Realising the potential of GB rail: report of the rail value for money study. Report, Department of Transport and Office of Rail Regulation (May).

Morse, A. C. E. 2011. Certificate and report of the Comptroller and Auditor General: whole government accounts 2009–10 (October).

Morton, A. 2011. Cities for growth: solutions to our planning problems. Report, Policy Exchange.

National Audit Office. 2011. Option appraisal: making informed decisions in government. National Audit Office Review (May).

Nature. 2010. An end to gridlock? *Nature* **468**, 599 (editorial).

Newbery, D. 2005. Infrastructure pricing and finance. In *HM Treasury Microeconomics Lecture Series, May 2004–June 2005*, pp. 22–39. HM Treasury.

Newbery, D. 2012. Energy and infrastructure. Submission to the LSE Growth Commission.

OECD. 2005. Economic survey of the UK (October).

OECD. 2007a. Infrastructure to 2030: Volume 1. Telecom, land transport, water and electricity.

OECD. 2007b. Infrastructure to 2030: Volume 2. Mapping policy for electricity, water and transport.

OECD. 2012a. OECD broadband portal (July).

OECD. 2012b. OECD internet economy outlook 2012.

Ofcom. 2012. Infrastructure report (November).

Office for Budget Responsibility. 2012. Fiscal sustainability report (July).

Ofgem. 2012. Electricity capacity assessment (October).

O'Hare, M. 1977. Not on my block you don't: facility siting and the strategic importance of compensation. *Public Policy* **25**(5), 407–458.

O'Hare, M. 2010. Environmental and other co-benefits of developing a high speed rail system in California: a prospective vision 2010–2050. Working Paper, UCB Center for Environmental Public Policy (December).

O'Hare, M., L. Bacow and D. Sanderson. 1983. *Facility Siting and Public Opposition.* New York: Van Nostrand Reinhold.

Patsy, R. 2012a. The Draft Energy Bill 2012. Standard Note SNSC-6324, House of Commons Library (May).

Patsy, R. 2012b. Smart meters. Standard Note SNSC-6179, House of Commons Library (May).

Pellegrin, S., and E. Sirtori. 2012. Methodologies to assess the impact of infrastructure projects in international development evaluations. Working Paper 02/2012, Center for Industrial Studies.

Petts, J. 1992. Incineration risk perceptions and public concern: experience in the UK improving risk communication. *Waste Management and Research* **10**, 169–182.

Portney, K. E. 1991. *Siting Hazardous Waste Treatment Facilities: The NIMBY Syndrome.* New York: Aubrun.

Redpoint–DECC. 2010. Electricity market reform analysis of policy options.

Regulatory Policy Committee. 2011. Challenging regulation: an independent report on the analysis supporting regulatory proposals, September–December 2010 (February).

Richardson, J., and H. Kunreuther. 1993. Experimental test of a Nash-efficient mechanism for collective choice with compensation. *Journal of Economic Behavior and Organization* **22**, 349–369.

Romani, M., N. Stern and D. Zenghelis. 2011. The basic economics of low-carbon growth in the UK. Policy Brief, Grantham Research Institute/Centre for Climate Change Economics and Policy (June). Available at www.lse.ac.uk/gran thaminstitute/publications/policy/docs/pb_economics-low-carbon-growth_ jun11.pdf.

Romp, W., and J. de Haan. 2007. Public capital and economic growth: a critical survey. *Perspektiven der Wirtschaftspolitik* **8**(s1), 6–52.

Rosewell, B. 2010. Planning curses: how to deliver long-term investment in infrastructure. Report, Policy Exchange (January).

Rosewell, B. 2012. Infrastructure and energy. Submission to the LSE Growth Commission.

Schively, C. 2007. Understanding the NIMBY and LULU phenomena: reassessing our knowledge base and informing future research. *Journal of Planning Literature* **21**(3), 255–266.

Serven, L. 2010. Is infrastructure capital productive? Report, The World Bank.

Skidelsky, R., F. Martin and C. W. Wigstrom. 2011. Blueprint for a British investment bank. Ebook, Centre for Global Studies (November). Available at http://globalstudies.org.uk/wp-content/uploads/2013/01/Blueprint-for-a -British-Investment-Bank-ebook1.pdf.

Smith, J. W. 2009. Governance and administration of national and local roads in Great Britain. Report, RAC Foundation (June).

Smith, J. W., A. Jan and D. Phillips. 2011. Providing and funding strategic roads: an international perspective with lessons for the UK. Report, RAC Foundation (November).

Stern, N. 2006. *The Stern Review on the Economics of Climate Change.* HM Treasury (October).

Stern, N. 2010. Presidential address: imperfections in the economics of public policy, imperfections in markets, and climate change. *Journal of the European Economic Association* **8**, 253–288.

Stern, N. 2011. (Re)constructing success: a way forward for the Green Investment Bank? BIS Blog (December). Available at http://webarchive.nationalarchives .gov.uk/20121205183318/http://blogs.bis.gov.uk/blog/2011/12/ 19/reconstructing-success-a-way-forward-for-the-green-investment-bank/.

Stewart, J. 2010. The UK national infrastructure plan 2010. European Investment Bank Papers: Public and Private Financing of Infrastructure.

Sullivan, A. 1992. Siting noxious facilities: a siting lottery with victim compensation. *Journal of Urban Economics* **31**(3), 360–374.

Wagenvoort, R., C. de Nicola and A. Kappeler. 2010. Infrastructure finance in Europe: composition, evolution and crisis impact. *European Investment Bank Papers* **15**(1), 16–39.

Water UK. 2010. Meeting future challenges: a blueprint for policy action. Report (July).

White, A. L., and S. J. Ratick. 1989. Risk, compensation, and regional equity in locating hazardous facilities. *Papers of the Regional Science Association* **67**, 29–42.

A Blueprint for an Infrastructure Bank

By Novella Bottini, Miguel Coelho and Jennifer Kao

5.1 INTRODUCTION

As discussed in chapter 4, an Infrastructure Bank (IB) could provide stable, predictable and appropriately scaled long-term support for infrastructure on the basis of robust banking principles and additionality. The IB would be different from existing financial institutions in a number of key ways. First, it would act as a vehicle to reduce policy risk. Indeed, the IB could serve as a vehicle to generate credible commitment to maintaining consistent policy frameworks across parliaments. Moreover, governments would be less likely to chop and change policies if a publicly owned long-term investment bank were involved. Second, it would have special convening powers and strong networks to put together different coalitions and sources of finance. And lastly, the IB would develop banking and sectoral skills in new and important areas (Stern 2011).

5.2 MANDATE AND OPERATING PRINCIPLES

The core of the IB's mandate would be to promote medium- and long-term growth through facilitating investment in infrastructure projects of national strategic importance. The IB would aim to provide additionality by 'crowding in' the right type of capital, enabling other types of finance to flow.

Under the mandate of facilitating medium- and long-term growth, the IB would act in accordance with predefined operating principles and objectives against which its executive board could be judged. Crucially, it would need a wide measure of independence from government to fulfil its mandate. In particular, there should be a clear distinction between oversight of mission and purpose, and day-to-day operational control.[1]

---

[1] In almost all the countries reviewed, similar institutions have been established by (or exist and operate by) virtue of an act of parliament or the equivalent. These include Kreditanstalt für Wiederaufbau (KfW) in Germany, Caisse des Depots (CDC) in France, Cassa Depositi e Prestiti (CDP) in Italy, the Small Business Administration (SBA) in the US and the Business Development Bank of Canada.

The IB would most likely assume the role of senior partner lender/investor in a given project alongside the private sector and other institutional investors. Using a partnership model would enable the IB to tap into the expertise of its partners, including external fund managers who would be expected to assume responsibility for performing due diligence on individual projects and overseeing day-to-day project activities.

The bank would be expected to act as a fully commercial entity but would not be required to pay a dividend to its shareholders (that is, taxpayers). Among overseas national banks, only the Nordic Investment Bank pays a dividend, perhaps as a means of assuring taxpayers in the separate countries that it covers that they are getting a return for the capital they invest in the bank.

The role of the bank could possibly be time limited. However, this requires the establishment of a credible exit strategy. In addition, even if there is an exit strategy in place, there is a danger that it will not be implemented because of pressure applied by groups with vested interests.

5.3 GOVERNANCE

The government would be the IB's sole shareholder and would set its strategic objectives—it would have no influence over individual investment decisions or how the IB manages its funds.[2] The strategic policy orientations defined by the Independent Strategy Board (as per the governance model proposed in chapter 1) would be reflected in the operating principles and objectives of the bank.

The IB could have an eclectic board of governors, composed of representatives from government, commercial banks, regulators, business, academia and trade unions. This board would set strategic priorities and assess the performance of the bank against its objectives. It would also be responsible for ensuring that the IB remained compliant with EU state-aid rules.[3] To give frequent advice on technical matters there

---

[2]For example, the UK Department for Business, Innovation & Skills is the Green Investment Bank's sole shareholder, and in consultation with the Green Investment Bank Policy Group it approves the founding articles of the Green Investment Bank, the Green Investment Bank charter and the bank's strategic priorities.

[3]In this way, the IB's board of governors would be similar to the Board of Supervisory Directors of the KfW and the Board of Directors of BNDES (the Brazilian Development Bank). Within the Green Investment Bank, this body is split into two components: the Green Investment Bank Policy Group (comprised of representatives from relevant government departments) and the Green Investment Bank Corporate Board (which includes experts from business and academia). The Nordic and European investment banks, whose shareholders are different countries, have a board of governors (made up of the finance

should be a number of technical advisory groups whose memberships would be drawn from a wide range of sources, including academia and social partners.

As well as a board of governors the IB would have an executive board that would comprise the senior management of the bank. The chief executive would be appointed by a supervisory board and would be expected to report to it regularly. The board of governors, the supervisory board and the advisory council would not be expected to interfere in any way in the day-to-day operations of the bank. These bodies would be responsible for setting the strategic direction of the bank. All banking decisions would be the responsibility of bankers.

To further ensure that the work of the IB is strategically aligned with government policymaking, an advisory council could be established on which ministers, members of parliament and senior civil servants would sit. It would assess the existing strategic objectives of the IB and make recommendations to the board of governors about changes to them. The KfW's Mittelstandsrat (small and medium enterprises advisory council) assumes a similar role in Germany (Dolphin and Nash 2012; Skidelsky *et al.* 2011).

5.4 INSTRUMENTS

Traditional Financial Instruments

The IB would select infrastructure projects on the basis of robust financial rules and provide financial support primarily by issuing bonds. These bonds would not have an explicit government guarantee but they would be likely to attract a high credit rating because the bank would be in public ownership, the mix of assets that it would acquire would be of high quality, and the danger of default would therefore be extremely low. Bonds issued by the European Investment Bank have no government guarantee and have always had an AAA rating. If IB bonds also acquired an AAA rating, they could be expected to typically yield a little more than UK government bonds but less than corporate bonds.

An increase in the contribution from the total investment or global sovereign wealth fund markets of UK pension funds could provide great support in funding infrastructure networks (Glaister 2012; CBI 2012). However, the current risk profile of most infrastructure assets is not

---

ministers of the member states) and a board of directors (comprised of members state representatives selected by respective governments).

sufficiently attractive for private investment. Given this situation, government action is needed to increase the attractiveness of infrastructure investment: for example, it could try to lift project ratings, and it could introduce specific measures to encourage UK pension funds to enter the market.[4]

An AAA rating would make IB bonds attractive to UK pension and insurance funds and to overseas investors in the UK bond market. When defined-benefit pension funds close, and the money flowing into them through contributions dries up, they shift assets to more closely match their liabilities. This means that they increase their holdings of bonds, primarily index-linked bonds, and particularly long-duration bonds. The extra yield that IB bonds would offer compared with government bonds—at very little extra risk—would definitely appeal to these funds.

It would be wrong to give the impression that this is 'free' money, as the government is prone to do when it talks about pension funds investing directly in infrastructure. If pension and insurance funds buy IB bonds, they will have to sell other assets to do so—including UK government bonds and equities. This will push down the prices of these assets and increase their yields. As a result, the cost of funding for the UK government and for UK firms will go up. This is inevitable; the IB would add to the demand for funds, and increased demand means higher prices. This is not, though, an argument against the IB. The rationale for the IB is that there are market failures in the UK in the provision of finance for infrastructure. A corollary of this argument is that more funds are therefore being channelled to other areas, including the equity and bond markets, artificially lowering yields there. The government and firms that raise funds on the equity market have benefited in the past from the market failures in finance for infrastructure; there is no good reason why they should continue to do so (Dolphin and Nash 2012).

Innovative Financial Instruments

Some new investment models allow banks to continue to finance the greenfield (construction) phase of a particular project while at the same time allowing them to exit projects earlier than they did in the past. Such models could be built using a 'split-finance' model, as suggested by Bhattacharya *et al.* (2012) and CBI (2012). Banks—thanks to their market expertise, due diligence and risk-bearing capacities—would be able

---

[4]Examples of investments from institutional investors include Gatwick Airport and HS1. The CBI recommends increasing the attractiveness of infrastructure investments through providing a package of benefits, such as tax incentives (CBI 2012).

to finance the more risky construction phase of a project and leave the investment once the project reaches a stable operation level, at which point they can be refinanced in the capital markets. This strategy would benefit both banks and institutional investors: banks would be able to comply with their capital requirements under Basel III and institutional investors would benefit from the long-term stable returns offered by the management phase of the project without directly bearing any of the initial construction risk.

However, institutional investors could face construction risk indirectly. Any delay or overspending in the first phase can lead to over-leveraged assets in the second phase, when institutional investors enter the project. If institutional investors are involved in the discussions over the project's construction phase, this risk could be mitigated. This could be done by structuring the financing of the entire project through a 'secondary debt' structure. Through this financial tool, banks and institutional investors commit funds to cover both the greenfield and brownfield (management) phases of a project.

Over the long term, this model should help to attract non-bank institutional investors into the greenfield phase. However, this would happen only once institutional investors became open to increasing their risk exposure in exchange for higher returns (CBI 2012).

Non-financial Instruments

The IB could be a key convener and syndicator of programmes in a way that involves the private sector as well as other public institutions, such as national development banks and sovereign wealth funds (i.e. co-financing arrangements and/or co-ownership with other institutions). This would be reflected in the composition of its institutional bodies, whose members would have a wide range of experiences and abilities—from building and running institutions to project finance and market transactions capabilities—as well as technical and academic expertise in specific sectors, in sustainable and responsible financial services and in development banking. Moreover, the bank would favour continuous communication with the private and public sectors through the publication of periodic reports and the organization of seminars and conferences.

While the IB would not devise infrastructure strategy, it could play a crucial role as a centre for project coordination, evaluation and implementation through building the right capacity and specific skills to meet infrastructure challenges in new and important areas. This advisory function would be core to the IB's ability to catalyse private co-investment.

Lastly, the IB could serve as a coordination centre. Economic infrastructure cuts across several government departments and it can therefore be difficult for prospective investors to gain access to timely information about investment opportunities. The IB would simplify this process by providing reliable information on the key investment features of the project, such as the planned timing for each phase (construction, post construction and operation), the forecast demand and risks, and so on.

5.5 PRACTICAL CONSIDERATIONS

Three practical considerations that impact on the bank's establishment need to be considered: (1) bank funding, (2) the integration of bank activity into the public accounts, and (3) compliance with EU law.

First, the IB would need an initial one-off injection of capital. This could come from a number of sources including general government spending, selling the government's stakes in Royal Bank of Scotland and Lloyds, national savings, a one-off levy on commercial banks, or a targeted round of quantitative easing (Dolphin and Nash 2012). The volume of bonds issued by the IB will depend on the size of its capital base and its permitted leverage ratio. The Nordic Investment Bank and the European Investment Bank have relatively conservative leverage ceilings of 2.5 times their capital base.

If the IB were to operate with the same ratio and was capitalized with £20 billion over four years (i.e. £5 billion per year), it would be able to build an asset sheet with £50 billion. With estimated UK infrastructure needs totaling £310 billion (HM Treasury 2012), and more than two-thirds (around £206 billion) of that being financed by private capital, the bank would be able to provide 25% of this amount in a relatively short period of time.[5]

Second, the IB would be part of the public sector in the UK. This implies that its financial liabilities—the money it raises in capital markets though bond issuance—would be counted towards public sector net debt while the bulk of its assets would not be netted off (only liquid assets are taken into account in the calculation of net debt). The creation of an IB would therefore lead to a substantial increase in public sector net debt as currently measured. Its activities would also increase measured public sector net borrowing. One solution would be to exclude the self-financing activities of the IB from the calculation of public sector debt and borrowing, on the same grounds that temporary financial interventions (even though

---

[5] A similar approach was proposed by Dolphin and Nash (2012).

they are likely to stretch over many years) are now excluded—this is what the German KfW and the Green Investment Bank are currently doing (Dolphin and Nash 2012; Helm *et al.* 2009).

Finally, the UK government would have to gain approval from the European Commission before an IB could be established. The EU has strict state-aid rules that prevent national governments from providing various forms of aid to companies. In the case of an IB, the European Commission would need to be assured that any lending done by the IB was not simply undercutting commercial banks, and thus effectively subsidizing the rates at which companies could borrow. The EU's state-aid rules also carry a number of exemptions, generally in areas where it is widely accepted that market failure is prevalent in all advanced economies. These include financing aimed at promoting SMEs, innovation and environmental protection. Increasingly, investments that can be demonstrated to have local economic benefits are also looked upon favourably, particularly if these benefits will accrue in deprived regions. Higher levels of state investment in business and infrastructure in deprived regions are permitted by the European Commission. The KfW, for example, offers more favourable loan terms for SMEs in regions that qualify for regional aid. If the IB's remit is confined to funding infrastructure spending, this should not be an impossible process to complete, given the UK's long-standing under-investment in infrastructure in comparison with similar nations. In addition, facilitating infrastructure projects within the broader aim of rebalancing the economy away from London and the southeast would also make it easier to sell the idea of an IB to the European Commission, which is concerned with lifting the performance of slow-growing and low-income regions.

5.6 PAST AND PRESENT UK INSTITUTIONS

The Green Investment Bank

The Green Investment Bank (GIB) was launched in 2012 as part of the government's commitment to setting the UK on course to deliver long-term sustainable growth in keeping with the UK's climate change objectives (Dolphin and Nash 2012). Initially, the GIB only had funding of £3 billion (from the government), but once public debt starts to decrease, it will be able to raise funds in capital markets (subject to limits imposed by the government). The GIB will invest up to £100 million in commercial and industrial energy efficiency projects, as well as make major co-investments with private finance in offshore wind projects. Even then, though, the GIB will be some way short of a full-scale national bank.

Skidelsky *et al.* (2011) notes that it could be the 'nucleus of something more ambitious'.

The GIB provides lessons for the IB (Tott 2011). Over £200 billion in green infrastructure investments will be needed over the next decade. However, bank lending constraints and the risk aversion of institutional investors are particularly potent when it comes to green technology, where projects can involve new technologies and business models with an insufficient track record. Compounding the reluctance of investors to invest is the fact that the original business innovator may not reap the full benefits of the technological innovation, despite having to incur the upfront costs of innovation and development. Instead, follow-on businesses may capture the benefits without having to incur any of the costs or risks. Through acting as a pioneer financier, the GIB aims to 'crowd in' additional investment through creating new financing structures to overcome the high costs of due diligence for new projects and technologies. Moreover, the GIB aims to overcome credit constraints caused by information asymmetries by developing track records for projects and technologies. The GIB's investment activity will follow a set of explicit purposes and is likely to have synergies with other types of infrastructure policy.

The Industrial and Commercial Finance Corporation

After the Second World War, the Bank of England and the then 'big five' clearing banks created the Industrial and Commercial Finance Corporation (ICFC) to address the structural small business financing gap. Through a regional branch network, the ICFC combined technical specialists with local business expertise to support local investments. In order to gain independence from the clearing banks, the ICFC turned to the market to raise funds. This led to a shift away from projects with moderate long-term returns to projects that provided high short-term returns. In addition to highlighting the important role that local networks and technical expertise play in government interventions, the ICFC experience demonstrates the ability of private capital to drive investment activity towards investments with higher short-term returns (Tott 2011; Skidelsky *et al.* 2011).

An International Example: The European Bank for Reconstruction and Development

The European Bank for Reconstruction and Development (EBRD) is an international financial institution that mobilizes foreign and domestic capital to foster transition towards 'open and democratic market economies' (EBRD 2012f).[6]

The EBRD's operating region stretches from central Europe to central Asia and has recently expanded to North Africa and the Middle East. The EBRD provides funds for well-structured, financially robust projects through additionality in order to avoid crowding out private capital (EBRD 2012f). Moreover, it select the projects it will finance following sound banking principles, i.e. it ensures that the potential returns on a project are commensurate with its risks. The EBRD shares this project risk by acting with private sector entities, multilateral lenders and national export credit agencies. Unlike a commercial bank, the EBRD does not provide retail banking services. However, EBRD products are priced on a commercial basis.

The EBRD's shareholder countries and organizations form a solid capital base that allows the bank to act as an effective 'demonstrator' on the frontier of commercial possibilities (EBRD 2012f). The EBRD is AAA rated due to the security of its capital base and the quality of its loan portfolios. This enables the bank to raise funds cheaply in capital markets and to pass on the benefits of low-cost financing to its borrowers.

In addition to its regional and sectoral strengths, the bank is unique among international financial institutions in its ability to use a broad and flexible range of financing instruments in both the public and private sectors in order to support the different stages of transition.

For each project it finances, the EBRD assigns a team of specialists with specific sectoral, regional, legal and environmental skills to provide technical assistance to banks, businesses and municipalities. Due to its deep regional and sectoral knowledge, the EBRD also plays a critical role in policy dialogue with governments and international financial institutions.

The EU/EBRD Municipal Finance Facility provides an example of the EBRD's engagement with infrastructure investment. The scheme is aimed at encouraging bank lending to small and medium-sized municipalities (SMMs) and their utility companies in EU accession countries (EBRD 2010c). The EBRD aims to provide up to €75 million in long-term (10–15 years) lines of credit and €25 million for risk sharing on up to 35% of the partner bank's risk on a loan portfolio to SMMs. Pricing takes into account the credit risk of the partner bank, which make loans of up to

---

[6]For an overview of other international infrastructure banks such as the European Investment Bank, the Brazilian Development Bank and the Nordic Investment Bank in the five Nordic countries (Sweden, Norway, Denmark, Iceland and Finland), see Dolphin and Nash (2012) and Skidelsky *et al.* (2011).

Table 5.1. EBRD financial involvement in transport, power and energy, and municipal and environmental infrastructure projects.

Year	Country	Sector	No. of projects	Total project cost (€m)	EBRD finance (€m)	EBRD finance (%)
2009	Albania	Transport	6	327	134.2	41
2009	Albania	Power and energy	7	513.1	112.5	22
2009	Russia Federation	MEI	35	3519	804	23
2009	Russia Federation	Transport	29	4115	1494	36
2009	Russia Federation	Power and energy	15	4651	973	21
2009	Turkmenistan	Transport (port devel.)	1	32.2	20.5	64
2009	Turkmenistan	Power and energy (oil)	1	355.8	41.1	12
2010	Latvia	MEI	2	216	44	20
2010	Latvia	Transport	5	150	45	30
2010	Latvia	Power and energy	3	502	133	26
2010	Moldova	MEI	5	100.9	43.1	43
2010	Moldova	Transport	6	159.3	73.8	46
2010	Moldova	Power and energy	3	68.8	33.4	49
2010	Slovenia	MEI	NA	48	15	31
2010	Slovenia	Transport	NA	218	86	39
2010	Slovenia	Power and energy	NA	107	65	61
2012	Armenia	MEI	3	47	19	40
2012	Armenia	Transport	3	200	62	31
2012	Armenia	Power and energy	4	156	92	59
2012	Lithuania	MEI	10	216	89	41
2012	Lithuania	Transport	2	218	76	35
2012	Lithuania	Power and energy	4	403	106	26
2012	Slovak Republic	MEI	7	126	43.9	35
2012	Slovak Republic	Transport	3	1379	234.8	17
2012	Slovak Republic	Power and energy	10	1592	313.4	20
2012	Turkey	MEI	6	902	213	24
2012	Turkey	Transport	2	83	37	45
2012	Turkey	Power and energy	4	804	203	25

MEI stands for municipal and environmental infrastructure. *Source*: the data collection of the authors, which is based on EBRD Strategy Reports for selected countries and years (EBRD 2009a–c, 2010a–c, 2011, 2012a–f).

€5 million with a maturity of 5–15 years available to SMMs for infrastructure investments. The EBRD acts as a loan guarantor through providing funding in the event of a loan default.

The EBRD Sustainable Energy Initiative provides an example of the bank's ability to attract both foreign and domestic capital in transition countries' infrastructure projects, as well as to finance a small share of the total project cost. The Sustainable Energy Initiative had an initial financing goal of €4.5–6.5 billion, with a target total project value range of €15–25 billion. In 2012 the EBRD financed 21% of projects in the sustainable energy area. Based on country and sectoral data for selected countries in the last four years, the EBRD has, on average, financed 34% of the total costs of transport, energy and power, and municipal and environmental infrastructure projects (table 5.1) (EBRD 2012e).

References

Bhattacharya, A., M. Romani and N. Stern. 2012. Infrastructure for development: meeting the challenge. Report, Center for Climate Change Economics and Policy.

CBI. 2012. An offer they shouldn't refuse: attracting investment to UK infrastructure. Report, Confederation of British Industry (May).

Dolphin, T., and D. Nash. 2012. Investing for the future: why we need a British investment bank. Report, Institute for Public Policy Research.

EBRD. 2009a. Strategy for Albania 2009–2012. European Bank for Reconstruction and Development Document (approved by the Board of Directors on 17 November).

EBRD. 2009b. Strategy for the Russian Federation 2009–2012. European Bank for Reconstruction and Development Document.

EBRD. 2009c. Strategy for Turkmenistan 2009–2012. European Bank for Reconstruction and Development Document.

EBRD. 2010a. Strategy for Slovenia 2010–2013. European Bank for Reconstruction and Development Document (approved by the Board of Directors on 20/21 July).

EBRD. 2010b. Strategy for Moldova 2010–2013. European Bank for Reconstruction and Development Document (approved by the Board of Directors on 14 December).

EBRD. 2010c. EU/EBRD municipal finance facility. European Bank for Reconstruction and Development Document. Available at www.ebrd.com/pages/sector/financial/municipal.shtml (accessed in December 2012).

EBRD. 2011. Strategy for Latvia. European Bank for Reconstruction and Development Document (approved by the Board of Directors on 11 October).

EBRD. 2012a. Strategy for Armenia. European Bank for Reconstruction and Development Document (approved by the Board of Directors on 29 May).

EBRD. 2012b. Strategy for Lithuania. European Bank for Reconstruction and Development Document (approved by the Board of Directors on 13 November).

EBRD. 2012c. Strategy for the Slovak Republic. European Bank for Reconstruction and Development Document (approved by the Board of Directors on 13 November).

EBRD. 2012d. Strategy for Turkey. European Bank for Reconstruction and Development Document (approved by the Board of Directors on 17 April).

EBRD. 2012e. Sustainable energy initiative: scaling up finance to address climate change. European Bank for Reconstruction and Development (November).

EBRD. 2012f. What we do. Available at www.ebrd.com/pages/about/what.shtml (accessed in December 2012).

Glaister, S. 2010. Governing and paying for England's roads. Report, RAC Foundation (July).

Helm, D., J. Wardlaw and B. Caldecott. 2009. Delivering a 21st century infrastructure for Britain. Report, Policy Exchange.

HM Government. 2011. Update on the design of the Green Investment Bank.

HM Treasury. 2012. National infrastructure plan 2011 (November).

Skidelsky, R., F. Martin and C. W. Wingstrom. 2011. Blueprint for a British investment bank. Report, Centre for Global Studies.

Stern, N. 2011. Re)constructing success: a way forward for the Green Investment Bank? BIS Blog (December). Available at http://webarchive.nationalarchives .gov.uk/20120302091214/blogs.bis.gov.uk/.

Tott, N. 2011. The case for a British investment bank: a report for Labour's policy review. Available at www.yourbritain.org.uk/uploads/editor/files/BRITISH_ INVESTMENT_BANK.pdf.

CHAPTER SIX

Private Investment and Innovation

By Miguel Coelho, Jennifer Kao and Isabelle Roland

6.1 INTRODUCTION

Investment in equipment and new ideas (both technological and manage-rial) are crucial for economic growth. A favourable investment climate is important if UK businesses are to adopt new technologies and best prac-tices. Investment is also central to innovation and the process of 'creative destruction', or reallocation (whereby more efficient and innovative firms grow and less successful firms shrink and exit). Much of the aggregate difference in productivity across countries and in growth in productivity over time comes from this creative destruction (see, for example, Bartels-man *et al.* 2013). A supportive environment for investment and innova-tion is therefore paramount for a dynamic and productive economy. Even though investment and innovation are key market-driven processes, the policy environment—including policies that affect competition, market access, finance, taxation and regulation—plays an important supporting role.

Yet many UK businesses face a mix of structural, transitional and policy-related obstacles when it comes to raising finance from external sources. One consequence of this is that the UK has for decades invested

This chapter was produced by the LSE Growth Commission's Secretariat to inform the thinking of the commissioners. The analysis does not necessarily reflect the views of the commissioners. In contrast, the proposals are those of the Growth Commission report. We are grateful to a large number of people for kindly submitting written or oral evi-dence to the Secretariat and the Growth Commission. In no specific order, we are par-ticularly grateful to Albert Bravo-Biosca (NESTA), the US Small Business Administration, Thorsten Beck, Patrick Vanhoudt (EIB), John Kay, Mariana Mazzucato, Ralph De Haas (EBRD), Erik Berglöf (EBRD), the OECD, the Association for Financial Markets in Europe, Roger Witcomb (Competition Commission), Ayman Asfari, Keith O'Nions, Jon Moulton, Ian Davis, Hal Varian and officials at the Department for Business, Innovation & Skills. We are also thankful to Anna Valero for providing useful comments on previous versions of this paper, as well as to Jo Cantlay and Linda Cleavely for logistical support. The views expressed here do not necessarily reflect the views of the individuals or institutions mentioned above.

less than other advanced European countries at each stage of business development (NESTA 2012a). In 2008 the UK's share of total GDP devoted to R&D stood at 1.8%, a lower proportion than in the US (2.8%), Germany (2.7%) and France (2.1%). UK capital markets raised £2.9 trillion of capital in 2007, an increase of 355% over 1998 levels, but business investment in innovation increased by only 54% (NESTA 2012a). This trend may have been reinforced by the financial crisis. The World Economic Forum Global Competitiveness Report 2012–13 lists 'access to financing' as the most problematic factor for doing business in the UK. This is a troubling sign for the UK's innovative capacity, since access to external finance and investment is vital for productivity and is a sign of an optimistic, dynamic and entrepreneurial business sector (Beck 2012). Low investment and innovation generate lower levels of labour productivity or GDP per hour. There has been a long-standing productivity gap between the UK and three close comparator countries: France, Germany and the US (see chapter 2). In 2011 UK per hour GDP was 27% lower than it was in the US, 25% lower than in France and 22% lower than in Germany.

In this chapter we argue that some of the problems with investment and innovation are directly linked to a series of failures in the functioning of capital markets, including a lack of competition in banking and short-termist behaviour in financial markets in general. While there are certain financing issues that are pervasive for firms of all sizes, a key focus is on SMEs and SME-specific funding shortfalls. SMEs make up a large fraction of the UK economy, accounting for 99.9% of all UK businesses and over half of private sector employment and turnover in 2011 (BIS 2012). Even more important is the fact that young entrant firms—the source of many new radical ideas that shake up older firms—are likely to start as SMEs. Financing problems for start-ups and a lack of growth capital for young firms to enable them to reach scale will severely hold back aggregate productivity.

We also argue that poor management practices undermine private investment and productivity. In measures of management quality, the UK is mediocre by international standards, ranked significantly below the 'premier league' of countries, such as Germany, Japan and the US (Bloom *et al.* 2012a). This gap matters because recent evidence suggests that about a third of international productivity differences can be attributed to management (Bloom *et al.* 2013b).

Finally, we discuss the role of industrial strategy in supporting investment and innovation. Since the late 1970s industry-specific 'vertical' policies have been unpopular due to fears that the ambition of 'picking winners' will turn into an outcome of 'picking losers'. But some recent successes (such as foreign direct investment in the automotive sector) and the need to nurture more green industries have caused a rethink of a more activist industrial strategy. The convening power and coordination role of government can help to bring parties together to recognize and solve problems. Thus there is a role for strategic thinking, especially as the government touches on almost every industry in some way.

Other important impediments to private investment include a lack of skilled labour and relatively low levels of public investment in infrastructure. Efforts to increase human capital and improve infrastructure policies are likely to provide a boost to investment by firms. Issues related to human capital and infrastructure are discussed in chapters 3 and 4, respectively.

Section 6.2 gives a brief overview of investment and innovation in the UK, highlighting shortfalls in performance. Section 6.3 describes a number of financial market failures, particularly 'gaps' in the market for firms accessing finance (a brief overview of the financing conditions faced by UK firms is given in appendix 6A). Section 6.4 describes some of the key factors that lie at the root of these failures and hence contribute to poor performance in investment and innovation. Section 6.5 discusses shortcomings in UK management practices and their impact on productivity and growth. Section 6.6 discusses the potential benefits from an improved strategic approach to UK industrial policy. And finally, Section 6.7 details the recommendations that the Commission put forward in its report 'Investing for Prosperity—Skills, Infrastructure and Innovation'.

6.2 INVESTMENT AND INNOVATION IN THE UK

As figure 6.1 shows, UK investment levels as a share of GDP have historically been lower than those in France, Germany and Japan (and similar to those in the US). In addition, the composition of fixed asset investment has worsened from an innovation perspective. According to NESTA's Innovation Index, in the period from 2000 to 2007 investment in fixed assets became increasingly dominated by buildings and property rather than 'productive assets' such as machinery or technological equipment, which embody newer technologies (NESTA 2009, 2012a).

Moreover, the UK has not performed well in terms of intangible investment in recent years. Between 1995 and 2008, intangible investment increased in most rich countries. In contrast, the share of intangible investment in UK national output remained constant for most of the 2000s, having risen modestly between 1995 and 2000 (NESTA 2012a).

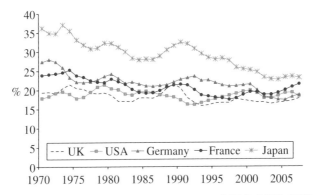

Figure 6.1. Investment as a percentage of GDP, 1970–2007.

Source: OECD (2009b). *Notes*. This indicator is calculated as the ratio of gross fixed capital formation to GDP. Data refer to fiscal year.

The UK is strong in the field of 'fast innovations', such as fund management, fashion, animation and architecture, where development cycles are relatively short and capital intensity is low (NESTA 2012a). In these fields, the UK possesses expertise in both the upstream (design, new product development, research) and downstream (production, sales, marketing) aspects of business. In addition, OECD data shows that the UK demonstrates above average performance in the pharmaceuticals, life sciences and aerospace sectors. However, in general, for industries that involve longer product cycles and require more capital, there are few sectors in which the UK is strong in both the upstream and the downstream aspects of the value chain (NESTA 2012a).

A great deal of UK scientific research is exploited in other countries, and 21% of business R&D in the UK is financed by foreign companies (NESTA 2012a). The UK punches above its weight in this area, with a strong science base and an internationally dynamic higher education sector with good support structures through the 'research excellence framework' administered by the Higher Education Funding Council for England. Fewer than 4% of the world's researchers are based in the UK and yet they manage to produce 6.4% of all scientific articles and receive 10.9% of citations. Commercialization of their insights and inventions has, however, been historically weak in the UK, with lower R&D and patenting intensity than in other rich countries.

The UK performs well in attracting inward investment, but international competition for hosting R&D is intensifying. In addition, the UK does not perform well in terms of its ability to grow great global firms.

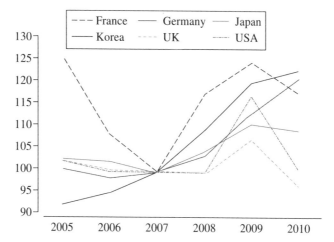

Figure 6.2. Government budget outlays or appropriations on R&D
(weighted by size of economy, 2007 = 100).
Source: NESTA (2012a), based on OECD data.

There is a tendency for British firms in high-tech and capital-intensive
sectors to be acquired by foreign businesses rather than raising finance
to grow. The purchase of UK businesses by foreign companies, which
in some cases leads to the transfer of operations out of the UK (e.g. in
the semiconductor sector), has weakened the productivity of the UK's
manufacturing sector (NESTA 2012a). There is evidence that the situation is worsening, too, as sectors where the UK performs relatively well
are coming under threat. An example is pharmaceuticals: in 2011, Pfizer
announced that it intended to close its UK R&D facilities, allegedly due to
a risk profile that had become unfavourable to private sector investment
and a retreat in public spending. While these facts may simply reflect
comparative advantage in the UK versus other countries, many of these
issues are likely to be caused by financing constraints.

We note that it has also been argued that direct government spending
on R&D is too small (NESTA 2012a). Under the 2010 spending review,
public sector gross investment for 2013–14 will be £1.4 billion for business, innovation and skills, compared with £1.9 billion for international
development and £4.4 billion for health (HM Treasury 2010). According
to OECD data, other countries, including the US, France, Germany and
Korea, not only spent more on R&D than the UK before the crisis but they
also increased their innovation budget much more quickly after it (see
figure 6.2).

6.3 Failures in UK Financial Markets

Supply-Side Market Failures

While the credit crunch exacerbated problems in access to finance for UK SMEs, the existence of structural financing gaps due to market failures has been documented since as far back as 1931 (MacMillan Committee 1931). The Department for Business, Innovation & Skills (BIS) periodically conducts a demand survey among SME employers, the results of which suggest that market failures that prevent viable SMEs from accessing finance are still a problem.[1]

Debt financing gap. There is a debt financing gap for businesses that lack a track record and collateral. In general, it is costly for lenders to distinguish between high- and low-risk entrepreneurs (Beck 2012). To avoid the costs associated with collecting information on potential borrowers, lenders often require evidence of a financial track record and/or collateral to be provided. Despite advances in credit scoring techniques that have helped to lower the cost of assessing business proposals, these requirements remain a significant feature of current debt markets due to information asymmetries (HM Treasury 2004). This, in turn, negatively affects start-up businesses that require external sources of finance (BIS 2012).

Equity financing gap. Due to the transaction costs of undertaking due diligence, private equity investors tend to favour fewer, larger investments in later-stage businesses at the expense of early-stage venture capital for viable SMEs with high growth potential. The most recent assessment by the BIS (2009) confirms that in normal market conditions, a structural equity gap of between £250,000 and £5 million exists (the equity gap increases to £15 million for sectors that require complex R&D or large capital expenditure, often with long investment horizons). These equity gap boundaries relate to the maximum that angel investors would provide and the minimum amount that private sector venture capitalists were willing to invest (BIS 2012).

---

[1] The BIS found that although the percentage of SME employers seeking finance in the last twelve months rose from 23% in 2007/8 to 26% in 2010, there was evidence to show that demand for bank finance was declining. Of the SME employers that sought finance, 56% were looking for working capital while 21% wanted it for investment purposes (OECD 2012b). Evidence from the 2011 survey suggests that 74% of SMEs that sought finance managed to obtain it, but SMEs may not have obtained all the finance they required and market failures that restrict viable SMEs from accessing finance still exist (BIS 2009, 2010, 2012).

Growth capital gap. The Rowlands Review (BIS 2009) identified a gap in the provision of growth capital for established businesses looking to expand. Raising growth capital has been a long-standing challenge: banks have typically been averse to providing growth capital due to the scarcity of data on financial returns to such investment. Of the directors that participated in the 2012 ECI Growth Survey, 64% indicated that raising growth finance was difficult or very difficult, and this meant that there was a heavy bias towards depending on internal cash flow rather than seeking external finance (ECI Partners 2012). The Rowlands Review estimates that there exists a growth capital gap of between £2 million and £10 million. This reflects the £2 million ceiling of existing government interventions and the £10 million threshold below which private equity firms, including venture capitalists, rarely invest due to the structure of their business models (BIS 2012). The Business Finance Taskforce recommended establishing a new Business Growth Fund (BGF) to fill the gap in the availability of long-term equity growth capital that was identified in the Rowlands Review. The BGF became operational in April 2011 and the investment it provides takes the form of equity or equity-like capital (minority stakes). The BGF's shareholders committed a total of £2.5 billion to fund investments and six regional offices were set up across the UK.[2]

Demand-Side Market Failures

There are informational failures that affect the demand side of the market: SMEs may not recognize the potential benefits of external finance, they may believe that only debt finance is suitable, and they may lack the skills to put their projects forward to investors in a professional way. Furthermore, businesses are increasingly reluctant to approach banks due to perceived tight credit conditions: it is feared that making an approach would lead to an increase in the cost of existing borrowings or to reductions in overdraft limits (NESTA 2011b). BIS (2012) found that the value of applications by SMEs for new term loan and overdraft facilities in the six months prior to February 2011 decreased by 19% compared with the same period a year earlier. Moreover, in order to decrease the risk of adverse changes in the price or availability of credit, small businesses are cautious about making new investments. Instead, they are choosing to repay bank debt and increase cash holdings. The CBI's 2011 SME Trends Survey of

---

[2]According to the first review of the BGF's activities, eleven investments have been made since October 2011.

manufacturers demonstrates that the proportion of manufacturers planning to invest only to replace existing capital in the year ahead rose to the highest level registered since such a survey was first conducted in October 1998 (CBI 2011).

In most of the countries in which large sums of public money were used to rescue banks during the financial crisis, the government requested that banks supply the SME sector with sufficient credit, with some governments requiring banks to report their level of support for SMEs. Several OECD countries introduced credit monitoring and mediation systems. SMEs that are denied credit by banks can call in these monitors or mediators, who then attempt to reconcile the differences between the parties. Despite the fact that mediators do not have any formal authority to reverse a bank's initial decision, these measures have proved to be an effective way of easing access to credit for SMEs in several countries, particularly in France and Belgium (OECD 2010). Unlike traditional guarantee programmes, which have mostly been used by medium-sized enterprises, mediation has mostly been used by smaller enterprises. Importantly, the experience of these systems has highlighted some demand-side factors that play an important role in credit rejections: communication problems between entrepreneurs and banks, a lack of clarity in the business plans put forward to banks, and a lack of skills among entrepreneurs when it comes to drafting viable business plans.

6.4 THE ROOTS OF UK FINANCIAL MARKET FAILURES

6.4.1 *Lack of Competition in Banking*

The lack of competitive pressures on UK banks has resulted in a lack of incentives to provide innovative services for SME customers. There are two dimensions to this: high concentration in retail banking, and weak effective competition (in the form of high barriers to entry and exit and poor conditions for consumer choice).

High Concentration in the Retail Banking Market

Concerns about the effectiveness of competition in the retail lending market are long standing.[3] According to Vickers (Independent Commission

---

[3] There have been several studies on this topic since 2000: Cruickshank's (2000) report into competition in UK banking, the Competition Commission's (2002) inquiry into SME banking, the OFT's (2006) Survey of SME Banking, the OFT's (2010) 'Review of barriers to entry, expansion and exit in retail banking', and the Final Report of the Independent Commission on Banking (2011).

on Banking 2011), most of the problems highlighted by Cruickshank (2000) on competition in UK banking remain.

Numerous studies have expressed concern about the high levels of concentration in UK SME banking. In 2002 the Competition Commission found that the four largest clearing groups (Barclays, HSBC, Lloyds TSB and Royal Bank of Scotland) accounted for over 90% of liquidity management services in each region. By 2007 the OFT concluded that competition had increased, with the strongest challengers being HBOS and Alliance & Leicester, but the four largest banks still accounted for nearly 80% of liquidity management services in 2008 (OFT 2010).

Furthermore, the financial crisis has led to an increase in concentration in the retail banking market through mergers and exits from the market. In particular, the mergers of Lloyds TSB with HBOS and Santander with Alliance & Leicester have eliminated the strongest challengers to the four largest banks identified by the OFT before the crisis.[4] According to the Independent Commission on Banking (2011), concentration is now higher than it was before the crisis in many retail banking sub-markets, including SME banking (see figure 6.3). SME banking was the most concentrated market in 2010, with a Herfindahl–Hirschman Index of 1,910.[5] In 2010 the four largest banks had an 85% share of the market for business current accounts.[6]

Weak Effective Competition in the Retail Banking Market

Concentration is one criterion for assessing the competitiveness of the SME lending market. While there is a tendency for markets to be less competitive when they are more concentrated (see Degryse and Ongena 2008), the link between concentration and competition is not straightforward. In principle, competition can be strong in concentrated markets and weak in markets that are not highly concentrated, although this is likely to be the exception rather than the rule. Other reasons for the lack of effective competition in retail banking include barriers to entry and exit and to consumer choice.

---

[4]Notably, the Lloyds TSB/HBOS acquisition was not referred to the Competition Commission despite the fact that the OFT had found that the test for reference on competition grounds was met for personal current accounts, banking services to SMEs and mortgages.

[5]According to the OFT merger assessment guidelines, any market with a Herfindahl–Hirschman Index exceeding 1,000 (respectively, 2,000) may be regarded as concentrated (respectively, highly concentrated).

[6]Note that these figures do not take into account the impact of the Lloyds Banking Group and Royal Bank of Scotland state-aid divestitures.

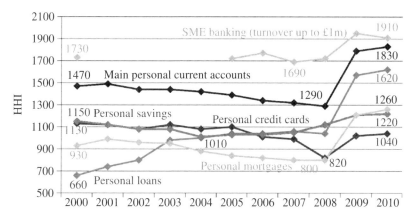

Figure 6.3. Concentration levels in retail banking measured using the Herfindahl–Hirschman Index.

Source: Independent Commission on Banking (2011).

Barriers to entry and exit. High barriers to entry and exit can result in weak competition even if the market is not highly concentrated. Recent work by the OFT (2010) concluded that new entrants face difficulties in attracting customers and gaining market share. The most challenging barrier to entry was the difficulty in attracting personal and SME customers, due to the latter's preference for banks with a large branch network, strong brand loyalty and low switching rates. According to an OFT survey, for 17% of SMEs one of the main reasons for choosing a specific bank was that its branch was located closest to their business (OFT 2006). Already holding a personal current account with a particular bank was cited as one of the main reasons for adopting that bank as their business bank by 34% of SMEs. This suggests that banks that are not active, or do not have a strong presence, in personal banking face a significant barrier in attracting SME customers.

In addition, the 'too big (or too important) to fail subsidy' may also represent an important barrier to exit. A large body of evidence suggests that large banks benefit from implicit subsidies due to the fact that their creditors anticipate government bailouts (see, for example, O'Hara and Shaw 1990; Morgan and Stiroh 2005; Schmidt and Walter 2009; Gandhi and Lustig 2010; Bank of England 2010). Banks that are perceived to be too big to fail are protected from market discipline and derive benefits from their status in the shape of lower funding costs for reasons that have nothing to do with fundamentals. This may place new entrants and smaller banks at a disadvantage. The recent financial crisis has worsened this competitive distortion. The Bank of England Financial Stability Review of December 2010 provided estimates of government subsidies for banks and building societies split by size for 2007, 2008 and 2009. In all three years small banks were estimated to have received the lowest subsidy in proportion to their size.

Consumer choice. For competition to be effective, consumers must be well informed and be able to switch between providers without incurring substantial transaction costs. Competition between banks can therefore also be undermined by the actual and perceived difficulties for customers in identifying the best banking products for their needs and switching between providers. Given consumers' low willingness to switch, banks have weak incentives to provide better offers. An OFT study of personal current accounts in 2008 showed that a significant proportion of consumers believe that it is difficult and risky to switch accounts. These perceptions were found to contribute significantly to low switching rates. Few consumers spend time actively monitoring the relative competitiveness of their accounts. Similarly, the survey showed that many consumers are not aware of, or do not properly understand, the key fees attached to their personal current accounts. Similar problems apply in the market for business current accounts. As a result, switching rates in SME banking are very low.[7]

6.4.2 Lack of Economies of Scale in SME Financing

A key reason for the gap in SME lending may be the lack of economies of scale and the limited fee-generating capacity in these types of activity. According to Skidelsky *et al.* (2011), the lack of economies of scale in the administration of loans to SMEs is a primary reason for banks' lack of interest in lending to them. There are important economies of scale in bank lending activities, e.g. in the production of information about borrowers, but economies of scale cannot be exploited at the typical

---

[7]In response to concerns raised by the OFT on the low levels of switching in retail banking, and following the recommendations of the Independent Commission on Banking's Final Report, a new account switching system will be put in place by the Payments Council in September 2013 to benefit personal and small business customers. Importantly, this service includes a guarantee that both consumers and small businesses will be able to switch all aspects of their current account from one financial institution to another in seven working days; and a redirection service for customers' payments into and out of their account, including direct credits, debits, standing orders and regular card payments.

borrowing scale of SMEs.[8] Consequently, banks will prefer large loans to larger firms. The lack of economies of scale is a problem everywhere, not just in the UK, but market participants suggest that UK banks tend to focus excessively on fee-generating activities (such as mergers and acquisitions activities). Since there is limited potential for small clients to generate fees in the current SME banking model, large and established companies get precedence.

The Breedon Review (2012) advocates the creation of an aggregation and securitization platform for SME loans (the Agency for Business Lending), for which there is increasing support. In the same vein, the Association for Financial Markets in Europe has proposed setting up a platform for SME securitization that will need initial government funding. Such a platform would remove the requirement for investors to analyse the credit quality of many small issuances from individual SMEs. This could help banks to relax financing constraints when lending to SMEs (European Commission 2007) and contribute to the creation of a corporate bond market for SMEs in the UK. Although SME loan securitization has become more widespread in the EU, the market is still immature, especially when compared with other sectors such as mortgages, where securitization has enabled banks to increase the production and affordability of mortgage loans.[9] In addition, data from the Association for Financial Markets in Europe/the European Securitisation Forum show that the UK lags behind other EU member states, with one of the lowest amounts of SME securitization at the end of 2010 (European Investment Fund 2011).

A related development is the pledge by the Business Finance Taskforce to improve the access of SMEs, and particularly medium-sized businesses, to syndicated debt markets (Business Finance Taskforce 2010). In the UK most SMEs use a single bank to cover their entire needs for debt financing. The use of club and syndicated loans is less widespread in the UK than

---

[8]However, it is also true that some technologies applied to lending to SMEs benefit from the effects of economies of scale, e.g. credit scoring. Credit scoring systems rely on statistical models and hence a large number of clients and loans.

[9]According to the European Commission (2007), it is estimated that only around 1–2% of securitizable SME claims in bank balance sheets in the EU have been securitized. By contrast, around 10% of outstanding residential mortgage loans were securitized. The SME securitization market is developing more slowly than other market segments for a variety of reasons, including the high degree of diversity in SME loan instruments, and the different types of collateral and legal forms of SMEs (European Commission 2007). This diversity makes it more difficult to securitize SME loans than other more standardized asset classes. In addition, securitization of SME loans implies high market entry costs, which can be prohibitive for regional or smaller credit institutions, which are those that tend to have high market share in the SME lending market.

in other countries. Since syndicated loans can be resold on secondary markets, this may help increase the liquidity of the SME loan market and make SME loans more attractive to investors.

6.4.3 *Short-Termism*

Short-termism may be characterized as a propensity to underinvest in physical assets or intangibles and/or as hyperactive behaviour by executives: namely, a tendency to focus on restructuring, financial re-engineering, or mergers and acquisitions to the detriment of the development of the fundamental capabilities of the business (Kay 2012).

The short-termism debate is not new. Excessive discounting of future outcomes was already a familiar topic among classical economists. Short-termism is a market failure, resulting in underinvestment, especially in long-duration projects and projects with high build or sunk costs, such as infrastructure and high-tech investments. These are often projects with the highest long-term (private and social) returns. Concerns with short-termism exist in equity markets, business and banking, and we discuss each of these areas in turn. We also consider the issue of growing short-termism in institutional investment, which may be a manifestation of developments in equity markets. Finally, we discuss the government's plan to create a Business Bank, which could be used to leverage the advantages of institutional investment to address the long-standing gaps in the supply of SME finance.

6.4.3.1 *Short-Termism in Equity Markets*

Emphasis on Short-Term Relative Performance

There is increasingly clear evidence that equity markets systematically discourage long-term investment, particularly in risky endeavours like R&D or other forms of innovation (see, for example, Asker *et al.* 2011; Aghion *et al.* 2013; Haldane and Davies 2011). Discussing these issues in the context of UK equity markets, the Kay Review has recently noted that the appointment and monitoring of active asset managers is too often based on short-term relative performance, whereas companies and savers should be largely interested in long-term absolute performance (Kay 2012). In other words, there is a conflict between the business model of asset managers and the interests of UK businesses and investors.

According to the Kay Review, competition between asset managers on the basis of relative performance is a zero-sum game. The activities of asset managers can only benefit savers taken as a whole to the extent that they focus on improving the performance of investee companies. The pre-eminence of relative performance appears to be reinforced by regulatory requirements on the asset management industry. Respondents to the Kay Review mentioned that greater obligations on trustees to seek professional advice—as well as stronger transparency and disclosure requirements—had resulted in more extensive benchmarking, performance monitoring and use of external consultants, all of which reinforce the tendency to focus on short-term relative performance.

Investors Lack the Incentives or the Ability to Counteract Short-Termism

Rajan (2006) argues that investors may have weak private incentives to actively prevent investment managers from focusing on short-term returns. Current investors in a fund benefit when new investors join because the fund's average costs decrease. By contrast, the movement of investors between funds has little social value (and potentially has negative value) as there is very little robust evidence that past fund performance is an indicator of future results. Consequently, current investors have weak incentives to restrain managers from focusing on the short term, and the private gains from attracting new investors to the fund through its superior short-term performance exceed the social gains. Finally, even if investors were willing to restrain managers' short-term focus, they may not have complete control over the latter: for example, because of weaknesses in corporate governance.

Hyperactivity Bias

The Kay Review also noted a bias towards action that is found at almost every point in the equity investment chain (Kay 2012): corporate executives dedicate a lot of attention and time to reorganizations, acquisitions and disposals; traders earn returns based on the volume of activity in the securities in which they deal; analysts are rewarded if their advice generates buy or sell recommendations; investment bankers and advisers generate earnings from transactions; and independent financial advisers are remunerated by commissions. This hyperactivity bias is a symptom of short-termism.

6.4.3.2 *Short-Termism in Business*

Even if capital markets were rational, it is possible that distortions in corporate management would lead to short-termism and underinvestment. Stein (1989) develops a model of inefficient managerial behaviour in the face of a rational stock market. In the model, managers try to mislead the market about the worth of their firms by forgoing good investment opportunities in order to boost current earnings. Two relevant areas are short-termism in mergers and acquisitions decisions and short-termism in executive pay.

Short-Termism, Mergers and Acquisitions (Hyper-)activity and Foreign Acquisitions of UK Businesses

There appears to be a tendency for British businesses to sell up rather than raise finance to grow, and to acquire rather than develop existing operations. Several leading British companies ceased to exist due to bad mergers and acquisitions decisions: they were either sold to foreign firms or made bad diversification decisions. Famous examples include the sale of the glassmaker Pilkington to Japan's Nippon Sheet Glass in 2006 and the takeover of Imperial Chemical Industries (ICI) by AkzoNobel, a Dutch conglomerate, in 2008.

NESTA (2012a) also identifies a tendency among British firms in high-tech and capital-intensive sectors to be bought by overseas businesses instead of raising and utilizing growth capital. While inward foreign direct investment can bring great benefits to the UK economy, the acquisition of UK businesses by foreign companies sometimes results in the transfer of much or all of the acquired operations out of the UK. The semiconductor sector is an example of this phenomenon. NESTA provides evidence that this tendency has weakened the productivity of the UK manufacturing sector. According to NESTA, industries in which this does not happen, including aerospace and pharmaceuticals, are those where government has provided strong support in developing a complete innovation system. NESTA therefore suggests that competition authorities intervene in takeovers of intellectual property-based firms through requiring 'binding commitments on [innovative] capacity as a condition for takeovers to proceed' (NESTA 2012a).

Similarly, the Kay Review deplores the fact that some companies place too much emphasis on acquisitions relative to developing the competitive advantage of their existing business operations (Kay 2012). Kay argues that the short-term incentives of market participants, particularly those advising companies on takeover activity, have led to mergers and acquisitions that have destroyed long-term value for investors. This tendency for British businesses to sell rather than raise finance to grow, and to acquire rather than develop existing operations, may be due to short-termism in the financial sector, but also to agency problems in corporations, including managers' 'empire building' incentives (see, for example, Jensen and Meckling 1976; Jensen 1986)

Short-Termism and Executive Compensation

In the financial services industry competition between banks and other financial institutions for bankers and traders is intense. As a result, bankers and traders receive pay that is focused too much on short-term revenues and performance. Consequently, huge risks have built up in the financial system. This short-termism is believed to be one of the causes of the recent financial crisis. Globally, financial regulators are introducing new rules that determine the allowable structure of bankers' pay. But the concern that executives put short-term results ahead of long-term value creation is not specific to financial services. A compelling narrative in the accounting scandals leading up to the Sarbanes–Oxley Act of 2002 in the US was that pressure to deliver short-term results resulted in profits being booked early and results being manipulated. In the scandals caused by major accidents in industries such as oil, it was again concluded that pressure for short-term results led executives to excessively discount possible future costs by neglecting due testing and delaying safety-driven interruptions to production. Similarly, executives that agree to take part in price-fixing cartels overly discount the costs of the fines and law suits that their businesses might incur in the future. There are clearly many instances across numerous industries when firms focus on the short term at the expense of future profits. This raises the question of why firms choose to offer remuneration contracts that can induce managerial myopia in the first place.

The academic literature has generated several competing explanations as to why firms would find it optimal to hire executives with contracts that tolerate short-termism. Bolton *et al.* (2006) argue that stock prices may deviate from fundamentals and include a speculative element that is increased by short-term actions. Therefore, shareholders may use contracts for their chief executive officers that induce them to take short-term actions that will maximize shareholders' profits from sales to overconfident investors. Froot *et al.* (1992) make a similar argument.

Thanassoulis (2012) argues that firms must use some form of variable remuneration to induce effort, and this introduces a myopia problem. Executives have an incentive to inflate early expected earnings at the expense of future profits. To manage this short-termism some bonus pay must be deferred. Convergence in size among firms makes the cost of managing the myopia problem grow faster than the cost of managing the effort problem. Ultimately, the optimal contract can jump from one that deters myopia to one that tolerates it.

The idea that including stock options in executives' compensation packages aligns the interests of shareholders and managers has also been questioned. Lazonick (2010) and Parris *et al.* (2010) argue that stock buybacks, legitimized by the ideology that firms should maximize shareholder value, are a symptom of managerial myopia and undermine long-term investment and R&D. Lazonick's analysis of different industries suggests that the sharp increase in executive pay via stock options is happening at the expense of innovation in the US economy. He argues that large US information and communications technology (ICT) companies, such as Microsoft, Cisco, IBM and Intel, invest more profits into stock repurchases than they invest in R&D. Similar behaviour is found in pharmaceuticals. Large firms, such as Johnson & Johnson, Pfizer and Amgen, often justify the high prices of their drugs in the US by pointing out their need to recover large R&D expenditures—while simultaneously reinvesting profits into stock repurchases.

Linking pay to longer-term performance may not be the panacea either. Inderst and Pfeil (2013) examine whether financial institutions should be required to defer bonus pay in order to align incentives with the longer-term risk of transactions. They derive conditions for when such mandatory deferred compensation curbs risk taking and improves the quality of assets, but they also show that such regulatory interference can have the opposite effect and lead to deferred, but more high-powered, incentives and thus, ultimately, to lower asset quality.[10]

6.4.3.3 Short-Termism in Banking

Given that SMEs are more vulnerable to problems of asymmetric information than large firms, and that they are much more bank dependent, relationship lenders have an important role to play in the provision of external finance to SMEs (Carbo-Valverde *et al.* 2009; Canales and Nanda 2012). In their capacity as relationship lenders, banks develop close relationships with borrowers over a long period of time, a costly process which facilitates monitoring and screening and can overcome problems of asymmetric information (Boot 2000). In recent years, however, banking seems

---

[10]In the model, deferring compensation allows the principal to observe a more informative signal on the quality of a closed deal. However, deferring compensation is costly as the agent is more impatient than the firm. Unintended consequences are possible when deferred compensation is too costly for what it delivers in terms of additional information.

to have evolved towards more arms-length and transaction-oriented banking (trading) and away from traditional intermediation.

These movements have ramifications for long-term growth. According to recent work by Beck *et al.* (2012), the growth effects of finance come mainly from the intermediation function. Based on a sample of seventy-seven countries for the period 1980–2007, the authors find that intermediation activities increase growth and reduce volatility in the long term. An expansion of the financial sector along other dimensions (non-intermediation activities, including professional and business services) has no long-run effect on real sector outcomes. Following Beck (2012), recent policy approaches towards the financial system have focused more on the size of the sector rather than on its intermediating function, which may have led to short-run growth at the expense of high volatility.

Moreover, the emphasis on arms-length and transaction-oriented banking impacts the availability of the relationship lending services that are so important for SMEs. In what follows we examine two symptoms of short-termist behaviour in SME banking: excessive reliance on credit scoring, and the 'advice gap'.

Lack of Relationship Lending: Excessive Reliance on Credit Scoring

Short-termism is reflected in banks' 'lending technologies', particularly credit scoring systems that emphasize short-term financial indicators rather than long-term industrial performance indicators such as productivity growth. According to market participants, the UK banking sector is unique in Europe in terms of the importance it gives to the credit scoring system. This issue has been raised by several institutions: for example, the European Commission's FINNOV (Finance, Innovation & Growth) collaboration and the OECD. The academic literature on lending technologies and their impact on credit availability for SMEs is sparse (see, for example, Berger and Frame 2007; DeYoung *et al.* 2008) and tends to focus on the benefits of credit scoring for small businesses. Berger and Frame (2007) argue that small-business credit scoring has improved access to credit for small businesses in the US in a number of dimensions, including

(1) an increased supply of credit,

(2) increased lending to relatively opaque, risky borrowers,

(3) increased lending within low-income areas,

(4) lending over greater distances and

(5) increased loan maturity.

In the UK, however, there is mounting evidence that the credit scoring system does a poor job when it comes to financing small and innovative businesses. Given the high transaction costs of conducting due diligence on each and every individual SME, banks tend to be reliant on credit scoring, such as having a good track record and a high level of collateral. This 'tick box' approach automatically shuts out many SMEs, particularly start-ups, because they enjoy neither. Analysis by Experian and NESTA suggests that banks' credit scoring ratings systematically favour low-growth businesses over high-growth ones, all other things being equal (NESTA 2011a).

The appeals process launched by the Business Finance Taskforce in April 2011 showed that credit scoring is an important reason for the decline of loan applications by start-ups (see appendix 6B for more details). According to the Business Finance Taskforce, this is because the personal credit scoring of entrepreneurs is examined as much as the credit scoring of their businesses. This suggests that it is personal credit scoring (which is mainly done externally to the banks) rather than the banks' own credit scoring process that needs to be reviewed.

Lack of Relationship Lending: An Advice Gap

NESTA (2011b) argues that small businesses suffer from an advice gap, despite the presence of services such as corporatefinance.org.uk (a network of independent accountants and business advisers) and the Forum of Private Business. Survey data gathered for SME Finance Monitor shows that most small business managers seek little or no external advice. Many exclusively depend on their accountant for advice. Small businesses that see their applications for loans or overdrafts rejected often complain about poor advice from their banks. Those problems are currently being addressed by the UK's five largest banks through the Business Finance Taskforce. The key area for improvement identified by the Business Finance Taskforce review of the appeals process was the importance of a return to old-fashioned banking relationships.[11]

First, banks need to retrain their own staff so that they are qualified to make credit judgements and lending decisions. The review highlights that branch staff often do not possess the necessary skills to make credit judgements and instead rely on the 'tick box approach' of credit scoring.

---

[11] According to Accenture (2011), the availability of innovative and relationship-based services is an increasingly important reason given by SMEs for switching banks. In addition, the successful entry of Handelsbanken into the UK market is evidence of the attractiveness of, and need for, relationship lending.

In other words, branch staff have often become salespeople rather than lenders. Second, businesses also need training in how to approach banks and put their business cases forward. Third, the review highlights the need for early and continued dialogue between lenders and SMEs through relationship managers. And finally, customer feedback suggests that many smaller businesses are unaware of what type of finance options might be available to them. There is a need for banks to refer businesses that have been declined credit to other forms of finance. Businesses, in turn, need to be educated about the availability of alternative sources of finance. More details about the Business Finance Taskforce's review of lending technologies are given in appendix 6B.

Relationship Lending and Competition in Banking

Section 6.4.1 identified the long-standing lack of competition in the SME banking market as a major problem, and this section has identified a potential lack of relationship lending in the UK, which may negatively affect SMEs (Carbo-Valverde *et al.* 2009). The question of whether competition and relationship lending are compatible aims therefore arises.

The theoretical literature on the relationship between competition and relationship lending delivers conflicting results. The 'information hypothesis' argues that competitive banking markets can weaken relationship lending because they prevent banks from extracting the informational rents generated by investing in their relationships with borrowers. This deters banks from investing in soft information (see, for example, Petersen and Rajan 1995; Ogura 2010). By contrast, the 'market power hypothesis' states that less competitive banking markets are associated with more credit rationing and a higher price for credit—constraints that traditionally disproportionately affect SMEs. In addition, some authors argue that competition from outside banks (or arm's length lenders) may induce local banks to develop their competitive advantage in providing relationship banking services to small and informationally opaque borrowers in order to insulate themselves from pure price competition from those competitors (see, for example, Boot and Thakor 2000; Yafeh and Yosha 2001; Hauswald and Marquez 2006).

The empirical evidence delivers more positive results on the role of competition. Across a wide swath of sectors, competition has been found to improve productivity and firm performance, partly by improving managerial practices within firms (see, for example, Van Reenen 2011a). Banking is unlikely to be an exception here. Many studies find a positive relationship between interbank competition and relationship lending

(Petersen and Rajan 1995; Fischer 2000; Ogura 2007, 2010), while some do not (Memmel *et al.* 2007; Neuberger *et al.* 2008). A weakness of the empirical literature is that competition is often measured by an index of market concentration, which is a crude proxy. By contrast, Carbo-Valverde *et al.* (2009) employ the Lerner index, which measures the degree of excess profits and is arguably a much better proxy of monopoly power. The authors find that higher competition (i.e. a lower Lerner index) seems to improve credit availability for Spanish SMEs.

Presbitero and Zazzaro (2011) investigate the possibility that the relationship between competition and relationship lending depends on the organizational structure of the local credit market. In particular, they find that increased competition is particularly effective in stimulating relationship lending when markets are not concentrated in a few large incumbents. This is consistent with the finding that small banks have an advantage when lending to small firms due to their ability to engage in relationship banking and because of their decentralized lending structures (Canales and Nanda 2012).[12]

Competition is generally a beneficial force for improving industry performance, and the evidence here suggests that fears that greater competition will undermine relationship lending are mistaken. In fact, competition is likely to simulate more relationship lending to innovative SMEs.

6.4.3.4 *The Case of Institutional Investment*

Institutional investors have specific characteristics that give them a potentially crucial role in channelling the nation's savings into long-term investment that supports sustainable growth. Firstly, they represent 'patient capital': institutional investors (particularly pension funds and life insurers) are 'natural' long-term investors due to the often long-term nature of their liabilities. Secondly, they have an important role in corporate governance: due to their long-term investment horizons, institutional investors may help align managers' incentives with the long-term interests of the investee companies. Thirdly, their size: much of the financial wealth of UK households is in pension funds and insurance companies. The total assets of insurance companies, pension funds and trusts were valued by the ONS to be around £3,000 billion at the end of 2010, and their decisions therefore play a critical role in the process of allocating

---

[12]Strahan (2008), however, notes that large banks may be able to reap the same benefits as smaller banks (without losing the diversification advantages of large size) by breaking their operations up into small affiliate banks.

capital within the economy. However, there are a number of signs pointing to growing short-termism among institutional investors.

Signs of Short-Termism in Institutional Investment

Declining investment holding periods. Most OECD stock markets, including the London Stock Exchange, have displayed declining investment holding periods in the last few decades (OECD 2011d). While this trend is partly driven by the growing importance of investors that trade with a high frequency, such as hedge funds, there is evidence that even long-term investors have increasing portfolio turnover rates. According to Mercer (2010), 8.2% of managers of UK equity strategy funds had portfolio turnover rates that exceeded the expected level during 2006–9. During the same period, 40.5% of managers of European (including UK) equity strategy funds had portfolio turnover rates that exceeded expectations. Furthermore, pension funds are gradually becoming the most important investors in hedge funds, so they have also contributed to the rapid increase in the frequency of trading observed in recent years.

Increasing allocation to hedge funds. Pre-crisis, the largest portion of capital for hedge funds came from non-institutional investors such as high-net-worth individuals and family offices, but institutional investors have now become the leading investors in these funds (KPMG/AIMA 2012). Not only were there a lot of redemptions from hedge funds by non-institutional investors during the crisis, but the proportion of institutional assets being allocated to the global hedge fund industry has grown significantly in the years since the financial crisis. According to a survey by Natixis (2012), a long-only strategy of traditional assets is no longer viable, as traditional assets are too highly correlated and deliver low returns. Therefore, institutional investors have started looking into liquid alternative investments as a way of managing portfolio risk, mitigating the impact of market volatility on portfolios and achieving higher returns.

Increasing investment in short-term assets. The latest statistics on the net investments of insurance companies, pension funds and trusts released by the ONS in September 2012 show that investment in short-term assets (those maturing within one year of their originating date) continued to be positive at Q2 2012. At Q1 2012, net investment in short-term assets was estimated to be £24 billion: the highest level since records began in 1983. Since Q3 2010 there have been six quarters of net investment in short-term assets and only one quarter of net disinvestment

(Q3 2011). This contrasts with the period Q4 2008–Q3 2010 during which six of the eight quarters showed net disinvestment in short-term assets. Although these are recent developments, they should be monitored in the future.

Low allocations to long-term infrastructure assets. The surge in private infrastructure investment only started recently (about five years ago) as this sector has historically mainly relied on public sources of financing. In the UK the level of infrastructure investment is estimated to be less than 1% of pension funds' assets, compared with 8–15% in Australia and Canada (OECD 2011c). Insurance companies' levels of investment in infrastructure are also very low. However, according to the OECD future infrastructure investments will have to rely to a much greater extent on the private sector because of both the sheer size of the investment needs and strained public finances (OECD 2007).

Infrastructure investments seem naturally well suited to pension funds and life insurers as they can produce predictable and stable cash flows over the long term, matching long-term liabilities and reducing portfolio volatility. Nevertheless, institutional investment in infrastructure has so far been modest. Important factors identified by the OECD (2011d) that limit the involvement of institutional investors in the financing of infrastructure projects include the following.

- Investment regulations that discourage allocations to unlisted instruments.
- Weaknesses in governance and insufficient project scale.
- An inadequate general investment policy framework resulting in a lack of adequate investment opportunities.

Some of these issues are addressed in the chapter on public investment in infrastructure (chapter 4).

Decreasing allocation to equities. In continental Europe, insurance companies and pension funds have traditionally had a much more conservative asset allocation than their counterparts in the UK, and a large share of investment has gone into government bonds. In the UK, the investments of both insurance companies and pension funds have been highly geared towards equities (see, for example, OECD 2011a). However, pension funds' exposure to equities as a percentage of total assets has been decreasing since the mid 1990s—a trend that may be partly driven by regulatory and accounting constraints (as discussed below).

There also appear to be changes in the composition of equity investments. The last ONS survey of the balance sheets of insurance companies, pension funds and trusts (for the end of 2010) showed that, for the first time, the value of overseas ordinary shares held by these institutions exceeded the value of UK ordinary shares held. Since 2010 there has been further disinvestment in UK corporate securities and investment in overseas securities.

Failure to exercise a voice in corporate governance. The lack of active engagement by institutional investors in the corporate governance of their investee companies is a long-standing issue that was highlighted in the Myners Review as far back as 2001 (see Myners (2001) and, for further details, appendix 6C). Recently, the issue has been flagged up again by the Kay Review of UK equity markets (Kay 2012) and the OECD review of corporate governance and the financial crisis (OECD 2009a).

The Origins of Short-Termism among Institutional Investors

There may be factors that are distorting decision making by institutional investors and preventing them from investing with a sufficiently long-term view.

Long-standing agency problems. The origins of short-termism for pension funds mainly lie in agency problems. Most funds, especially smaller ones that lack in-house expertise, rely extensively on external asset management firms, which may not always pursue the best interests of the ultimate asset owners. In addition, incentives and monitoring structures may be ill designed.[13]

Long-standing regulatory pressures. Regulatory constraints can have a significant impact on the proportion of assets that can be directed towards long-term investing. Regulations in continental Europe have traditionally been stricter than those in the UK, but prudential and accounting standards may still create distortions in institutional investors' asset

---

[13]The main agency problems relate to differences in time horizons and the monitoring of agents. Investment managers and other advisers are likely to wish to optimize short-term returns because they are monitored over a much shorter horizon than the investment horizon of the fund owners. Furthermore, the performance of investment managers is often evaluated in relation to a performance benchmark or index such as the S&P 500. Myners (2001) argues that this tends to produce investment decisions—particularly regarding asset allocation—that are based on what other funds are doing. Once most pension funds are not invested in a given asset class, it becomes very difficult for one manager to break ranks and invest differently, however good the prospects for that asset class might be.

allocation decisions. For example, the implementation of the UK Pensions Act in 1997 and the announcement of mark-to-market accounting as part of FRS 17 in 2000 had a significantly negative impact on the proportion of funds that pension funds allocate to equities. The Pensions Act 1997 required defined-benefit funds to meet the 'minimum funding requirement'. This increased their incentives to invest in safer assets because this is the best way to ensure confidence about meeting defined pension liabilities. Mark-to-market accounting (introduced in FRS 17) encourages investors to focus on short-term changes in market value rather than on the long-term prospects of an investment, which may also induce them to minimize risk taking.

Pressures resulting from the crisis and new regulations. The financial crisis caused extreme market volatility in 2008–9, and UK pension funds found themselves underfunded by about 15% by the end of 2009 (OECD 2009a). According to the World Economic Forum (2011), the crisis created pressures to both de-risk and re-risk. As a result, investment management has become either hyperactive or excessively passive, neither of which is conducive to long-term and engaged investment on the part of institutional investors.

Pressures to de-risk. Regulated pension funds' underfunded positions constrain their ability to adopt a long-term investment strategy. Long-term investing requires the ability to hold on to assets in the face of market volatility. UK pension funds face pressure from the regulator to maintain funded status in the short term and to make up for any shortfall in funding. These constraints, combined with the reporting of pension results to the market on a short-term basis, encourage some pension funds to set a lower risk appetite. Accordingly, for the more traditional parts of their portfolios, funds have incentives to increase the proportion of assets allocated to liquid, high-grade debt instruments.

The introduction of Solvency II (an updated and expanded version of the Solvency I regulatory requirements for insurance firms in the EU that is expected to come into effect in 2013) may also reinforce this bias for short-termism as it will penalize insurers for holding assets with high volatility, such as equity. Investments in common stock or illiquid assets require an institution to hold significantly more capital in reserve than does investment in high-grade corporate bonds. The need to maintain a high capital ratio therefore acts as strong encouragement to insurance companies to invest in low-risk assets. One may therefore expect a migration away from equity and towards fixed-income assets, discouraging life insurers from making longer-term investments in illiquid markets.

Pressures to re-risk. On the other hand, it is critical for funds to have sufficient capital to meet their shorter-term obligations. Therefore, there is pressure to increase risk in their portfolios. This search for returns may have contributed to the recent increase in exposure to hedge funds that was mentioned above.

Demographic pressures. Finally, life insurers and pension funds are subject to structural demographic pressures. As a result, the liability profiles of many pension plans are moving towards shorter durations, which will encourage these institutions to further de-risk and to place less emphasis on long-term investment strategies.

6.4.3.5 *Addressing Short-Termism with a Business Bank*

One recent attempt by the government to leverage the advantages of institutional investment to address the long-standing structural gaps in the supply of SME finance has been the creation of the Business Bank (HM Treasury 2012a). Armendariz de Aghion (1999) formally shows that a public financial institution may be an effective way of combatting the short-termist tendencies of a decentralized banking system that under-invests and fails to disseminate expertise in long-term industrial finance.

Under the Business Bank, £1 billion of government funding will be combined with private sector participation (i.e. investment from pension funds and other long-term institutional investors) to support up to £10 billion of additional business lending to manufacturers, exporters and high-growth companies. With an aim to become fully operational by autumn 2014, the Business Bank will operate through the wholesale markets and will not replace or subsidize retail banks (HM Treasury 2012a). The government has been clear that the role of the institution is to encourage, rather than compete with, private sector solutions for SME financing. The Business Bank's lower cost of capital and its remit to consider social returns would allow it to make loans that would typically be avoided by commercial banks. In particular, it would be able to take a wider economic view of the benefits of investing in certain sectors.

The Business Bank may provide a demonstration effect to the financial market, boosting confidence. This may be particularly relevant as major structural changes are needed, including banks intermediating more equity and debt capital financing, and more innovative ways of financing SMEs. For example, the Business Bank could follow in the footsteps of the US Small Business Administration (see box 6.1 below) and contribute to the growth of a corporate bond market for SMEs in the UK by participating in SME loan securitization, such as the securitization platform strategy advocated by the Breedon Review (2012). By removing the need for investors to assess the credit risk of many small issuances from individual SMEs, such a platform could relax SME financing constraints as well as kick-start institutional investment in SMEs (Dolphin and Nash 2012).

The Business Bank will house, review and rationalize existing government schemes under the Department for Business, Innovation & Skills aimed at boosting SME lending. By bringing all policies and schemes under the management of a single institution, policy continuity, consistency and scale may be improved substantially. Moreover, the Business Bank's singular strategy of raising funds on capital markets specifically to address structural financing gaps for SMEs may allow it to avoid the pitfalls of similar, less effective former and existing government policies. In 2011 the government established 'Project Merlin', under which banks agreed to provide £190 billion of new credit to businesses (Bank of England 2011b). However, the scheme targeted gross, not net, lending. While banks were making new lending available, businesses were massively repaying existing debts, so that net lending was actually negative. Launched in March 2012, the National Loan Guarantee Scheme was designed to make cheaper finance available to companies by providing government guarantees on unsecured borrowing by banks (HM Treasury 2011). This was followed by the July 2012 Funding for Lending Scheme, under which the Bank of England made cheap finance available to banks if they pledged to use it to increase lending to firms and households (HM Treasury 2012b). A drawback of both the National Loan Guarantee Scheme and the Funding for Lending Scheme is that they rely on banks' voluntary participation.

In a similar vein, the Business Bank may mirror the strategic coordination abilities of the German Kreditanstalt für Wiederaufbau (KfW) and the US Small Business Administration through having a role in wider business support, procurement assistance, training and advice.

Box 6.1. A case study: the US Small Business Administration.

The US Small Business Administration (SBA) is a government agency rather than a bank, and its main purpose is to direct finance to small businesses and start-ups (Dolphin and Nash 2012). The SBA also acts as a 'national ombudsman' for small business concerns; it is based in Washington, DC.

The SBA uses federal funding and government guarantees to provide affordable and long-term finance to its customers. Like the KfW, the SBA channels finance through financial intermediaries in the form of debt financing, surety bonds and equity. The SBA's primary programme (the 7(a) loan programme) was set up to address the lack of long-term funding for SMEs and is largely revenue neutral. The SBA largely operates on a guarantee-based model and only channels finance to creditworthy businesses (those with a poor credit history are therefore unable to access SBA-issued loans). The SBA guarantees up to 85% for loans worth less than $150,000, with the intermediary being responsible for the remaining liability. The SBA charges a small fee for this service.

Furthermore, the SBA has contributed to the growth of the US SME loan securitization market. In 1975 a secondary market in SBA 7(a) guaranteed loans emerged. In 1984 Congress passed the Small Business Secondary Market Improvement Act, which provided for the central registration and servicing of loans sold in the secondary market by a single fiscal and transfer agent. This legislation allowed the pooling of SBA loans and helped to increase efficiency and provide better liquidity in this sector. Since 1992, SBA-approved finance has allowed the securitization of the unguaranteed amount of loans originated by nonbank, non-depository lenders, further enhancing the liquidity of this sector.

One issue the Business Bank will need to address is whether it should have an industrial policy mandate and target sectors in which the UK has a competitive advantage. Despite industrial policy being a very controversial topic, some recent work does suggest a role for industrial policies (Aghion *et al.* 2012). Corry *et al.* (2011) suggest that an effective long-run growth policy requires government to consider: (1) where there are likely areas of growth and (2) where the UK has some comparative advantage. While it may be difficult to guess future growth sectors, healthcare, education, green technologies, business services and digital businesses stand out as potential candidates. Similarly, the UK has clear comparative advantages in areas such as bio-pharmaceuticals, higher education, financial and business services, creative industries and some areas of ICT (e.g. ARM).

An additional area of concern is the type of institutional architecture that strikes a balance between maintaining operational independence and ensuring strategic alliance with government policy (Skidelsky *et al.* 2011). According to Dolphin and Nash (2012), the most effective way to achieve this is through ensuring that there is a clear division between 'where the input of the government ends and the work of the bankers begins'. In an assessment of public investment banks, Skidelsy *et al.* (2011) conclude that

> a mandate-driven institution with governmental or parliamentary involvement at the strategic level and full autonomy on an operational level has proven to be a model which successfully marries the need for public control over public capital with the need for the maintenance of sound banking principles for market credibility.

The Nordic Investment Bank (NIB) offers a classic example. The board of governors comprises the finance ministers of the bank's member states and it sets the policy decisions for the bank. A Control Committee ensures that this policy is aligned with the NIB's mandate. Assisted by the Management Committee, the Credit Committee, the Finance Committee and the ICT Council, the NIB's president is charged with managing the bank's day-to-day operations. An in-house team sources potential projects and assesses each potential loan in reference to the bank's mandate. This governance and operational strategy attempts to ensure that the NIB remains a politically independent organization with no political influence over individual loans. For example, it is not uncommon for the bank to withhold financial support for member-state government initiatives that do not further the bank's mandate. However, board members have the right to veto loans targeted at his or her country to ensure that that the bank's policies are in line with the national industrial policies of his or her respective state (Skidelsky *et al.* 2011).

Other existing national investment banks, such as Germany's Kreditanstalt für Wiederaufbau (KfW) and the Brazilian Development Bank (BNDES), can offer lessons for the design and operation of the Business Bank (Dolphin and Nash 2012). The KfW was established after the Second World War with the aim of rebuilding Germany through disbursing Marshall aid. The KfW is primarily focused on SME financing, but it also actively invests in infrastructure, housing, entrepreneur and start-up promotion, energy efficiency and environmental protection and innovation. The bank's SME loan financing reached €28.5 billion in 2010 (approximately 94% of the bank's lending commitments). The bank works collaboratively with (rather than in competition with) existing banks: through the bank's 'on-lending' process, SMEs apply for regular bank loans, which the KfW then refinances at favourable interests rates with longer maturities (KfW loans typically have a maturity of 10–20 years and have repayment-free periods). The intermediary bank and the KfW share the liability. The

German government's AAA rating allows the KfW to raise funds at preferential rates and channel the low cost of capital from its bank intermediaries to the borrowers. The KfW is a commercially driven institution that aims to make sound investments: though it is not profit maximizing, it is profit making.

The German federal government owns 80% of KfW's equity while the German Länder own the rest. The KfW's governance structure consists of two executive bodies and two advisory bodies. The executive board is charged with the 'day-to-day management of the bank, the conduct of its business and the administration of its assets' (Dolphin and Nash 2012). The executive board is accountable to the second executive body—the board of supervisory directors—which comprises federal government ministers, members of parliament, representatives from commercial and savings banks, and industry, business and trade union representatives. The SME advisory council provides strategic advice and monitors the bank's work in promoting German SMEs.

The BNDES was established in 1952 with the aim of promoting the objectives of the Brazilian government. It is characterized by having a broad investment portfolio (through its 'corporate integration' approach), which includes investments in Brazilian infrastructure, industry, SMEs, technological innovation, sustainable development, exports and overseas investments. The BNDES focuses primarily on large-scale capital-intensive projects and long-term business finance. Moreover, the bank provides favourable fixed-interest loans to businesses in sectors in which Brazil holds a comparative advantage. Like the KfW, the BNDES relies on intermediaries to channel funds to borrowers. The bank assumes either full liability for credit risk or will work with intermediaries to co-finance loans. In addition to raising funds on capital markets, the BNDES benefits from government tax breaks and a workers' assistance fund. However, the BNDES is largely a self-financing institution and is able to generate the majority of its funds from returns. This is largely due to the bank's diverse, high-performing portfolios, its clear corporate strategy, and its effective risk-management processes.

6.4.4 Excessive Reliance on Debt: Overhang, Forbearance and Debt Bias

Debt Overhang and Forbearance Limit the Capacity of Banks to Make New Loans

UK financial institutions are heavily leveraged and suffer from debt overhang. The accompanying lack of recapitalization prevents banks from extending credit to the UK economy. The phenomenon of forbearance aggravates the situation. While forbearance provides relief to struggling debtors and supports balance sheets in the short term, it also has a negative impact on banks' income and constrains new lending. Forbearance could also generate uncertainty over banks' capital positions, thereby limiting their ability to attract new funding. This may constrain new lending by banks whose capital buffers are already limited.

Despite the difficulties involved in measuring the precise scale of forbearance, there is some evidence that it is happening in the UK. A recent review by the FSA found that around a third of UK commercial real estate loans and 5–8% of UK mortgages are subject to forbearance. These levels are material. Mortgages subject to forbearance exceed total net new mortgage lending to UK households over the past three years (Bank of England 2012b). And there is evidence that this is constraining banks' ability to make new loans. In 2011 the UK banks with the highest levels of forbearance supplied significantly fewer new mortgage loans than the banks with lower levels of forbearance (Bank of England 2012b).

A decrease in credit supply can further weigh on economic growth. An example of this effect was witnessed in the 1990s during the Japanese 'lost decade'. There is a body of evidence that suggests that forbearance by Japanese banks significantly dragged down investment and the employment levels of 'healthy' industries (see Caballero *et al.* 2008). Chari *et al.* (2002) make a similar point about the Great Depression in the US.

Debt Overhang and Forbearance Constrain Business Investment and Productivity

According to the Bank of England (2012c), business investment remains around 15% below its pre-recession peak. At the same time, the level of productivity has on average been around 10% below its pre-crisis trend since mid 2010. Numerous factors may help to explain this, including weak business investment and reduced innovation. In addition, forbearance may be contributing to the financial sector's failure to reallocate capital resources efficiently across sectors of the UK economy. The Bank of England (2012e) provides some initial evidence that the financial system has failed to reallocate capital resources across sectors in response to heterogeneous sectoral shocks since mid 2007. Evidence of capital misallocation includes a marked increase in the dispersion of output growth, price inflation and rates of return on capital at a sectoral level. As the health of the financial system improves, capital will be reallocated efficiently across sectors, especially towards tradables. However, this process may be lengthy and in the meantime businesses with the potential to invest are unable to finance themselves, while 'zombie firms' are allowed to continue operating. This could help explain the strikingly low rate of corporate births and deaths during the crisis and the continued weakness in business investment and productivity. Company liquidations have increased only slightly since the start of the recession, even though company accounting data suggest that the share of companies making losses has increased sharply since 2007.

Tax Distortions Create a General Debt Bias

We have seen that SMEs tend to rely on bank lending, since access to other types of finance is limited. However, an issue across firms of all sizes is a bias towards debt finance due to tax incentives.

This debt bias exists internationally (see IMF 2009, 2011). In most countries, financing investment by debt offers tax advantages, e.g. by allowing interest payments to be tax deductible. This bias is hard to justify on legal, administrative or economic grounds (IMF 2011). In addition, there is evidence that this bias creates significant economic distortions, including inefficiently high debt-to-equity ratios. More importantly, though, it may constrain economic growth by leading to overinvestment by mature firms and underinvestment by innovative growth firms (IMF 2011). Since credit constraints mostly affect the latter type of firms, a general deduction for interest will not benefit them but will benefit firms that have easy access to debt, i.e. large and mature firms.

6.5 MANAGEMENT, PRODUCTIVITY AND GROWTH

The large productivity differences between nations are mirrored in the huge variation in productivity between firms and establishments within countries, even in narrowly defined industries. Syverson (2011), for example, estimates that there is a fourfold difference in labour productivity between plants at the 90th and 10th percentiles of the distribution in a typical four-digit UK manufacturing industry. Although some of these differences can be accounted for by inputs such as capital, skills and technology, a large residual remains (Syverson 2011). Moreover, there is evidence that these differences are persistent (Ábrahám and White 2006). The importance of examining differences in productivity cannot be overlooked: invariant to place, time and industry, a robust finding in the literature is that producers with higher productivity have a greater chance of survival (Syverson 2011).

Many writers have posited that differences in management quality lie behind this large and persistent heterogeneity in performance, but only in the last decade have management practices been measured in a systematic way across firms and countries to examine this hypothesis (see, for example, Bloom *et al.* 2012a). This work involves a mixture of in-depth 'double blind' open question surveys (Bloom and Van Reenen 2007) and traditional survey tools.

In an example of a 'double blind' open question survey, Bloom *et al.* (2012a) use interview-based evaluation to rate key management practices from 1 ('worst practice') to 5 ('best practice'). Key management practices are based on three operations-based dimensions: (1) performance monitoring, (2) target setting and (3) incentives/people management. 'Best' management practices are defined as those that continuously monitor and analyse performance information, set the right targets, track the right outcomes, take the appropriate action if the targets and outcomes are inconsistent, prioritize hiring, reward high performers, and punish low performers. A badly managed organization is one that fails to track performance, has ineffective targets, and has no incentive system to address employee underperformance. Alternatively, a well-managed organization continuously monitors its employees, attempts to improve its practices, imposes comprehensive and 'reach' targets, and has an effective incentive system to reward employees who perform well and to retrain and/or remove those that underperform (Bloom *et al.* 2012a). In a management assessment based on traditional survey tools, Bloom *et al.* (2013a) studied a large management survey of over 30,000 US manufacturing establishments conducted by the US Census Bureau. Management practices were assessed using similar monitoring, targets and incentives measures to those developed by Bloom and Van Reenen (2007), and were weighted into a single measure of 'structured management'.

It turns out that what was long suspected was true: a large fraction of productivity differences is related to management, and this appears to be causal according to randomized controlled trials of exogenous improvements in management quality (Bloom *et al.* 2013c). In a management field experiment on Indian textile firms, free consulting on management practices was provided to a set of randomly chosen treatment plants. By comparing the productivity of the treatment plants, Bloom *et al.* (2013c) find that adopting good management practices improved productivity by 17% through improved quality, efficiency and inventory management within the first year.

What is true between firms also appears to be true between countries. Bloom *et al.* (2013b) suggest that about a third of the cross-country differences in productivity can be traced back to simple measures of management quality (which is likely to be an underestimate as these are measured imperfectly). Looking across twenty developing and developed countries, researchers have found that firms with management practices that emphasize monitoring, targets and incentives are more profitable, more productive, grow more quickly and survive longer (Bloom *et al.* 2012a).

Several factors appear to be systematic drivers of better management. Stronger product market competition, openness to foreign investment, better human capital (of workers and managers) and good governance (e.g. selecting chief executive officers through a meritocratic process) all appear to be very important. This is true in simple correlations and by exploiting more sophisticated policy experiments. For example, China's entry into the World Trade Organization in 2001 was a large competitive shock for European textile and clothing producers, and it appeared to generate large improvements in managerial quality, innovation and productivity within surviving firms (see Bloom *et al.* 2012b). The threat of extinction was a motivator for improvement.

The finding that competitive markets are associated with better management practices can be explained through several channels (Bloom *et al.* 2012a). For example, selection forces may dominate as badly run institutions and organizations exit more quickly in competitive markets. Alternatively, competition may sharpen incentives to improve practices as managers become more worried about keeping their jobs, and improved efficiency practices may have large impacts on market share. While one cannot infer a causal relationship between manager and worker education and 'better' management practices, there is reason to believe that

(1) managers that are more highly educated are more aware of the benefits of certain management practices and

(2) better management practices are more easily implemented among an educated workforce.

Bloom *et al.* (2012a) argue that basic business education (i.e. capital budgeting, data analysis, standard human resources practices) could have significant beneficial effects on management in many countries.

There is also evidence that privately owned institutions significantly outscore publicly owned institutions, even after controlling for country and state (Bloom *et al.* 2012a). A possible explanation for this is that publicly owned institutions have weaker incentive management practices (in many cases, promotion is based on time served, and persistent underperformance is not adequately addressed through retraining or removal). Researchers have also found that foreign multinationals often outperform domestic firms (the differences extend to export status, with non-exporters scoring lowest in average management scores, non-multinational exporters scoring second lowest and multinationals scoring highest). In addition to being better managed than domestic firms, foreign multinationals are able to disseminate their better practices abroad.

In measures of management quality, the UK is mediocre by international standards, ranked significantly below the 'premier league' of countries, such as Germany, Japan, Sweden and the US (see, for example, Bloom *et al.* 2012a). Bloom and Van Reenen (2007) find that US firms are better managed than European firms, on average, but more variation is found between firms than between countries. The explanation for the weak UK position is a 'long tail' of badly managed firms. In the US, for example, such firms appear to be forced to rapidly shrink and/or are driven out of business much more ruthlessly. The two main weaknesses in the UK appear to be relatively low levels of human capital and a preponderance of 'family firms'. Being owned by a family is not necessarily a problem, but managerial problems often appear when the chief executive officer of a second- or third-generation family-owned firm is automatically a family member, typically the eldest son. Bloom and Van Reenen (2007) found similar rates of family ownership among middle-sized manufacturing firms in Germany as there is in the UK, but British family-owned firms were three times more likely to use primogeniture to choose their chief executive officer than their German counterparts. The greater preponderance of family firms in the UK than in, say, the US is down to a mixture of long-term cultural factors and also the fact that inheritance tax is 100% deductible for business assets passed down to family members. This is a reason for considering a change in this tax rule.

6.6 INDUSTRIAL STRATEGY

Since the late 1970s, industry-specific 'vertical' policies, or 'any kind of public intervention going beyond horizontal supply-side policies with the aim to influence sectoral developments and the composition of aggregate output', have been unpopular, due to fears that the ambition of 'picking winners' turns into an outcome of 'picking losers', therefore distorting competition (Aghion *et al.* 2012). But some recent successes (such as foreign direct investment in the automotive sector) and the need to generate more green industries (such as targeted intervention to support the growth of alternative technologies in the production or use of energy) have caused a rethink towards a more activist industrial strategy. Moreover, academics have become wary of laissez-faire policies that lead developed countries to specialize in upstream R&D and in services while outsourcing manufacturing to developing countries. Scholars point to countries, such as Germany and Japan, that have benefited from maintaining intermediate manufacturing facilities (Aghion *et al.* 2012).

Empirical studies of the effects of industrial policy have generally found negative results. Krueger and Tuncer (1982), for example, find that following the introduction of industrial policy in Turkey in the 1960s, protected industries were associated with lower productivity than those not protected by the trade regime. However, it is acknowledged that there are success stories: Southeast Asian countries, for example (e.g. South Korea), and China in particular. Studying a panel of medium and large Chinese enterprises for the period 1998–2007, Aghion *et al.* (2012) find that subsidies targeted at competitive sectors and used to maintain or increase the level of competition lead to positive and significant effects on productivity, productivity growth and product innovation. In a closely related study, Nunn and Trefler (2010) use cross-country industry-level panel data to analyse whether tariff protection that is skewed in favour of skill-intensive activities and sectors affects a country's productivity growth. Their results suggest that skill-intensive targeting may positively affect growth in the subsidized (and non-subsidized) sectors.

More recent econometric work has attempted to provide rigorous microeconomic evaluations of the causal effect of industrial policies using natural experiments. For example, Criscuolo *et al.* (2011) exploit changes generated by European state-aid rules that have exogenously induced some areas to be eligible for industrial subsidies. They conclude that the industrial subsidies given to firms for investment in economically disadvantaged areas of Britain have a positive effect on employment (through reductions in unemployment), investment and net entry. Like similar studies conducted on firms in the US, Spain, Israel and Italy (Wallsten 2000; González *et al.* 2005; Lach 2002; Bronzini and Iachini 2010), this study shows that industrial policies have stronger effects on smaller firms. The authors also conclude that such subsidies have no additional effects on total factor productivity after controlling for investment effects, and may even lead to lower measured aggregate productivity due to the increased share of employment in low-productivity firms.

Evidence suggests that there is a role for strategic thinking, especially as the government touches on almost every industry in some way

243

(Van Reenen 2011b). The convening power and coordination role of government can help bring parties together to recognize and solve problems (see, for example, Rodrik 2007).

6.7 RECOMMENDATIONS ON PRIVATE INVESTMENT AND INNOVATION

6.7.1 *Core Recommendations*

Increasing Competition

One important route with longer-lasting benefits could be through spurring increased competition in retail banking. The direction of travel in recent years—since HBOS was absorbed by Lloyds–TSB in 2008—has been in the opposite direction, but there is a mounting case for formulating a plan to reduce concentration in the retail banking sector. This would be a radical intervention, so before taking the step of referring such a proposal to the new Competition and Markets Authority with a narrow and time-limited remit, we recommend the measures that follow.

Liberalizing entry conditions, including speeding up the process for obtaining a banking license, is essential. The OFT has committed to work with the Prudential Regulation Authority to review the application of prudential requirements to ensure that new entrants and smaller banks are not disproportionately affected by, for example, requirements to hold more capital than incumbents. It is important that all of this is completed in a timely fashion.

In addition to the recently introduced automatic redirection service, further measures to reduce switching costs between banks are vital, including greater transparency. It should be as easy to transfer a bank account as it has now become to transfer a mobile phone number between operators.

Increased competition in banking would have a variety of benefits. It would encourage banks to seek out profitable lending opportunities more assiduously. It could also stimulate relationship lending as retail banks focus on more mundane finance rather than 'casino' activities. We documented these potential benefits in more detail in section 6.4.3.3.

Business Bank

The Commission supports, with some provisos, current moves towards the creation of a Business Bank. At present, the remit of the bank is to deliver the existing programmes of the Department for Business, Innovation & Skills (BIS) with £1 billion (leveraged up to £10 billion) for additional lending to manufacturers, exporters and high-growth firms. The rationale is that the bank will be able to access funds on more favourable terms than commercial banks (especially those currently saddled with a legacy of poor past investment decisions) and will therefore have a lower cost of capital.

The Business Bank's lower cost of capital and its remit to consider social returns would allow it to make loans that would typically be avoided by commercial banks. In particular, it would be able to take a wider economic view of the benefits of investing in certain sectors, including cases where there are potential long-term social returns from developing new technologies. This would mean a particular focus on lending for innovation investments to new and growing firms, which experience the most acute financial market failures and where the externalities will be greatest. Since this would include green technologies, there would be a case for folding the Green Investment Bank into the Business Bank.

The Business Bank should play an important role in creating a corporate bond market for SMEs. This would require a platform for SME loan securitization along the lines advocated by the 2012 Breedon Review. By removing the requirement for investors to analyse the credit quality of many small issuances from individual SMEs, such a platform would relax SME financing constraints and kick-start institutional investment in these firms.

The Business Bank does carry risks. To be effective, its governance has to be removed from immediate political pressures and it needs to operate on the basis of clearly defined economic objectives. We recommend that it is run by an appointed independent board to oversee operational decisions independently from the BIS. It should also operate under a charter that clearly articulates its mission and ensures that the bank is held accountable for delivering that mission.

The proposal for a Business Bank also has to be a long-term commitment supported by cross-party consensus to avoid the perennial process of abolition, reinvention and rebranding that has characterized much government policy in the past. These features are shared with our proposals for infrastructure institutions (including the Infrastructure Bank), but the skills required for the Business Bank are quite distinct so the institutions should be kept separate.

6.7.2 Other Policies

Making the Financial System More Stable

The Commission endorses the Vickers Report on banking regulation and encourages the government to implement both the letter and spirit of its recommendations (Independent Commission on Banking 2011). Some commissioners wanted to go further and recommend the structural separation of the investment and retail arms of banks along the lines of the US Glass–Steagall Act, but the consensus was to wait and see how the current set of Vickers and Basel III reforms worked before deciding whether to press ahead with something more radical and potentially disruptive. Although such reforms would help to make banking safer and more stable, higher capital requirements will often, in the short-term, mean less lending, particularly to risky projects. Recent announcements that suggest a less stringent timetable for implementing the Basel III reforms therefore seem to be a sensible move, so long as the delay is not too lengthy.

Holding Assets for Longer

To combat short-termism, the Commission recommends that equity voting rights be linked to investment duration, with rights becoming stronger the longer the holding period. This would follow the spirit of the US Securities and Exchange Commission's proposal for a minimum one-year holding period before shareholders become able to amend or request an amendment to a firm's governing documents concerning nomination procedures for directors. A concern with this is that it could lead to control by insiders, or 'tunnelling', as happens in many southern European and developing countries. We view this as less likely to happen in the UK, with its strong rule of law, protection of minority investors and transparent contracting environment. Clearly, though, the design of this proposal must be carefully crafted.

Tax Policy and Innovation

Debt finance is less attractive for an innovative firm than an equity stake because of the inherent riskiness of future revenue streams. The UK's current tax system creates a bias towards debt and against equity that distorts investment incentives generally and investment in innovation in particular.

Following the recommendations of the Mirrlees Review (2011), we support the introduction of an 'allowance for corporate equity' (ACE). This would offer a tax break on issuing equity to ensure equal treatment of equity- and debt-financed investments. There is a range of options under an ACE for creating a level playing field between debt and equity. Any resulting loss of corporate tax revenue could, in principle, be offset elsewhere in the tax system. For example, the Mirrlees Review proposes using a broad-based tax on consumption rather than increasing the corporate tax rate.

The Mirrlees Review estimates that introducing an ACE could boost investment by around 6.1% and boost GDP by around 1.4%. This is mainly because an ACE lowers the cost of capital. In addition, an ACE would help to rebalance the UK economy away from debt finance and towards equity finance. A corporate tax system of this kind has now been introduced in several countries. In addition to stimulating investment, an ACE has the potential to increase financial stability by reducing the bias towards debt finance.

The share of GDP devoted to business R&D has been rising in almost all OECD countries since the Second World War, but it started falling in the UK in the 1980s. We view the R&D tax credit system introduced in the 2000s as a positive development that helped to arrest this decline. HM Revenue & Customs defines R&D for tax purposes in a fairly narrow and formal way due to legitimate concerns over tax avoidance, so there needs to be ways of supporting investments in innovation directly without further complicating the tax code. One route is through the Business Bank, as it can take a wider view of the social returns to innovative projects. This would help to address weaknesses in the commercialization of inventions from the science base. The Business Bank could also be permitted to use a variety of venture capital-style financing approaches as well as making standard business loans.

Funding for innovative start-ups often comes from alternative sources, such as venture capital, angel funding and private equity in high-tech sectors. This is welcome and it is well known that clusters like Silicon Valley have a deep seam of such liquidity. Unfortunately, such 'agglomerations' of high-tech activity are extremely hard for governments to manufacture, although it can certainly hold them back through onerous regulations. Finance often follows after high-tech clusters have got going due to other factors, such as the presence of world-class universities like Stanford and Berkeley in California's Bay Area. Finance helps the next stage of development but it is not the prime mover. Hence, we do not support introducing additional tax breaks for such alternative investments.

Industrial Strategy

It is vital that industrial strategy does not divert attention from the importance of 'horizontal' policies, such as promoting competition, R&D, infrastructure and skills, which benefit all sectors of the economy. Nevertheless, spotting cases where there is an impediment to the growth of a sector is an important role for the government. Supportive interventions need not take the form of direct subsidies—removing specific regulatory barriers is more important.

Underpinning new thinking on industrial strategy should be a view of where the UK has some actual or latent comparative advantage. For the sectors or firms thus identified, it must then be considered whether these are in areas of global growth. This means taking an appropriately dynamic perspective. For example, investment in low-carbon technologies is likely to be an important area in the future. We recommend a tight focus on what factors inhibit the growth of such sectors and what policies could encourage their growth. Moreover, it is important that this thinking is conducted transparently, with the supporting analysis subject to independent scrutiny.

One example of how highly focused government intervention can help would be the relaxing of severe planning restrictions that are inhibiting the expansion of high-tech clusters in some parts of the country (such as Cambridge and Oxford) where the UK has strong comparative advantage in its universities. Planning restrictions on housing for workers, land-use restrictions and slow roll-out of ultra-fast broadband are particular constraints on these dense centres of new economic activity. The infrastructure institutions we propose should help, but additional political attention needs to be focused on relaxing regulations that are impeding growth. Other examples that should be the subject of focused government intervention include management training in the creative sectors, visa restrictions that are harming universities, and prevarication over expanding airport runway capacity, which harms our comparative advantage in international business services.

What kinds of institutions can help to develop and deliver a better industrial strategy? We recommend creating an independent National Growth Council, which would bring together expertise across all disciplines to review relevant evidence and to recommend growth-enhancing policy reforms that could be subject to rigorous evaluation. This body should also challenge government on why successful policies are not introduced and/or why unsuccessful ones are not closed down. The National Growth Council would work with the BIS on formulating the evidence base needed to underpin a good industrial strategy.

The lending strategies of the Business Bank and the Infrastructure Bank should be supportive of this type of industrial strategy. This could be important for industries where there is good evidence that access to finance is holding back investment and innovation. This is particularly

Table 6.1. The financing options open to firms of different sizes.

	Definition (turnover)	Bank lending	Equity markets	Private placements	Bond markets
SMEs	Under £25 million	Yes	Limited	No	No
Mid-sized companies	£25 million–£500 million	Yes	Limited	Limited	No
Large companies	Above £500 million	Yes	Yes	Yes	Yes

Source: BIS (2010).

true where large upfront investments are needed in an emerging area, such as developing low-carbon technologies.

Policies to Improve Management Quality

Policies should be pursued that encourage good management practices. High levels of competition, meritocratic appointment of chief executives, proper management training and foreign direct investment all lead to improved management performance, but additional specific and directed efforts are warranted given the importance of management. For example, while business education is growing, it is still quite limited in the UK and is undermined by tough immigration controls. There is also evidence that family-run businesses suffer from managerial deficits, so targeted support for management training could be useful for this group. The inheritance tax regime, which gives tax breaks to those who pass business assets between generations, should also be re-evaluated as it discourages reallocation of assets away from family ownership.

APPENDIX 6A: THE FINANCING CONDITIONS FACED BY UK FIRMS

In this section we set out the financing conditions faced by UK firms, which largely depend on firm size. Table 6.1 sets out the financing options open to firms of different sizes.

It is clear that the sources of finance available to SMEs are more constrained than those available to their larger counterparts, and the situation has worsened since the financial crisis. Limited access to equity markets is a particular concern. Equity finance is considered 'patient' capital, in that it can wait for long-term economic returns on investments and thereby meet the long-term financial needs of a young firm and allow it to innovate.

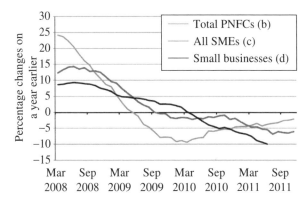

Figure 6.4. The net fall in UK SME lending.

Source: Posen (2012), based on Bank of England, British Bankers' Association and BIS calculations.

With a focus on SMEs, recent developments are examined for each type of finance in turn.

Bank Loans

Bank loans are the primary source of finance for UK SMEs; however, SME lending has declined since the financial crisis (figure 6.4). This is due to a mixture of supply-side and demand-side factors: on the supply side, banks have become more risk averse and firm credit quality has worsened due to lower sales; on the demand side, there has been increased deleveraging and lower demand for bank credit as business confidence and investments have fallen (BIS 2012). The Breedon Review (2012) notes that the UK has one of the highest SME loan rejection rates in the EU.

The cost of loan finance has increased via increased interest rates, shortened maturities and increased requests for collateral and guarantees, forcing many SMEs to switch to costly alternatives, such as asset-based finance, which is discussed below (OECD 2012a). Though SME interest rates trended downwards between 2008 and 2011, the interest rate spread between loans to SMEs and those to large enterprises increased (Posen 2012) (figure 6.5).

However, according to the Business Finance Taskforce, most data (survey-based or sourced directly from businesses or banks) suggest that weak demand is the main driver of the reduction in bank lending. First, the utilization of agreed but unused lending facilities across the range of British businesses has returned to pre-crisis levels, after peaking in 2009. Second, application levels have decreased significantly (by as much as 50% in some segments). The reasons for this are to be found in businesses'

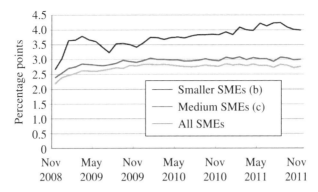

Figure 6.5. Spread over bank rate of indicative median
interest rates on new SME variable-rate facilities.

Source: Posen (2012), based on Bank of England and BIS calculations.

reactions to the economic downturn, including running down stocks, cutting investment and repaying more debt than is contractually required. While there is also evidence of a squeeze on the supply side, the Business Finance Taskforce does not believe it was constraining demand at the time of its report (2010).

A further explanation for reduced lending has been the retrenchment of a number of foreign banks from the UK SME market. In October 2010 net lending from foreign banks was declining at a rate of £1.5 billion per month, and the number of active players had decreased significantly compared with the pre-crisis period.

Equity Finance

Private equity: business angels. Angel investors are important to provide seed capital to early-stage SMEs (Mason and Harrison 2011; OECD 2011b). In addition to providing money, angel investors offer expertise (both strategic and operational) and social capital. Business angels have become an increasingly important source of external finance in the UK, contributing around £300 million in 2012, a comparable amount to venture capitalists (BIS 2012). According to the OECD (2011b), the UK (and particularly Scotland) has one of the most active angel markets in Europe. However, business angels have increasingly been moving their investment activity upstream in recent years (NESTA 2012b).

Private equity: venture capital. Venture capital typically serves early-stage, risky firms that need significant levels of initial capital or require complex R&D (BIS 2012). Venture capital requires a profitable exit strategy and is therefore less appropriate for businesses with longer time horizons and greater capital requirements. The UK has one of the best-performing venture capital markets in Europe (BIS 2012) but it still lags behind that in the US. The recent financial crisis has led to a decline in the number and value of venture capital investments (in 2009, UK venture capital investments were at their lowest level since the dotcom bubble burst and they have not improved since (NESTA 2011b)). BIS (2012) reports that venture capital only represents 4% of private equity by value, while the long-run ten-year trend stands at 6%. Moreover, venture capital firms have been moving to later investment stages, where risk is lower.

Public equity. Raising finance through the issuing of shares via exchange-regulated markets generally applies only to larger firms, and it has not been an important source of capital for new investment in the UK for many years; the Kay Review (Kay 2012) notes that many large, quoted UK businesses are self-financing. Though listed firms are primarily large, SMEs can access public equity through exchange-regulated markets such as the AIM (Alternative Investment Market) or the PLUS quoted market. During the recent financial crisis, the liquidity of AIM was heavily constrained and this significantly limited the trade of listed shares and new admissions. New listings peaked in 2005, fell to their lowest level in 2009, and then began a slow recovery in 2010 (BIS 2012).

Growth capital. This is funding that allows established firms to expand; it has structural properties that make it unfit for low-risk, fully secured banks and high-risk, high-return private equity providers. The recent financial crisis has seen banks substitute growth capital funding with traditional short-term or working-capital debt finance. Moreover, increased risk aversion encourages private equity investors to invest in larger firms and larger transactions (such as buyouts, where risk is easier to calibrate and the returns are attractive) (BIS 2009).

Debt Markets and Bonds

Debt capital markets. Private placements, corporate bonds and commercial paper are skewed towards large businesses because of barriers that prevent smaller firms from participating.

There are four primary barriers for private placement investors:

(1) the lack of ratings among SMEs and the dearth of in-house credit-assessment capabilities among UK-based investors;

(2) maturity mismatch, since many institutional investors prefer instruments with significantly longer maturities (e.g. 10–15 years or more) than the borrowing requirements of most companies;

(3) regulation that places an emphasis on liquidity; and

(4) price, as UK investors require an illiquidity premium.

The main barrier for private placement issuers is cost. Advisory and legal fees can be high, especially as there is no standardized private placement documentation in the UK (as there is in the US). Upfront legal fees can amount to over £120,000, as individual agreements need to be drafted for each transaction.

The need for institutional investors to invest in liquid securities poses the biggest restriction to access to the public bond markets. Consequently, the size of most wholesale bond issuances is restricted to greater than £150 million. The requirements of defined contribution pension schemes combined with the fact that investors are often benchmarked against indices, skews the market towards bond issuances that are liquid, large and highly traded. As a result, mid-sized businesses can issue public bonds only if they can find investors who are less concerned about liquidity, credit rating or size of issue (Breedon Review 2012).

Mezzanine finance. This form of debt shares some characteristics with equity but ranks below senior debt in terms of security/risk. The Breedon Review (2012) reports that only 1% of businesses used mezzanine finance in 2010, despite the fact that over a third of mid-sized businesses understand how mezzanine finance works. This may be driven by behavioural constraints: businesses are aware of this debt option but they lack familiarity with it as a source of finance.

Other Sources of Finance

Although loans and overdrafts provided by the large banks still appear to be the default form of external finance for the great majority of businesses, some new sources of finance are becoming more important. However, they have also been negatively affected by the financial crisis.

Asset-backed finance. This includes hire purchase and leasing arrangements and provides longer-term finance (typically 3–5 years) to around 20% of all SMEs. Since the financial crisis, leasing has slowed down in overall new business figures, though the overall stock of lease finance has remained stable (NESTA 2011b).

253

Asset-based finance. Asset-based finance encompasses secured business loans, where borrowers use their assets (such as stock or invoices) as collateral. Data from the Asset Based Finance Association show that loaned sums have decreased across most SME categories since the financial crisis. The number of clients using asset-based finance has also been falling. However, the smallest businesses that still make use of asset-based finance appear to be making far heavier use of invoice discounting and factoring than was previously the case. NESTA (2011b) argues that this may be because the access of these smaller businesses to conventional overdrafts for working capital has become more restricted or costly and that they are therefore seeking alternative sources of external finance.

Equity crowdfunding. This is an innovative method of raising finance, involving the offering of securities by a privately held business to the public, usually through an online platform. The method allows anyone to acquire a stake in a privately held business by allowing that business to offer a certain proportion of its equity for a set portion of capital (NESTA 2012b). Despite the financial crisis, crowdfunding has expanded rapidly in recent years. Technological advances and the growth of social media have made it easier for entrepreneurs to access a large pool of potential investors at relatively low cost.

Public Support to Early-Stage Capital

Over the years, UK governments have introduced a number of interventions to improve access to finance for early-stage businesses, including the establishment of several government-backed venture capital schemes and tax breaks. Table 6.2 provides a summary of these types of schemes. NESTA (2012a) reports that the efforts of the UK government over the last two decades have stood out from those of other countries due to a focus on early-stage finance and the large number of small-scale interventions.

Support has been shored up since the financial crisis through the establishment of the Innovation Investment Fund, new Enterprise Capital Funds, the Enterprise Guarantee Scheme, the Business Finance Partnership, the Business Angel Co-investment Fund, an increase in the size of the Enterprise Investment Scheme and the launch of the Seed Enterprise Investment Scheme (see NESTA (2012a) for more details).

These interventions have had a positive impact, but NESTA argues that efforts to help innovative businesses by directly promoting the venture capital industry are running into diminishing returns. In addition, there

Table 6.2. Publicly backed finance for early-stage businesses.

Fund type	Total funds available (during investment period)	Investment size range	End of investment period	Geographical scope
EGFs	£36.5m	Up to £200k	2014–16	Regional
ECFs	£185m	£500k–£2m	2011–13	National
SCF	£72m	£100k–£1m	Currently investing	Scotland
BACF	£50m	£100k–£1m	Currently investing	England
VCT	£150m pa	Businesses can raise up to £5m via the scheme in a 12-month period	NA	National
EIS	£260m pa	Businesses can raise up to £5m via the scheme in a 12-month period	NA	National
SEIS	£20m pa	Businesses can raise up to £150k via the scheme	NA	National

EGFs, Early Growth Funds; ECFs, Enterprise Capital Funds; SCF, Scottish Co-investment Fund; BACF, Business Angel Co-investment Fund; VCT, Venture Capital Trust; EIS, Enterprise Investment Scheme; SEIS, Seed Enterprise Investment Scheme. *Source*: NESTA (2012a).

is concern that the venture capital model itself is broken as a way of investing in high-growth start-ups, due in part to poor returns. Similarly, generous government support to angel finance may also have reached its limits for now (NESTA 2012a).

APPENDIX 6B: UK BUSINESS FINANCE TASKFORCE REVIEW OF LENDING TECHNOLOGIES

The chief executives of the major UK banks and the British Bankers' Association agreed in July 2010 to set up a task force to review the role of banks in supporting the UK economy and its recovery. The task force was set up in response to concerns about the supply and price of credit, and because of the widespread perception that banks were not doing enough to support businesses, with a particular focus on SMEs. The banks that are part of the Business Finance Taskforce have committed to seventeen actions across three broad areas: improving customer relationships, ensuring better access to finance, and providing better information and promoting understanding.

In October 2010 the Business Finance Taskforce set up a Lending Code of Practice to improve customer service standards, and an appeals process was launched in April 2011. Under the appeals process, any business with a group turnover of less than £25 million which is declined any form of lending can appeal that decision to their bank. A full review of the case by an external party who has not been involved with the original rejection is then launched. In the first year of the process 86% of all loan applications at participating banks were agreed and only 14% of all applications were declined; 2% of declined applications were taken to appeal and 39.5% of appeals resulted in the bank and the customer reaching a satisfactory lending agreement. These numbers were equivalent to extra lending of over £10 million to SMEs.

Approximately 33% of appeal cases were launched by SMEs (businesses with a turnover of up to £50,000). Interestingly, the overturn rate was also largest for smaller firms. This reflects both the effect of the use of automated credit scoring systems and the limited amount of time spent by relationship managers on applications for smaller-scale loans. When dealing with larger companies and loans, banks typically exercise more discretion. Importantly, the main reason for credit being declined is credit scoring (in almost 40% of cases). Credit scoring as a reason for decline is also higher for start-ups and those switching banks. According to the Business Finance Taskforce, this is because the personal credit scoring of small entrepreneurs is examined as much as the credit scoring of their businesses. This suggests that it is personal credit scoring (which is mainly done externally to the banks) rather than the banks' own credit scoring process that needs to be reviewed.

APPENDIX 6C: THE MYNERS REVIEW AND THE UK STEWARDSHIP CODE

In March 2000 HM Treasury commissioned Paul Myners to undertake a review of institutional investment in the UK. The review identified a number of weaknesses in the governance and decision-making processes of institutional investors. Areas of particular concern were the skills and expertise of trustees, performance measurement and reporting, the clarity of investment time horizons, shareholder engagement, and the clarity of the role of, and relationships between, trustees and investment consultants.

In light of these deficiencies, Myners recommended that pension fund trustees should draft and follow a voluntary set of principles that would improve governance and decision making. In 2002 the Institutional Share-holders Committee published 'The responsibilities of institutional share-holders and agents: statement of principles', which it converted to a code in 2009. Following the 2009 Walker Review of governance in financial institutions, the Financial Reporting Council took responsibility for the code. In 2010 the Financial Reporting Council published the first ver-sion of the UK Stewardship Code. The code, which was last updated in September 2012, sets out the principles of effective stewardship for insti-tutional investors and promotes greater professionalism in the gover-nance of institutional investors. It has now gained widespread acceptance in the UK.

These initiatives have made the governance of UK pension schemes far more professional, and the UK serves as a model for other countries. The latest version of the Stewardship Code makes clear that the con-cept of stewardship encompasses strategic engagement by institutional investors, and not just monitoring companies' compliance with corporate governance. This is in line with the recommendations of the Kay Review.

References

Ábrahám, Á., and K. White. 2006. The dynamics of plant-level productivity in US manufacturing. Working Paper 06-20, Center for Economic Studies.

Accenture. 2011. Next generation SME banking: how banks can apply innovation to seize the SME revenue growth opportunity. Report.

Aghion, P., M. Dewatripont, L. Du, A. Harrison and P. Legros. 2012. Industrial policy and competition. Working Paper 18048, National Bureau of Economic Research.

Aghion, P., J. Van Reenen and L. Zingales. 2013. Innovation and institutional ownership. *American Economic Review* **103**(1), 277–304.

Armendariz de Aghion, B. 1999. Development banking. *Journal of Development Economics* **58**, 83–100.

Asker, J., J. Farre-Mensa and A. Ljungqvist. 2011. Comparing the investment behavior of public and private firms. Working Paper 17394, National Bureau of Economic Research.

Bank of England. 2010. Financial stability report (December).

Bank of England. 2011a. Financial stability report (June).

Bank of England. 2011b. Government welcomes banks' statements on lending 15% more to SMEs, and on pay and support for regional growth. Bank of England Newsroom and Speeches, 2011 Press Notices.

Bank of England. 2012a. The distributional effects of asset purchases (July).

Bank of England. 2012b. Financial stability report (June).

Bank of England. 2012c. Inflation report (November).

Bank of England. 2012d. Monetary policy roundtable. Quarterly Bulletin 2012 Q3.

Bank of England. 2012e. Productivity and the allocation of resources. Speech given by Ben Broadbent (External Member of the Monetary Policy Committee) at Durham Business School (September).

Barrell, R., S. Kirby and R. Whitworth. 2011. Real house prices in the UK. *National Institute Economic Review* **216**(1), F62–F68.

Bartelsman, E., J. Haltiwanger and S. Scarpetta. 2013. Cross-country differences in productivity: the role of allocation and selection. *American Economic Review* **103**(1), 305–334.

Beck, T. 2012. Finance and growth: lessons from the literature and the recent crisis. Submission to the LSE Growth Commission.

Beck, T., H. Degryse and C. Kneer. 2012. Is more finance better? Disentangling intermediation and size effects of financial systems. Mimeo, Tilburg University.

Berger, A. N., and W. S. Frame. 2007. Small business credit scoring and credit availability. *Journal of Small Business Management* **45**(1), 5–22.

BIS. 2009. *Rowlands Review: The Provision of Growth Capital to UK Small and Medium Sized Enterprises.* Department for Business, Innovation & Skills.

BIS. 2010. Financing a private sector recovery. Report, Department for Business, Innovation & Skills (July).

BIS. 2012. SME access to external finance. Economics Paper 16, Department for Business, Innovation & Skills.

Bloom, N., and J. Van Reenen. 2007. Measuring and explaining management practices across firms and countries. *Quarterly Journal of Economics* **122**(4), 1341–1408.

Bloom, N., C. Genakos, R. Sadun and J. Van Reenen. 2012a. Management practices across firms and countries. *Academy of Management Perspectives* **26**(1), 12–33.

Bloom, N., M. Draca and J. Van Reenen. 2012b. Trade induced technical change? The impact of Chinese imports on innovation, IT and productivity. Discussion Paper 1000, Centre for Economic Performance. Available at http://cep.lse.ac.uk/pubs/download/dp1000.pdf.

Bloom, N., E. Brynjolfsson, L. Foster, R. Jarmin, I. Saporta-Eksten and J. Van Reenen. 2013a. Management in America. Working Paper 13-1, Center for Economic Studies. Available at www2.census.gov/ces/wp/2013/CES-WP-13-01.pdf.

Bloom, N., C. Genakos, R. Sadun and J. Van Reenen. 2013b. Management as a technology. Mimeo, London School of Economics and Political Science. Available at http://cep.lse.ac.uk/textonly/_new/staff/vanreenen/pdf/mat_2012mar10.pdf.

Bloom, N., B. Eifert, A. Mahajan, D. McKenzie and J. Roberts. 2013c. Does management matter? Evidence from India. *Quarterly Journal of Economics* **128**(1), 1–51.

Bolton, P., J. Scheinkman and W. Xiong. 2006. Executive compensation and short-termist behaviour in speculative markets. *Review of Economic Studies* **73**(3), 577–610.

Boot, A. W. A. 2000. Relationship banking: what do we know? *Journal of Financial Intermediation* **9**, 7–25.

Boot, A. W. A., and A. V. Thakor. 2000. Can relationship banking survive competition? *Journal of Finance* **55**(2), 679–713.

Breedon Review. 2012. *Boosting Finance Options for Business.* Department for Business, Innovation & Skills.

Bronzini, R., and E. Iachini. 2010. Are incentives for R&D effective? Evidence from a regression discontinuity approach. Mimeo, Bank of Italy.

Business Finance Taskforce. 2010. Supporting UK business: the report of the Business Finance Taskforce (October).

Caballero, R. J., T. Hoshi and A. K. Kashyap. 2008. Zombie lending and depressed restructuring in Japan. *American Economic Review* **98**(5), 1943–1977.

Canales, R., and R. Nanda. 2012. A darker side of decentralised banks: market power and credit rationing in SME lending. *Journal of Financial Economics* **105**, 353–366.

Carbo-Valverde, S., F. Rodriguez-Fernandez and G. F. Udell. 2009. Bank market power and SME financing constraints. *Review of Finance* **13**(2), 309–340.

CBI. 2011. Smaller manufacturers reappraise business plans as optimism falls. Confederation of British Industry Media Centre (August).

Chari, V. V., P. J. Kehoe and E. R. McGrattan. 2002. Accounting for the Great Depression. *American Economic Review* **92**(2), 22–27.

Cheshire, P., and S. Sheppard. 2005. The introduction of price signals into the land use planning decision-making: a proposal. LSE Research Online.

Competition Commission. 2002. The supply of banking services by clearing banks to small and medium sized enterprise. Report (March).

Corry, D., A. Valero and J. Van Reenen. 2011. UK economic performance since 1997: growth, productivity, and jobs. Report, Centre for Economic Performance (November).

Criscuolo, C., R. Martin, H. Overman and J. Van Reenen. 2011. The causal effects of an industrial policy. Discussion Paper 1113, Centre of Economic Performance. Available at http://cep.lse.ac.uk/pubs/download/dp1113.pdf.

Cruickshank, D. 2000. Competition in UK banking: a report to the Chancellor of the Exchequer (March).

Degryse, H., and S. Ongena. 2008. Competition and regulation in the banking sector: a review of the empirical evidence on the sources of bank rents. In *Handbook of Financial Intermediation and Banking* (ed. A. V. Thakor and A. Boot). Elsevier.

DeYoung, R., D. Glennon and P. Nigro. 2008. Borrower–lender distance, credit scoring, and loan performance: evidence from informational-opaque small business borrowers. *Journal of Financial Intermediation* **17**(1), 113–143.

Dolphin, T., and D. Nash. 2012. Investing for the future: why we need a British investment bank. Report, Institute for Public Policy Research.

ECI Partners. 2012. ECI growth survey 2012.

European Commission. 2007. Fifth round table between bankers and SMEs 2006–2007: SME securitisation. Directorate-General for Enterprise and Industry.

European Commission. 2012. In-depth review for the United Kingdom. Commission Staff Working Document.

European Investment Fund. 2011. European small business finance outlook. Working Paper 12, European Investment Fund.

Financial Services Authority. 2012. Retail conduct risk outlook 2012. Report (March).

Fischer, K.-H. 2000. Acquisition of information in loan markets and bank market power: an empirical investigation. Johann Wolfgang Goethe University.

Froot, K. A., A. F. Perold and J. C. Stein. 1992. Shareholder trading practices and corporate investment horizons. *Journal of Applied Corporate Finance* **5**(2), 42–58.

Gandhi, P., and H. Lustig. 2010. Size anomalies in US bank stock returns: a fiscal explanation. Working Paper 16553, National Bureau of Economic Research.

González, X., J. Jamandreu and C. Pazó. 2005. Barriers to innovation and subsidy effectiveness. *RAND Journal of Economics* **36**, 930–950.

Haldane, A., and R. Davies, 2011. The short long. Speech given at the 29th Société Universitaire Européenne de Recherches Financières Colloquium: New Paradigms in Money And Finance? (May).

Hauswald, R., and R. Marquez. 2006. Competition and strategic information acquisition in credit markets. *Review of Financial Studies* **19**(3), 967–1000.

HM Treasury. 2004. Graham review of small firms loan guarantee recommendations (September).

HM Treasury. 2010. Spending review 2010 (October).

HM Treasury. 2011. National loan guarantee scheme (December).

HM Treasury. 2012a. Autumn statement 2012 (December).

HM Treasury. 2012b. Funding for lending scheme (July).

IMF. 2009. Debt bias and other distortions: crisis-related issues in tax policy. International Monetary Fund, Fiscal Affairs Department (June).

IMF. 2011. Tax biases to debt finance: assessing the problem, finding solutions. Staff Discussion Note, International Monetary Fund (prepared by Ruud A. de Mooij, May).

Independent Commission on Banking. 2011. Final report (September).

Inderst, R., and S. Pfeil. 2013. Securitization and compensation in financial institutions. *Review of Finance* **17**(4), 1323–1364.

Jensen, M. C. 1986. Agency costs of free cash flow, corporate finance, and takeovers. *American Economic Review* **76**(3), 323–329.

Jensen, M. C., and W. Meckling. 1976. Theory of the firm: managerial behavior, agency costs, and capital structure. *Journal of Financial Economics* **3**(4), 305–360.

Kay, J. 2012. *The Kay Review of UK Equity Markets and Long-Term Decision Making*. Department for Business, Innovation & Skills.

KPMG/AIMA. 2012. Global hedge fund survey 2012: the evolution of an industry. Report (May).

Krueger, A., and B. Tuncer. 1982. An empirical test of the infant industry argument. *American Economic Review* **72**(5), 1142–1152.

Lach, S. 2002. Do R&D subsidies stimulate or displace private R&D? Evidence from Israel. *Journal of Industrial Economics* **50**, 369–390.

Lazonick, W. 2010. The Chandlerian Corporation and the theory of innovative enterprise. *Industrial and Corporate Change* **19**(2), 317–334.

Love, I., and M. S. M. Pería. 2012. How bank competition affects firms' access to finance. Working Paper 6163, World Bank.

MacMillan Committee. 1931. Report of the Committee on Finance and Industry (June).

Mason, C. M., and R. T. Harrison. 2011. Annual report on the Business Angel market in the United Kingdom: 2009/10 (May). Report prepared for the Department for Business, Innovation & Skills.

Memmel, C., C. Schmieder and I. Stein. 2007. Relationship lending: empirical evidence for Germany. Discussion Paper Series 2: Banking and Financial Studies no. 14, Deutsche Bundesbank.

Mercer. 2010. Investment horizons: do managers do what they say? Report for the Investor Responsibility Research Center Institute.

Mirrlees, J., S. Adam, T. Besley, R. Blundell, S. Bond, R. Chote, M. Gammie, P. Johnson, G. Myles and J. Poterba. 2011. *Tax by Design: The Mirrlees Review.* Oxford University Press.

Morgan, D., and K. Stiroh. 2005. Too big to fail after all these years. Staff Report 220, Federal Reserve Bank of New York (September).

Myners, P. 2001. *Institutional Investment in the UK: A Review.* The Myners Report. HM Treasury (March).

Natixis. 2012. UK institutional investors turn to alternatives for the long term to combat volatility and reduce risk. Report (September).

NESTA. 2009. The innovation index: measuring the United Kingdom's investment in innovation and its effects (November).

NESTA. 2011a. Vital growth: the importance of high-growth businesses to the recovery (March).

NESTA. 2011b. Beyond the banks: innovative ways to finance Britain's small businesses (September).

NESTA. 2012a. Plan I: the case for innovation-led growth.

NESTA. 2012b. The venture crowd: crowdfunding equity investment into business (July).

Neuberger, D., M. Pedergnana and S. Räthke-Döppner. 2008. Concentration of banking relationships in Switzerland: the result of firm structure or banking market structure? *Journal of Financial Services Research* **33**(2), 101–126.

Nunn, N., and D. Trefler. 2010. The structure of tariffs and long-term growth. *American Economic Journal: Macroeconomics* **2**(4), 158–194.

OECD. 2007. Infrastructure to 2030. Volume 2: mapping policy for electricity water and transport (June).

OECD. 2009a. Review of corporate governance and the financial crisis: key findings and main messages (June).

OECD. 2009b. *Factbook 2009—Economic, Environmental and Social Statistics.*

OECD. 2010. Assessment of government support programmes for SMEs' and entrepreneurs' access to finance and the global crisis (November).

OECD. 2011a. Asset allocation of pension funds and public pension reserve funds. In *Pensions at a Glance 2011: Retirement-Income Systems in OECD and G20 Countries.*

OECD. 2011b. Financing high growth firms: the role of angel investors (January).

OECD. 2011c. Fostering long-term investment and economic growth: summary of a high-level OECD financial roundtable. *OECD Journal: Financial Market Trends* **2011**(1), 9–29.

OECD. 2011d. Promoting longer-term investment by institutional investors: selected issues and policies. OECD Discussion Note drafted for the Eurofi High-Level Seminar on the Benefits and Challenges of a Long-Term Perspective in Financial Activities (February).

OECD. 2012a. Financing SMEs and entrepreneurs 2012 (April).

OECD. 2012b. Household saving rate. In *National Accounts at a Glance 2011* (December).

OFT. 2006. Survey of SME banking (July).

OFT. 2008. Personal current accounts in the UK: an OFT market study (July).

OFT. 2010. Review of barriers to entry, expansion and exit in retail banking (November).

Ogura, Y. 2007. Lending competition, relationship banking, and credit availability for entrepreneurs. Working Paper 07-E-036, Research Institute of Economy, Trade and Industry.

Ogura, Y. 2010. Interbank competition and information production: evidence from the interest rate difference. *Journal of Financial Intermediation* **19**(2), 279–304.

O'Hara, M., and W. Shaw. 1990. Deposit insurance and wealth effects: the value of being 'too big to fail'. *Journal of Finance* **45**(5), 1597–1600.

Parris, S., W. Lazonick, M. Mazzucato and P. Nightingale (eds). 2010. FINNOV: state of the art report (August).

Pessoa, J., and J. Van Reenen. 2013. UK economic performance. Submission to the LSE Growth Commission.

Petersen, M., and R. Rajan. 1995. The effect of credit market competition on lending relationships. *Quarterly Journal of Economics* **110**(2), 407–443.

Posen, A. S. 2012. Deepen and diversify: UK financial infrastructure to enable small business growth (February). Presentation at the TUC Panel 'Banking after Vickers'.

Presbitero, A. F., and A. Zazzaro. 2011. Competition and relationship lending: friends or foes? *Journal of Financial Intermediation* **20**(3), 387–413.

Rajan, R. G. 2006. Has finance made the world riskier? *European Financial Management* **12**(4), 499–533.

Rodrik, D. 2007. *One Economics, Many Recipes.* Princeton University Press.

Schmidt, M. M., and I. Walter. 2009. Do financial conglomerates create or destroy economic value? *Journal of Financial Intermediation* **18**(2), 193–216.

Skidelsky, R., F. Martin and C. W. Wigstrom. 2011. Blueprint for a British Investment Bank. Report, Centre for Global Studies.

Stein, J. C. 1989. Efficient capital markets, inefficient firms: a model of myopic corporate behavior. *Quarterly Journal of Economics* **104**(4), 655–669.

Strahan, P. E. 2008. Bank structure and lending: what we do and do not know. In *Handbook of Financial Intermediation and Banking* (ed. A. V. Thakor and A. Boot). Elsevier.

Syverson, C. 2011. What determines productivity? *Journal of Economic Literature* **49**(2), 326–365.

Thanassoulis, J. 2012. Industry structure, executive pay, and short-termism. Working Paper, University of Oxford.

Tucker, P. 2011. A few remarks on current monetary policy in a rebalancing economy. Report, Bank of England (November).

Van Reenen, J. 2011a. Does competition raise productivity through improving management practices? *International Journal of Industrial Organization* **9**(3), 306–317.

Van Reenen, J. 2011b. From plan B to plan V. Mimeo, London School of Economics and Political Science. Available at http://blogs.lse.ac.uk/politicsand policy/archives/8131.

Wallsten, S. 2000. The effects of government–industry R&D programs on private R&D: the case of the Small Business Innovation Research Program. *RAND Journal of Economics* **31**, 82–100.

World Economic Forum. 2011. The future of long-term investing.

World Economic Forum. 2012. The global competitiveness report 2012–2013.

Yafeh, Y., and O. Yosha. 2001. Industrial organization of financial systems and strategic use of relationship banking. *European Finance Review* **5**, 3–78.

Beyond GDP

By João Paulo Pessoa

7.1 INTRODUCTION

Discussions about economic growth typically centre on changes in the GDP of a country. GDP measures production and it is important for several reasons: to guide macroeconomic policies,[1] for example, to account for productivity, and because it is intrinsically linked to other variables, such as employment. However, it is not a direct measure of living standards, meaning that improvements in GDP (or GDP per capita) might not reflect gains experienced by a representative subset of society.

A representative growth measure of material well-being should reflect changes in the material living standards of a typical group within a country: GDP fails on both counts. Firstly, because we should be analysing changes in measures of income, consumption and wealth, instead of measures of production, since they are the relevant variables when it comes to the material well-being of individuals. Secondly, because GDP (or, more precisely, GDP per capita) is an average measure and there are better indicators of what is experienced by a typical household (or individual) in a society. This last point will become clearer in section 7.2.

Additionally, GDP is a gross measure and does not take into account taxes or depreciation, both of which affect living standards and should be considered when analysing growth. If a significant part of production moves towards capital replacement rather than consumption, then society is not fully benefiting from GDP growth. The argument for taxes is similar, i.e. if an increase in GDP is accompanied by an increase in taxes, then it is possible that living standards remain unchanged.

I am grateful to a large number of people for kindly submitting written or oral evidence to the LSE Growth Commission. I thank James Lewis and Nathan Thomas from the Office for National Statistics for providing some of the data used in this chapter. In no specific order I am also grateful to Tony Atkinson, Paul Schreyer and Jean-Paul Fitoussi, as well as to Jo Cantlay and Linda Cleavely for logistical support. The views expressed here do not necessarily reflect the views of the individuals or institutions mentioned above.

[1] See European Central Bank (2012) for a discussion of monetary and fiscal policies.

In this chapter we propose that much greater emphasis should be given to changes in median equivalized disposable household income (or simply median income) for the purpose of evaluating material living standards. We argue that this measure does not share all of the disadvantages of GDP and, hence, it better represents what a typical household experiences. This recommendation is based on Stiglitz *et al.* (2009).

Distributional issues and non-material well-being are also important aspects of the analysis of living standards. Although they are not the main focus of this chapter, we recognize these issues and dedicate sections 7.3 and 7.4 to briefly describing an income measure that internalizes distributional issues that are not captured by median income, and to highlight some core aspects of non-material well-being. In section 7.5 we discuss the capacity of societies to sustain well-being over time, i.e. sustainability.

7.2 OUR PROPOSED MEASURE: MEDIAN EQUIVALIZED DISPOSABLE HOUSEHOLD INCOME

Given the issues with GDP that were discussed in the previous section, it should not be surprising to find that better measures are available for evaluating changes in the material well-being of a country. As recommended by Stiglitz *et al.* (2009), we think a good candidate is median equivalized disposable household income, henceforth simply called median income.

It is a (net) income measure and, hence, it better reflects changes in the material living standards of a society than does (gross) production. Additionally, it is based on the median income (and not on the mean): median income is more closely aligned with what a typical individual (or household) experiences in a country, as discussed in Stiglitz *et al.* (2009).

Another advantage of median income is the fact that it is an equivalized household measure. Considering households instead of individuals internalizes the fact that people generally live together in households and not as single individuals. And equivalization implies that it is adjusted so that households with different sizes and compositions can be compared in a reasonable manner.

Equivalence scales take a family configuration as a reference point. The income of larger households is adjusted downwards while the income of smaller ones is adjusted upwards. Examples of equivalization scales are the McClements scale and the OECD-modified scale (the latter of which is used in our analysis; see appendix 7A for details about these scales).

Median income also includes values for benefits in kind that are received by a household, especially those services that are provided by the government, like health and education.

Our analysis is based on income series provided by the ONS and used in their annual reports about the effects of taxes and benefits on household income (see, for example, ONS 2012a). These series are derived from the Living Costs and Food Survey. Other possible series are also available.[2]

The ONS does not produce an equivalized income series that includes benefits in kind (median income). They argue that equivalization scales are not appropriate for such values because expenses like health and education do not have significant economies of scale. On the other hand, other papers considered by the OECD in their analysis (Fesseau and Le Laidier 2010) do equivalize monetary values for benefits in kind. We follow this last approach and calculate median income based on available ONS income series.[3]

Figure 7.1 shows GDP per capita and median income growth over time. The two measures are expressed as indexes. The index value minus one gives the cumulative growth rate for the period. For example, a value of 1.4 means that the variable grew by 40% through the period (1.4 − 1 = 0.4). See figure 7.2 for the levels of these variables.

We can see that median income grew more slowly than GDP per capita in the late 1980s and in the mid 2000s. The income lift that was seen in the middle of the last financial crisis was mainly due to the benefits-in-kind component of income (see figure 7.3 for a comparison between the growth of median income and median income not adjusted for benefits in kind). Hence, a typical household in the UK did not experience as much income growth as someone would infer by looking solely at GDP per capita. Cribb *et al.* (2012) find a similar trend for median income using a combination of the Family Resources Survey and the Family Expenditure Survey.[4]

Although these series are more informative than GDP in terms of material well-being, they are not perfect measures. Timely release is a clear disadvantage. These measures are based on household surveys that need

---

[2]There is a median income series (which does not include some measures of benefits in kind) that is sponsored by the Department for Work and Pensions and is used in the annual publication 'Households below average income'. This series is currently based on the Family Resources Survey but was previously based on the Family Expenditure Survey.

[3]Even though our median income series is not regularly produced by the ONS, they kindly generated it for this report.

[4]Their analysis does not consider values for most types of benefits in kind, and their series therefore looks more like our median income series without adjustment for benefits in kind, which can be seen in figure 7.2.

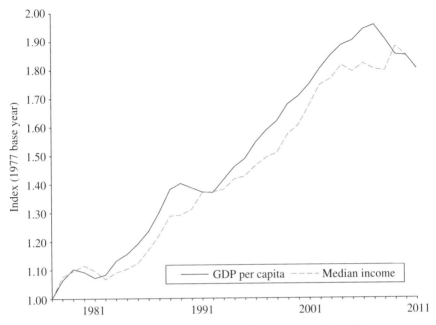

Figure 7.1. Real median income and GDP per capita indexes.

Source: ONS. *Notes*. Variables are deflated by the retail price index. Income is equivalized using the OECD-modified scale (using a household with two adults as the reference). From 1994 onwards, median income is based on the UK financial year rather than on the calendar year (e.g. 1994 corresponds to the fiscal year April 1994–March 1995).

time to be processed: both Department for Work and Pensions (2012) and ONS (2012a), which cover the 2010–11 period, were released in June 2012. In contrast, GDP figures are released within months.

Jenkins (2012) suggests two ways of obtaining more timely release of median income figures.

(1) Invest more in resources and personnel to make the gap between the surveys being conducted and the final series being released shorter.

(2) Place greater reliance on modelling and imputation (something that is also used in preliminary estimates of GDP), which would imply making use of micro-simulation models based on less up-to-date information to forecast the median for a short upcoming period (sometimes called 'nowcasting') before the surveys become available.

Another weak point is the lack of international standards to guide median income surveys (such as the ones that guide surveys on GDP and make its value comparable across countries). Even though the OECD and

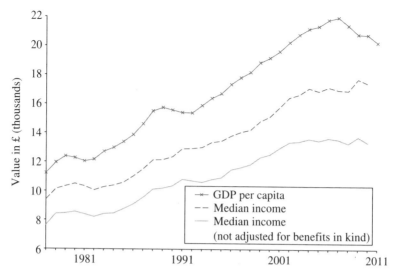

Figure 7.2. Real median income and GDP per capita
deflated by the retail price index in 2005 prices.

Source: ONS. *Notes*. Variables are deflated by the retail price index. Income is equivalized using the OECD-modified scale (using a household with one adult as the reference). From 1994 onwards, median income is based on the UK financial year rather than on the calendar year (e.g. 1994 corresponds to the fiscal year April 1994–March 1995).

Eurostat are putting some effort into remedying this situation, we are still some way from a worldwide standard similar to that for GDP.[5]

7.3 INEQUALITY

Stiglitz *et al.* (2009) also recommend giving more prominence to the distribution of income consumption and wealth. This would allow us to analyse not only a typical household but also the bottom and top income earners. It would also permit us to see what is happening to inequality in the UK, something that has become increasingly important since the late 1970s, as has been pointed out by several authors. For example, Van Reenen (2011) shows that wage inequality has increased not only in the UK but also in other OECD countries, and Cribb *et al.* (2012) find that income inequality increased throughout this period in the UK.

---

[5]The OECD has a project to use micro-information on income distribution to calculate figures for median household income that will be internationally comparable. Eurostat makes available international series for median household income in some countries (Eurostat 2011).

Although analysing median and mean measures together can give us a flavour of what is happening with the income distribution (and with inequality),[6] it is important to bear in mind that median income on its own does not take account of distributional issues. Other measures are therefore necessary.

Based on this last recommendation of Stiglitz *et al.* (2009), Jenkins (2012) and Atkinson (2011) propose a distributionally sensitive measure of national income based on Sen (1976). This measure is the product of real mean income and the Gini index of inequality (this lies between zero and one and increases with increasing inequality, implying that the income measure decreases with decreasing inequality). Jenkins (2012) points out that inequality-adjusted income has grown more slowly than unadjusted income in the UK since the early 1980s.

7.4   NON-MATERIAL AND SUBJECTIVE WELL-BEING

Well-being is multidimensional, so looking at only median income and GDP will be insufficient for evaluating all aspects that affect living standards. Other important components that shape individuals' quality of life are health, education and environment.

Health is fundamental to analysing a society's quality of life. Reliable statistics about mortality and morbidity rates are therefore needed and, although they are not as up to date as the income measures, the ONS provides information about both (see Beaumont and Thomas 2012).

It is well known that education is an important way of providing the competencies needed to foster economic growth. But education also increases well-being per se: for example, according to Stiglitz *et al.* (2009), many works associate better education with better health and lower unemployment.[7] Some education indicators refer to inputs (e.g. educational expenditure) while others refer to outputs (e.g. graduation rates). Many sources of data (such as the National Pupil Database provided by the Department for Education) are available to obtain such indicators (see ONS 2012b).

Environmental conditions have an immediate impact on a society's well-being: they affect human health and people's choices, and environ-

---

[6]Figure 7.1 shows that median income grew more slowly than GDP per capita in the late 1980s and the mid 2000s. This is an indication that inequality increased during these periods.

[7]And this is true even after controlling for the additional income that higher education brings.

269

mental imbalances may, in addition, lead to natural disasters such as floods and droughts. Many indicators can be invoked to measure the state of environmental quality (see ONS 2012c), but they are still of limited use when it comes to measuring quality of life.[8]

It is also worth pointing out that subjective measures of well-being need to be considered as well. This type of measure directly reveals individuals' perceptions about life satisfaction and thereby avoids 'paternalistic' assumptions of the type that attribute objective dimensions to life satisfaction without further consultation (like all the measures discussed previously). According to Layard (2005), there are sophisticated ways of measuring how satisfied (or happy) people are, and these measures should be of use to policymakers.

Finally, as highlighted in section 7.3, distributional issues have an effect not only on income but also on non-material well-being. It is important to account for inequalities between individuals' conditions (and not only for average conditions). A further challenge is to address the links between the various dimensions of well-being, something that is difficult to measure but extremely important in guiding policy decisions.

7.5 SUSTAINABILITY

It is important to measure well-being at a certain point in time, but also to assess society's ability to increase (or at least sustain) it over time. Stiglitz *et al.* (2009) recommend that sustainability should be measured separately from present well-being. This implies that a wealth (stock-based) approach should be used, something that is based on the principle that future well-being depends on the stocks of resources passed on to future generations. These stocks generally include exhaustive and renewable natural resources, and physical and human capital. Sustainability measures should, therefore, target these stocks (or at least their changes).

One alternative for measuring sustainability is to aggregate the many stocks according to one common metric (usually a monetary value), compiling one single stock of assets that affect the sustainability of a nation. This approach simplifies the final analysis but relies on relatively implausible assumptions such as perfect substitutability between different types of asset (e.g. oil reserves and human capital); it is also limited by the

---

[8]We should, for example, measure how many people are exposed to a given pollutant and not simply the quantity of that pollutant in the air.

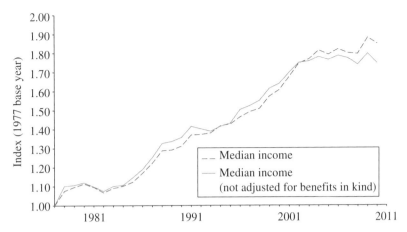

Figure 7.3. Real median income indexes.

Source: ONS. *Notes*. Variables are deflated by the retail price index. Income equivalized using the OECD-modified scale (using a household with two adults as the reference). From 1994 onwards, median income is based on the UK financial year rather than on the calendar year (e.g. 1994 corresponds to fiscal year April 1994–March 1995).

absence of markets for all types of stocks that need to be aggregated (e.g. quality-adjusted water availability).

Dashboards (or sets of indicators) are another alternative for assessing sustainability. They possess the advantage that they separately keep track of the many heterogeneous stocks that affect well-being, thereby avoiding the difficult task of summarizing all the stocks into a single metric. Nevertheless, this advantage may easily turn into a disadvantage because of the complexity of analysing a large and eclectic dashboard. A limited dashboard therefore appears to be the optimal solution.

The last recommendation of Stiglitz *et al.* (2009) is that the final dashboard should combine: (1) a monetary indicator that accounts for the economic aspect of sustainability and aggregates stocks for which reasonable valuation techniques exist (such as some natural resources and human and physical capital); and (2) a set of physical indicators for environmental pressure. A possible dashboard, suggested by UNECE/OECD/ Eurostat (2008), is given in table 7.1.

The World Bank produces statistics along the lines of point (1), while the Department for Environment, Food and Rural Affairs produces a dashboard composed of various indices of sustainability that is recognized as leading edge. Obviously, a difficulty not addressed by these indicators is the global aspect of sustainability, given that actions taken abroad might affect the UK and vice versa.

Table 7.1. Sustainability dashboard.

Indicator domain	Stock indicator	Flow indicator
Foundational well-being	Health-adjusted life expectancy	Index of changes in specific mortality and morbidity
	Percentage of population with post-secondary education	Enrolment in post-secondary education
	Temperature deviations from normal	Greenhouse gas emissions
	Ground-level ozone and fine particulate concentrations	Smog-forming pollutant emissions
	Quality-adjusted water availability	Nutrient loading to water bodies
	Fragmentation of natural habitats	Conversion of natural habitats to other uses
Economic well-being	Real per capita net foreign financial asset holdings	Real per capita investment in foreign financial assets
	Real per capita produced capital	Real per capita net investment in produced capital
	Real per capita human capital	Real per capita net investment in human capital
	Real per capita natural capita	Real per capita net depletion of natural capital
	Reserves of energy resources	Depletion of energy resources
	Reserves of mineral resources	Depletion of mineral resources
	Timber resource stocks	Depletion of timber resources
	Marine resource stocks	Depletion of marine resources

Source: Stiglitz *et al.* (2009) and UNECE/OECD/EUROSTAT (2008).

7.6 APPENDIX 7A: MEDIAN INCOME CONCEPTS

This appendix is a summary of the median income definitions explained thoroughly in ONS (2012).

Median income is given by

$$\text{median income} = \text{original income} + \text{cash benefits} + \text{tax credits}$$
$$+ \text{benefits in kind} - \text{direct taxes},$$

and each of the components of median income is discussed below.

Original income.   This is equal to the annualized income in cash of all members of the household before the deduction of taxes or the addition of any state benefits. It includes income from employment, self-employment, investment income, fringe benefits (such as company cars, private medical insurance and beneficial loans), private pensions and annuities (which includes all workplace pensions, individual personal pensions and annuities).

Cash benefits and tax credits.   Cash benefits and tax credits include the following.

(1) Contributory benefits: state pension, incapacity benefit, contribution-based jobseeker's allowance, bereavement benefits and statutory maternity pay.

(2) Non-contributory benefits: income support, child benefit, income-based jobseeker's allowance, housing benefit (council tax benefit and rates rebates are treated as deductions from council tax and Northern Ireland rates), statutory sick pay, carer's allowance, attendance allowance, disability living allowance, war pensions, severe disablement allowance, industrial injury disablement benefits, child tax credit, working tax credit, pension credit, over-80 pension, Christmas bonus for pensioners, government training scheme allowances, student support and winter fuel payments.

Direct taxes.   Income tax, council tax and Northern Ireland rates, as well as employees' and self-employed National Insurance contributions, are grouped as direct taxes. Taxes on capital, such as capital gains tax and inheritance tax, are not included in these deductions because there is no clear conceptual basis for doing so; in addition, the relevant data are not available from the Living Costs and Food Survey.

Benefits in kind. Benefits in kind include the National Health Service, state education, school meals and healthy start vouchers (including nursery milk), housing subsidy, railway travel subsidy and bus travel subsidy (including concessionary travel schemes).

Equivalization scales. The OECD-modified equivalization scale attributes different weights to each household member (1.0 to the first adult, 0.5 to subsequent adults and to children aged 14 and over, and 0.3 to children aged 13 and under). The values of the individuals are added together to give an equivalence number for the household, and this is used to divide the household income, resulting in the equivalized income. For example, a household composed of a married couple and three children under 13 with an annual income of £48,000, will have an equivalized income of $£48,000/(1 + 0.5 + 3 \times 0.3) = £20,000$.

The McClements scale is similar: it also possesses a household with two adults as its reference point but it assigns different weights to other members of the household than the OECD-modified scale does. For more details, see Anyaegbu (2010).

In order to compare median income and GDP per capita levels in figure 7.2, we rescale the income values using the OECD-modified scale such that a household with one individual is the new reference. This does not affect the growth rates shown in figures 7.1 and 7.3.

REFERENCES

Anyaegbu, G. 2010. Using the OECD equivalence scale in taxes and benefits analysis. *Economic and Labour Market Review* **4**, 49–54.

Anyaegbu, G. 2011. The effects of taxes and benefits on household income, 2009/10. Further analysis and methodology. Available at www.ons.gov.uk/ ons/rel/household-income/how-effective-are-taxes-and-benefits-in-reducing -inequality-in-the-uk/1980-2009-10/index.html.

Atkinson, A. B. 2011. Prosperity and fairness. Submission to the LSE Growth Commission.

Beaumont, J., and J. Thomas 2012. Measuring national well-being: health. Available at www.ons.gov.uk/ons/rel/wellbeing/measuring-national-well-being/ health/art-measuring-national-well-being---health.html.

Chiripanhura, B. 2010. Measures of economic activities and their implications for societal well-being. *Economic and Labour Market Review* **4**, 56–65.

Cribb, J., R. Joyce and D. Phillips. 2012. Living standards, poverty and inequality in the UK: 2012. Commentary C124, Institute of Fiscal Studies.

Department for Work and Pensions. 2012. Households below average income: an analysis of the income distribution 1994/1995–2010/2011. Available at http://research.dwp.gov.uk/asd/index.php?page=hbai_arc#hbai.

European Central Bank. 2012. Monetary and fiscal policy interactions in a monetary union. *ECB Monthly Bulletin* (July), 51–64.

Eurostat. 2011. Report of the taskforce: household perspective and distributional aspects of income, consumption and wealth. Sponsorship Group on Measuring Progress, Well-Being and Sustainable Development (November).

Fesseau, M., and S. Le Laidier. 2010. Social disparities between groups of households within a national accounts framework: a breakdown of household accounts. Paper prepared for the 31st General Conference of the International Association for Research in Income and Wealth.

Fleurbaey, M. 2009. Beyond GDP: the quest for a measure of social welfare. *Journal of Economic Literature* **47**, 1029–1075.

Jenkins, S. P. 2012. Distributionally-sensitive measures of national income and income growth. Submission to the LSE Growth Commission.

Layard, R. 2005. *Happiness: Lessons from a New Science.* London: Penguin.

OECD. 2011. How's life? Measuring well-being. Available at www.oecd-ilibrary.org/economics/how-s-life_9789264121164-en.

ONS. 2012a. The effects of taxes and benefits on household income, 2010/2011: further analysis and methodology. Available at www.ons.gov.uk/ons/rel/household-income/the-effects-of-taxes-and-benefits-on-household-income/2010-11/index.html.

ONS. 2012b. Measuring national well-being: education and skills. Available at www.ons.gov.uk/ons/rel/wellbeing/measuring-national-well-being/education-and-skills/art-education-and-skills.html.

ONS. 2012c. UK environmental accounts 2012. Available at www.ons.gov.uk/ons/rel/environmental/uk-environmental-accounts/2012/stb-ukea-2012.html.

Oulton, N. 2012. Hooray for GDP! Submission to the LSE Growth Commission.

Sen, A. 1976. Real national income. *Review of Economic Studies* **43**, 19–39.

Stiglitz, J., A. Sen and J.-P. Fitoussi. 2009. Report by the Commission on the Measurement of Economic Performance and Social Progress. Available at www.stiglitz-sen-fitoussi.fr/en/index.htm.

Thomas, J., and J. Evans. 2010. There is more to life than GDP but how can we measure it? *Economic and Labour Market Review 4*, 29–36.

UNECE/OECD/Eurostat. 2008. Report on measuring sustainable development: statistics for sustainable development, commonalities between current practice and theory. Working Paper ECE/CES/2008/29.

Van Reenen, J. 2011. Wage inequality, technology and trade: 21st century evidence. *Labour Economics* **18**, 730–741.

About The Centre for Economic Performance

The Centre for Economic Performance is one of the world's leading applied economics research centres. Our mission is to perform world-class policy-relevant research, particularly in the area of growth and inequality. We were founded in 1990 and are funded by the Economic and Social Research Council.

The Centre for Economic Performance studies the determinants of economic performance at the level of the individual, the company, the nation and the global economy. Its work covers labour markets, education, productivity, macroeconomics, international trade and well-being. It has contributed seven present or former members of the Monetary Policy Committee of the Bank of England.

About The Institute for Government

The Institute for Government is an independent charity helping to improve government effectiveness. We work with all the main political parties at Westminster and with senior civil servants in Whitehall, providing evidence-based advice that draws on best practice from around the world.